Nature's Self

Nature's Self

Our Journey from Origin to Spirit

by
Robert S. Corrington

ROWMAN & LITTLEFIELD PUBLISHERS, INC.

ROWMAN & LITTLEFIELD PUBLISHERS, INC.

Published in the United States of America
by Rowman & Littlefield Publishers, Inc.
4720 Boston Way, Lanham, Maryland 20706

3 Henrietta Street
London WC2E 8LU, England

Copyright © 1996 by Rowman & Littlefield Publishers, Inc.

All rights reserved. No part of this publication may be reproduced, stored in a retrieval system, or transmitted in any form or by any means, electronic, mechanical, photocopying, recording, or otherwise, without the prior permission of the publisher.

British Cataloging in Publication Information Available

Library of Congress Cataloging-in-Publication Data

Corrington, Robert S., 1950–
Nature's self : our journey from origin to spirit / Robert S. Corrington.
  p. cm.
Includes bibliographical references and index.
1. Self (Philosophy) I. Title.
BD450.C6414   1966   126—dc20   95-38603   CIP

ISBN 0–8476–8134–3 (pbk. : alk. paper)
ISBN 0-8476-8133-5 (cloth: alk. paper)

Printed in the United States of America

♾™ The paper used in this publication meets the minimum requirements of American National Standard for Information Sciences—Permanence of Paper for Printed Library Materials, ANSI Z39.48–1984.

Table of Contents

Preface	vii
Introduction: Nature's Self and the Ontological Difference	1
Chapter One: Finitude and Embodiment	23
A. Positioning and Origins	25
B. Depositioning and Loss	40
C. Repositioning and Return	50
Chapter Two: Fitful Transcendence	61
A. Public Intersections	62
B. Developmental Teleology and the Unconscious	73
C. The Spirit-Interpreter	85
Chapter Three: Potencies and Infinitesimals	97
A. Self-Othering	98
B. Fissuring	112
C. Providingness	123
Chapter Four: Nature's Self-Disclosure	131
A. Disruptive Grace	133
B. Eschatology and the Heart of Nature	143
C. Transfiguration	153
Bibliography	163
Index	179
About the Author	187

Preface

The current philosophical climate has failed to develop a judicious understanding of the human process and its unique semiotic features. At the same time, although often for different reasons, it has also failed to show the innumerable connections between the self and nature. Semiotic theory remains tied to poststructuralist notions of arbitrary reference, while naturalism goes to the other extreme and privileges a reductive and one dimensional understanding of nature's self. It is the concern of the present work to overcome the arbitrary dimension of contemporary philosophical semiotics, while rethinking nature from the standpoint of ecstatic naturalism, i.e., a naturalism that is non reductive and that illuminates the structures of renewal and transformation within nature itself. This entails a description of the fundamental divide within nature; namely, that between *nature naturing* and *nature natured*.

The focus in this analysis of the self shifts to the inner and outer drama of the movement of the self from its original position, tied to the lost object, through the powers of time and space where repositioning and depositioning occur, to the transfiguration that emerges when the self encounters the spirit that lies on the other side of temporality. Most contemporary analyses of the self are so ensnared in constructivist analyses and metaphors that they say almost nothing about how the self actually obtains as a foundling within nature itself. Nature's self is more than a social or personal construction. On the deepest level it is the locus for the eternal tensions manifest in nature's self-fissuring. Only by directly embedding the self in nature, which is merely the act of recognizing what has silently obtained all along, can the movement of the self be directed toward those healing energies that come from the spirit that is itself a product of nature.

If the present work has any effect in these strangely blind times, it will be to show the 'how' of the self in a nature that is beyond good and evil. The emergence of those meaning structures that are congenial to human need can only come from that most elusive child of nature, the spirit. The return of the spirit, when properly understood, is one of the most dramatic ways that the cunning of nature has of bringing itself back into the center of our thought and our lives.

Introduction
Nature's Self and the Ontological Difference

At the heart of the self is a cleft, a wound that emerges with the first dawn of consciousness and remains with the self until its death. This wound is not the Cartesian wound of a divided substance, with one substance in space and the other not, but a unique ontological wound that stems from the fundamental split within nature itself. This split is that between *nature naturing* and *nature natured*. The self is a gift of this self-fissure within nature, but receives this gift with an ambiguous configuration of melancholy and love. The substance tradition was dimly aware of the depth-dimension of this split but failed to probe into its inner logic. The semiotic tradition, even though it decisively moves beyond the concept of substance, shies away from this transfiguring momentum at the heart of all forms of semiosis.

The loss of the substantive self has been a liberating event in thought, but this loss brings with it a great deal of categorial confusion. The semiotic redefinition of the self, as an unlimited sign series, moves toward the social and presocial dimensions of the human process and gives us access to the scope and complexity of the self. Yet, the semiotic self remains cut off from nature and the ultimate fissure within the world if it denies the broken nature of its own trajectory through time. The Peircean tradition has become normative for many precisely because of its tremendous categorial and semiotic fecundity. Yet it too turns its back on the presemiotic fissure within nature and writes the self too large on the face of the world. The panpsychist move, found also in process perspectives, which sees all orders as to some degree mental, privileges the unique features of the human process and finds them manifest in lesser degrees throughout the innumerable orders of semiosis.

The current perspective on the self seeks to transfigure the Peircean tradition in terms of the centrality and mystery of the ontological difference. At the same time, it takes strong issue with many of Peirce's specific semiotic theories, while giving renewed attention to those of his theories that have been marginalized. In particular, his concept of the "ground" relation in semiosis will be reshaped to correspond to the phenomenological data concerning how the self moves between and among internal and external orders. Yet, as we will see, the spatial concepts of "internal" and "external" often cloud the issue and they must be used with great care. Be that as it may, the ground relation has a direct, if often hidden relation to the ontological difference.

The perspective of this work is that of ecstatic naturalism. Unlike more descriptive forms of naturalism that privilege efficient causality and methodologies like induction, the ecstatic form focuses on the presemiotic rhythms of *nature naturing* and shows how these mysterious potencies transform everything that they touch. At the same time, but using different categories, ecstatic naturalism works through the manifest orders of the world (*nature natured*) to show how they affect each other in terms of their efficacy or opacity. The human process lives out of the ever renewed bifurcation between *nature natured* and *nature naturing*. Yet this split is different in kind from that envisioned by the Cartesian tradition, which uses spatial constructs in a misguided way. As we will see, spatial concepts can be applied to the human process in an endless variety of ways, but certain aspects of the self are prespatial and, in the religious sense, postspatial.

In the spirit of Peirce, if not always within his own categorial scheme, ecstatic naturalism moves toward the "third" that can overcome the splits within the heart of the self. The primal wound of the human process cannot be overcome by anything *within* the self, but must find its healing from the power of the spirit-interpreter that lives between and among selves. The spirit, as noted by Peirce, is related to the semiotic ground relation and lives outside of the ontological triad of sign/object/interpretant. It is both a semiotic and presemiotic clearing 'behind' the self, and a transfiguring presence standing 'before' the self in the power of the "not yet." The spirit works tirelessly to overcome the ontological wound that haunts the self through its journey in time and space.

Phenomenologists have reminded us that the self becomes a clearing onto the world through its fundamental moods which serve as access structures. In a metaphoric sense moods stand in the between, holding self and world together so that the world can become translucent in particular ways. The primacy of mood is most clearly evident in the way in which the ontological difference appears before the self. The self emerges into its autonomy by rejecting and denying the underlying rhythms of *nature naturing*. The mood that surrounds the autonomous self is melancholy. Anxiety has often been privileged as the mood that opens us to the ontological difference, insofar as it breaks open the nothingness that itself points to the primacy of Being (Heidegger 1927). Yet anxiety remains too focused on the present and does not illuminate the more primal dimension of the lost object that lies in the past. In psychoanalytic terms, the lost object is found in the pre-Oedipal stage, where the self still lives in connectedness with the material maternal source of nourishment. The ontological analysis of the difference between *nature naturing* and *nature natured* corresponds in a surprising way with the language of psychoanalysis that speaks of the difference between the maternal pre-Oedipal and the post-Oedipal domain of paternal semiotic codes ("The name of the Father," Kristeva 1974). Ecstatic naturalism affirms this hidden connection between depth psychology and ontology.

If melancholy is that mood that points to the sense of the loss of the maternal (*nature naturing*), then love is the mood that points to the return of the maternal on the edges of personal and social life. Love has been understood to take three primal forms: eros, philia, and agape. Eros has been understood as the movement from the lower to the higher, in which the higher form draws the lover toward it because of its intrinsic and desirable features. Philia has been understood as the love of community members for each other. Agape has been understood, especially in Christian dogmatics, as the unearned gift of the perfect for the imperfect, even though the imperfect is not a worthy object of love. Ecstatic naturalism affirms a place for all three forms of love but questions the spatial images that serve to separate eros from agape. In what follows it is understood that we are speaking of eros/agape as a unity in which the self struggles to overcome its separation from the heart of nature (eros), while the heart of nature returns to the self from the future and the spirit (agape). Neither eros nor agape can exist alone. They represent two poles within the same phenomenon and interact dialectically. In one order of relevance eros may momentarily assume priority, while in another order of relevance, both connected to the same self, agape may assume priority. The mystery of love precludes a quantifiable analysis of the ratios of eros and agape, not to mention philia, within a given order of relevance.

The human process has innumerable moods (each serving as an access structure onto the world). But the primal emotive tension within the self is that between melancholy and love. The melancholy self is reminded of its loss, while the self of eros/agape lives in the primal and natural grace that gathers it into the heart of the ontological difference. This love is not in defiance of the world of embodiment, but transfigures the finite self so that it remains open to the presence of the spirit-interpreter, who points all selves toward the final transfiguration at the end of history. The myth of the resurrection of the body points toward a deeper ontological structure, a structure that we can only grasp in a fragmentary way. The deeper logic points to the way in which the final semiotic transfiguration grasps us on the edges of our 'normal' forms of semiotic interaction. In this sense, the resurrection is a continual presence/absence that emerges in the betweenness structures of semiosis.

What is the medium through which we gain access to the ontological difference? The most basic medium is that of the unconscious, which reaches down into the heart of nature. Here we can see how the language of depth psychology converges with the language of a semiotic ontology. The unconscious is the most basic link between the domain of *nature natured* and *nature naturing*. Both dimensions of nature have their place within the unconscious, but in different respects. The domain of *nature natured* is the domain of attained signs and interpretants. The unconscious 'contains' these in the form of memories, complexes, images, and constructs of all kinds. Dream material presents us with the semiotic contents of the self. The domain or dimension of *nature naturing* is the domain of presemiotic rhythms that appear before the self in terms of somatic states and highly charged dream contents. A given dream may contain elements from both sides of the ontological difference. In one dimension it will have signs and interpretants that have some obvious connection with the life history of the dreamer, while in another dimension it will have primal presemiotic imports that point to a domain of ultimate meaning and connectedness. This is not to say that such dreams are easily decoded and rendered intelligible. Indeed, the semiotic concepts of coding, transmitting, and decoding are pushed to their limits when we deal with the unconscious and its link to the ontological difference. It is to say that the unconscious is the primary means by and through which the sign-using self becomes open to the heart of nature in its self-fissuring.

The self is multipositioned, a view the substance tradition found difficult to articulate. In one sense, to talk of the self is to talk of all of its innumerable locations and relations, not to mention its internal features. We can add to this relational view the awareness that the self is also its many products, some random and some purposeful, that emerge from the self's actions. These products form a variegated world of their own. Given this productive and relational fecundity, how is it possible to make any sense of the traditional problem of self-identity? Just where and what is the self in the midst of its involvements? At the other extreme from the substance tradition are the postmodern semioticians who have given up on the issue of self-identity and who thus see the self as the mobile 'locus' of eliding and self-transforming sign systems. These systems have no anchor in either an integral self or a world outside of the self. It is as if the self is reduced to a moving clearing in which the signs of the world merely play out their roles in detachment.

Ecstatic naturalism occupies a third position in this debate. It firmly rejects the static and substance-derived view of the self that sees it as little more than a container of traits. In this view, identity is maintained by an underlying, yet always efficacious, center that serves as a kind of hidden magnetic field, shaping all internal and external structures into a clear contour. On the other side, ecstatic naturalism must also reject the anarchic view that sees the self as a self-emptying semiotic clearing in which all self-identity is elusive and deeply self-denying. The third and mediating view insists that the self is indeed multilocated, but that it has a cumulative directionality that can be mapped in a variety of ways. This directionality need not be conscious or intentional. As we will see, sheer semiotic drift and inertia are as much a part of the directionality of the self as are deliberation and creative contrivance.

The contour of the self is certainly elusive and much larger and more complex than any phenomenological analysis can possibly reveal. Yet this insight need not paralyze our inquiry. For the self constantly leaves traces and marks of its trajectory, whether through its products or through its semiotic codes, no matter how tenuous or ambiguous. At the same time, the self shows its most basic features in its struggles to return to the pre-Oedipal lost object. The self is neither a substance nor a mere body of unrelated signs. It is a cumulative momentum that responds to the lost object and that grooves and shapes all signs around a fundamental project, even if that project remains embedded in the unconscious and hence outside of conscious appraisal. As this treatise will show, self-identity can still be articulated within a multipositional view of the human process.

The unconscious is thus crucial for shaping and transforming self-identity. The post-Freudian psychoanalytic tradition has shed great light on the earliest stages of the self and its struggles with and against the nourishing mother (who appears as the material ground of Being for the child). The earlier Jungian tradition worked through some of the even more basic ontological structures of the unconscious and showed the link between the unconscious of the self and the unconscious of nature. This link must be moved more toward the center of any analysis of the human process, so that the correlation between self-identity and the infinity of nature can be shown. In a striking sense, the sign-using self is the self of nature. The ontological difference between the presemiotic potencies (*nature naturing*) and the attained orders of the world (*nature natured*) enters into the unconscious and gives it its unique form of dynamism and intensity. Yet the depth logic of the human unconscious simultaneously reverses this directionality and opens the self to the unconscious of nature. The mysteries of the self are in the end the mysteries of a self-fissuring nature.

Nature's self rides on the back of a self-transfiguring nature and derives its own rhythms and momentums from the unlimited domains of the world. In one sense, the self is as inexhaustible as the world, while in another sense, the self represents but one perspective on the world as a whole. The dialectical tension between transcendence and finitude points toward the ontological difference within nature. The self has an awareness of the presemiotic rhythms of *nature naturing*, even if this awareness is continually suppressed in favor of the manifest and more manageable codes of the domains of *nature natured*. The self is ejected from the heart of nature, rides precariously on both sides of the ontological difference, and forges a cumulative and multipositional identity that represents but one aspect of nature's semiotic plenitude. Philosophers are continually vexed by the utter complexity of the self and its relation to nature. Yet this complexity has its own inner logic that can be probed and partially displayed through a series of cumulative phenomenological descriptions.

What can we say about the multipositional nature of the self? First it must be born in mind that the concept of "position" need not be limited to the obvious spatial connotations. The self is not part of a three-or four-dimensional grid in which its features can be mapped and located with precision. Positions can be ambiguous and can push on the edges of spatiality. For example, the self is certainly positioned in political orders of relevance. In what sense is my position as a voter a spatial position? It makes more sense to say that my position in this case is a recurrent possibility that locates me as a member of a self-governing system. My actuality as a voter is not located in a container that can be opened or closed at will. Rather, it is a nonspatial 'place' that I enter into at appropriate times. Yet it is clear that the concept of "position" is still pertinent here. If this right were to be taken away from me, then I would have a very different social position and my sign systems and products would have a different meaning and cumulative force.

When the unconscious is considered, the concept of "position" takes on new meaning. Just 'where' is the depth meaning dimension of a dream located? And just 'where' is the possibility of transcendence located? Transcendence does have locations within the world, since it cannot be extra-worldly, but these locations are not obviously spatial or tied to an extended substance. The plot thickens when it is understood that the self is not the conscious source of all of its positions, and that it finds itself positioned by many semiotic and presemiotic powers beyond its ken or internal power. Positioning belongs with depositioning in a complex and often tragic dialectic. Repositioning occurs continually, and the full contour of positioning, depositioning, and repositioning lies beyond the conscious reach of any self. These shifts take place over and over again and add to the utter complexity of cumulative self-identity.

The correlation between the unconscious and consciousness frames the momentum of the self. Self-identity is part of a developmental teleology and emerges from the dynamic transposition of unconscious with conscious contents. Is this to say that the unconscious is itself purposive? The answer to this question must await the full treatment of the treatise itself, but some preliminary remarks can be made. The unconscious has a momentum that parallels the conscious mind. It is certainly the repository of contents that were once conscious, as well as of contents that were never fully conscious. At the same time, it has an uncanny ability to shadow the deliberations of the conscious mind and to provide a determinate negation of the conscious attitude. This compensatory relation to consciousness works itself out in a variety of ways, from somatic symptoms to dream material that directly contradicts the reigning self-image. Does this compensatory relation exhibit a deeper teleology?

If teleology is defined in static terms, in which a purpose is some kind of pregiven structure that must unfold by its own inner momentum, then the unconscious cannot be seen as a purposive agent. If, however, purposes are seen in developmental terms, allowing for change in direction and force, then the unconscious *is* teleological. Any change in the conscious attitude will have an effect on the momentums of the unconscious, and vice versa. If the conscious stance of the self takes on a more inclusive self-image, then the unconscious will have less 'need' to provide a precise determinate negation for the partial attitude. The more inclusive attitude has, by definition, incorporated aspects of the unconscious compensatory attitude. The purpose of the unconscious is to give as much scope and density to the conscious attitude as possible. Does this mean that the unconscious serves as a kind of internal providence giving the self a specific life plan? Ecstatic naturalism remains skeptical of any providential view that denies or overlooks the sheer drift and waste of the self. Any so-called life plan is a cumulative product that can always change direction under internal and external pressures (cf. Buchler 1955).

Consider how a dream series works to tie conscious aspiration to unconscious prospects, thereby showing a form of teleology at work. In this example of such a series, the dream ego (dreamer) finds himself rushing toward a stage in which he is to appear in a leading Shakespearean role. He has on the proper Elizabethan costume, but does not know his lines. He awakes in a panic. Months later, the dreamer again finds himself rushing toward a similar stage but has at least learned a small portion of his lines. Again, he awakes in a panic. After many more months have passed the dreamer once again finds himself walking toward the stage but this time he is dressed as Dr. Samuel Johnson. The stage manager tells him that he already knows about two-thirds of his lines and that he can invent the rest. The actors indicate that they will easily follow the innovations. He awakes full of confidence in his on-stage abilities. What happened to the conscious attitude during this dream series? Was it literally about the craft of acting or did it point to something else? It is rarely the case that such dream material is to be taken literally. Upon sustained reflection it became clear that the dream material was about the power of language and its possibilities outside of the dreamer's normal provenance of writing. The conscious attitude adjusted itself to each stage in the evolution of the dream material, a process which was mirrored in the evolving dream material itself. That is, the successful initial interpretation of a dream enabled the unconscious to move forward with a more developed meaning so that the import of the dream could be more deeply assimilated by the self in process. The dream series stopped when the dreamer decided to enter into the world of play writing. When a dream series stops it is fair to assume that its fundamental message has been understood, and that its developmental teleological momentum has been fulfilled.

Of course, the unconscious does not exist as some kind of free-floating sphere. The sociology of knowledge has reminded us that cultural codes and powers position both the conscious and unconscious dimensions of the human process. The logic of this process is an uncanny one in that it erases its presence precisely when it is exerting its greatest force. This leaves the self in what might appear to be a helpless position. This primal helplessness, in which the self must assimilate and undergo an encoding process not of its own making, makes it difficult to move toward some sense of transcendence. Yet the sheer power of social positioning, a power that penetrates right down into the depths of the unconscious, does not exhaust the resources of the self, nor does it reduce transcendence to a momentary form of escape or denial.

The momentum of the lost object returns out of the future (in the form of the spirit) to show how transcendence can be attained within the constraints of nature and cultural encoding. Transcendence is never free floating, nor can it emerge without a profound shift in the directionality of the self. But the spirit-interpreter does obtain within the self and holds the self into a deeper betweenness structure in which selves can become translucent to each other.

The unconscious manifests its own forms of developmental teleology. This logic holds for the correlation between the unconscious and consciousness. Indeed, it is impossible to separate these two dimensions of interaction. Whatever the unconscious does 'internally' it also does in relation to consciousness. This is not to say that the unconscious is some kind of goal directed mind, but that it has a rhythm that always moves dialectically with and against consciousness. The spirit-interpreter occupies a position at the point of connection between the unconscious and consciousness. The spirit-interpreter is not a conscious mind either, but has an uncanny ability to respond to the momentums coming from both consciousness and the unconscious. In Peircean terms, the spirit-interpreter keeps the flow of interpretants (new and emerging signs) moving from the unconscious (which lives as a kind of dynamic object) to consciousness, which functions as a series of sign systems 'awaiting' new and powerful interpretants.

Again we are compelled to ask the inevitable question: just 'where' is the self in this complex triad of unconscious, consciousness, and the spirit-interpreter? The answer is obvious, even if it requires detailed elaboration. The self is stretched across all three dimensions or domains and emerges from their interaction. Yet we are accustomed to see the self as a conscious and centered ego that serves as a clearing house for everything that comes across its desk. This static and spatially restrictive view masks the more complex reality. The self is both the point of intersection—which is itself both ego and the spirit-interpreter—and the many semiotic powers and codes that enter into the point of intersection. At the same time, the self is also its accumulated products as they make their way in the world. These products can be quite fleeting, such as a sneeze, or enduring, such as an aesthetic contrivance that comes to occupy a place in social history.

Thus far we have seen that the self is a much vaster and more complex phenomenon than had been intimated in the substance tradition. Yet it is also less attenuated and less diffuse than the postmodern tradition now assumes. The correlation of the unconscious with consciousness manifests a cumulative and developmental directionality that points to a larger meaning contour that can be portrayed and rendered at least partially transparent. The crystallization of signification through the spirit-interpreter brings the self to a greater sense of its overall cumulative momentum, even if it does not provide it with a clear and distinct blueprint of its future prospects. Social codes groove and shape the self, often converting it into a mere economic or sexual commodity. Yet even here, there are possibilities of renewal that emerge from the open spaces protected and preserved by the spirit-interpreter.

The semiotic ontology of positioning (which includes the modes of depositioning and repositioning) replaces the substance-derived anthropologies that would map the contour of the self through a survey of its internal states. As noted, the distinction between internal states and external relations is a complex one that cannot be drawn with any final precision. So-called internal contents often have a complex external history before they find themselves housed within a given individual. No internal content can isolate itself from external affiliations and involvements. By the same token, the self has an uncanny ability to become permeable to all kinds of external signs and interpretants, often internalizing them with little thought or awareness. Consider the generalized anxiety produced by a period of economic instability. Small and large signs of the economic reality buffet the self and remind it of its precarious tenure in a world that seems to have little prospect of overall stability. How often are these signs consciously entertained? More often than not, they pass directly into the unconscious and take up their underground residence. Yet they continue to exert an influence on the self, filling semiotic life with a kind of restlessness and melancholy whose source is not always obvious. Insofar as these particular signs are unconscious, they can have an astonishing force in the future momentum of the self. Unconscious sign systems have their own inertial power to shape any incoming interpretants.

The correlation between the self and nature takes place ✓ through the mediating link of semiosis. It is impossible to redefine and reshape our understanding of the self unless we move past the wrong kind of semiotic theory, namely, a theory that confines signification to human language and thereby fails to find any link between signification and the prelinguistic and prehuman ✓ orders. Before illuminating the contour of the self, some preliminary semiotic reconstruction is in order.

Sign systems exist in a blinding variety of guises throughout nature. Human languages are very late evolutionary products and have features that are both continuous and discontinuous with other semiotic systems. Many semiotic frameworks privilege those features that are discontinuous, thereby betraying and ignoring the deeper structures of language that have their roots in a self-transforming nature. The more compelling metaphysical view is one that understands all of nature's orders to be semiotic through and through. From the simplest causal transaction in the inorganic order (Deely 1991) to the most complex conscious sign system, nature is both the world of signs and the seed bed for future signs. Nature in its naturing is the seed bed for all forms of signification, even though *nature naturing* is presemiotic and prepositional. *Nature natured* is best understood as the semiotic ✓ pluriverse in which innumerable sign systems compete for scarce semiotic resources. When human interpreters confront the prehuman orders, they enter into vast sign series that have their own inner logic and history. Idealistic systems make too much of the image of nature as a self-recording monistic system, yet do they point to the semiotic and presemiotic realities that lie outside of human forms of signification.

The human process is what it is because it shares in the various forms of world semiosis. The self quickens and transforms possibilities, actualities, and potencies that come out of nature and its innumerable orders of relevance. It does not follow, however, ✓ that nature is somehow a domain of panpsychist drops of protoconsciousness. The process reading of nature privileges the order-specific features of the human process and reads them backwards, via analogy, into the heart of nature. The most that we can say is that nature has as one of its manifestations the mysterious irruption of centers of awareness that move the structures of signification to a new level of complexity.

To say that the self is nature's self is another way of affirming the sheer embeddedness of the self in a sovereign nature that seems to be indifferent to what appears to us to be its most semiotically dense product. Nature may or may not 'care' about its offspring, but it does provide the conditions for an intensification of centers of signification within the world. As we will see, one primary way to understand the sign-using self is in terms of semiotic density and scope. The self transforms the semiotic processes that surround it and brings some translucency and clarity to the inner dynamics of world semiosis.

No sign occurs alone. Just as there can be no purely isolated or unrelated order, so there can be no purely unique sign. Each sign is what it is because of vast antecedent structures that locate and shape it. Peirce's ontological triad (Corrington 1993) of sign/object/interpretant points to the sheer scope and complexity of the world of signification. Signs link together with other signs, in turn generating interpretants that have their own inner dynamism and vector directionality. Immediate and dynamic objects link together in ways that are shadowed by semiotic structures. The unfolding of interpretants is guided by the hidden hand of the dynamic object that exerts a kind of inertial force on the possible and actual interpretants that 'surround' it. Any given sign will point to its object and to both antecedent and hoped-for signs within its pertinent sign series. By the same token, its object will be self-moving to new possibilities and actualities. Interpretants circle around a moving object and work dialectically to both honor and expand the object that lies 'underneath' or 'within' them.

The restlessness of signs, objects, and their interpretants comes from two sources. Within the world of orders there are innumerable forces and counterforces that impact on semiotic structures. Yet there are deeper and more elusive momentums that come from the domain of *nature naturing*. These momentums are not purposive or even cumulative in their directionality. They serve to position, reposition, and deposition the semiotic orders of the world. The human process has a unique permeability to these presemiotic rhythms and responds to them with either denial or ecstasy. Semiotic frameworks that focus exclusively on human forms of signification (read as arbitrary cultural codes) fail to recognize the twin sources of semiotic momentum; namely, the extra human orders of the world and the potencies of *nature naturing*. The shift to a conception of world semiosis makes it possible to see how all orders belong to the momentums of other orders and to the potencies that reach down into the unconscious of nature.

INTRODUCTION 13

By now it should be clear that there is a direct connection between the unconscious of the human process and the unconscious of nature. The depth dimension of nature spawns signs, many of which can be consciously assimilated and appraised. Yet it is itself presemiotic and bereft of consciousness. The human process has an understandable need to see the universe in human terms, but this tendency must be challenged when the focus is on the depth momentum of nature. This follows from the commensurate logic pertinent to our dealings with the human unconscious. We have a tendency to domesticate the unconscious so that it is less frightening to consciousness and its goals. The otherness of the unconscious is a haunting presence that our normal semiotic systems and frameworks attempt to deny. Ecstatic naturalism affirms the otherness of both the human unconscious and the unconscious of nature. It does not follow from this that we can not gain access to some of the features of the unconscious, but that we must understand that these features will often appear in an uncanny and unfamiliar guise.

Again, the link between consciousness and the unconscious is through signs. However, there is a breakdown in the human/nature analogy. The human process has a form of consciousness that is not shared by nature itself. That is, nature is not some kind of consciousness of all consciousnesses. Nature is best understood to be an unconscious momentum that spawns finite and fragmented centers of consciousness. The key to the consciousness of nature will not be found until the divine natures are explored semiotically. This exploration will reveal a sense in which nature can become conscious of itself, but not in the sense denied above. Ecstatic naturalism insists that nature is indeed dark and taciturn, even though it hungers for an incarnation of power and meaning within certain semiotic orders. The spirit-interpreter operative in human communities is that dimension of nature that moves toward the translucency of semiosis, but the spirit itself (that is, the spirit that exists both outside *and* within human communities) is not a centered consciousness analogous to the human process. The spirit is in and of nature and becomes the spirit-interpreter whenever it becomes strongly and weakly relevant to human communities.

Put in metaphorical terms, nature's self is the place where the unconscious of nature becomes transfigured through a finite conscious center that can turn back toward the hidden conditions of its origin and find traces of its spawning source. Does nature 'use' the self in order to become translucent to itself? This highly romantic conception of the nature/self dialectic says far too much about the alleged purposes of nature, but does point to a phenomenological connection between finite centers of signification and their underlying principles and powers. The depth dimension of the human process is the depth dimension of nature, even though the continual denial of the lost object blocks the path of true insight.

There is an implicit link between the psychoanalytic concept of the lost object and Peirce's concept of the dynamic object. For Peirce, the dynamic object works 'behind' the various changing immediate objects to insure that there will be an ultimate convergence in the infinite long run—namely, that the last immediate object in the series (which contains all of the previous immediate objects) will converge with the consummated dynamic object and allow the object to be fully known. The focus on knowledge gives way to an analysis of participation when the concern is with showing how the lost object (the maternal) is deeply relevant to the human process. The self participates directly and indirectly in the lost object and thereby moves through a variety of states in which these degrees of participation have their own intrinsic effects.

The temporality of the self/lost object correlation is a complex one. There is a clear sense in which the lost object is both in and out of time. It is in time insofar as it has a concrete embodiment in the life history of the individual. The person has a direct participatory image of the lost object in a person from his or her past. This person need not be a biological mother of course, as male figures can take on the pre-Oedipal role of the lost object. In either case, the biological structures function to point to the cosmic structures of origin that cannot be confined to parents and/or their proxies. This insight has been missed by the post-Freudian tradition but has long been acknowledged in the Jungian tradition, where all personal images receive their own depth momentum from the originating powers of nature.

This dual layering in the lost object—that it is both a biological self and a prepersonal potency in nature—illuminates its complex temporal structure. The link to the biological self is a fully temporal link that is rooted in the past but lives in all three modes of temporality. The depth dimension of the biological, concresced (and partially veiled) by the 'parental,' opens to a pretemporal rhythm that is only indirectly related to the orders of time. The lost object comes to the self in both modes, temporal and pretemporal. Needless to say, the self is often deeply confused about this temporal layering and consequently places too much value on the more available biological structures. This in turn burdens the parental with a metaphysical hunger that cannot be assuaged by any intra-familial means.

Here we see where the basic subterfuge of life begins. In the struggle within and against the biological maternal, the self must struggle toward a successful substitute formulation in which the potencies of the maternal are transfigured into attained semiotic material that has only a tangential relational to the material conditions of origin. Of course, the concept "material" should not be taken too literally, but in the broader sense that includes all antecedent support conditions, whether constituted by so-called 'matter' or not. The human process thus enters into the ongoing wound that cannot be healed by a mere increase in semiotic activity.

The ontological wound of the self emerges with the first efforts at autonomy, efforts that are 'aided' by the self-fissuring of the ontological difference. The self is propelled toward autonomy by the sheer momentum of *nature naturing*, which is always self-othering. Any 'product' of *nature naturing* will be cast out into the wilderness of *nature natured*, where it must make its way among the other orders of the world. Psychoanalytic perspectives place too much emphasis on the act of matricide in which the child must produce a narcissistic tear between itself and the maternal. While this view is not strictly incorrect, it ignores the far deeper momentum of nature that drives all orders toward individuation. The self has no choice but to enter into the eternal rhythms of the ontological difference.

The ontological wound remains a permanent part of the self. Our semiotic activities can be seen to constitute a variety of mechanisms and strategies for closing over the wound that comes from nature itself. If we tie this wound too directly to the pre-Oedipal maternal biological situation, then we fail to recognize that all attempts at healing are doomed that merely point the self back to the immediacies of personal origin. The wound can only be healed (partially at best) through the prepersonal dimension of the maternal that comes to the self from the heart of the ontological difference. The unique pretemporality of this prepersonal overcomes the obsession with the personal.

The prepersonal maternal has another temporal dimension. In one dimension it is prior to the chronological split into past, present, and future. Yet in a deeper sense it enters into a posttemporal momentum that comes to the self from out of a transfigured future. The religious tradition refers to this unique temporality through the concept of the *kairos*. The time of the *kairos* is the fulfilled time of the future in which the potencies of nature are gathered together into a healing concrescence. The time of the *kairos* enters into chronological time (*chronos*) and opens it to its depths. It is in this unique form of time that we see the return of the maternal on the edges of chronological unfolding. Yet the maternal is not confined to time (in the mode of the posttemporal *kairos*). Space too is transformed under the impress of the maternal. The sacramental dimension of space is made manifest wherever the maternal returns on the edges of homogenized and quantified space.

The dialectic of participation is thus a complex one. The self participates in the personal and biological maternal in terms of chronological temporality and geometric spatiality. Yet this very form of participation represents a flight away from the deeper pre- and posttemporal dimensions of the maternal. Parallel to this is the flight away from the pre- and postspatial aspects of the maternal presence/absence. Is there a way past this tragic oscillation between two dimensions that seem to be forever antagonistic to each other? The answer comes from the maternal in its transfigured guise as the spirit. Whenever the maternal moves past the purely personal and biological it can flower into the rhythmic presence of the spirit as that spirit enters into personal and communal life. But this transformation is not a denial of the biological, nor a flight from the female and gendered aspects of origin. Rather, it is part of the depth logic of the personal that it illuminates the sources and potencies that give it power and meaning within the biological orders.

What then happens to our sign systems? Are they merely left on their own as artificial constructs designed to mask (and flee from) the maternal powers of origin? Some perspectives take this negative view on cultural forms of signification, relegating them to the paternal realm of arbitrary codes and processes. Ecstatic naturalism takes a very different approach in which the pertinent insights of psychoanalysis are chastened by a pragmaticist understanding of the inner logic and dynamic efficacy of sign systems within *all* forms of interaction, be they organic or inorganic. Even if our sign systems do represent a flight from the haunting presence/absence of the abjected maternal, they also represent a healthy manifestation of the forces of signification necessary in the domains of *nature natured*.

Sign systems point back to their hidden origin in the lost object and toward future interpretants that surround them as mobile possible worlds. In a metaphoric sense, signs evidence a melancholy for the unconscious potencies of nature and have a deep restlessness that stems from this lack. On the other side, signs have an equally deep need to intersect with other signs as if to deny the cleft of the ontological difference that continually opens up beneath them. Semiotic intersection has its own logic and moves any given sign into vast relational networks that give it an enhanced meaning and power within the domains of signification. Of course, a given sign may also experience a spoliation of its position and be forced out of a relational network. Semiotic death is as real and ubiquitous as semiotic renewal.

The innumerable orders of *nature natured* are constituted by attained signs and potential or virtual signs. These signs have their own validation structures, regardless of their relation to the lost object. Psychoanalytic perspectives rarely overcome the temptation to confine signs to internal imaginative acts of the self. Consequently, they actually pry the self loose from nature and isolate it even further from the sources of meaning and power. As soon as it is recognized that all signs are in and of a self-transfiguring nature, it follows that nature's self enters into these prepersonal semiotic systems and derives its own measure from world semiosis.

The current perspective thus honors the post-Freudian disclosure of the lost object, while also insisting that the true lost object is found in the heart of nature and in the ontological difference. Of equal importance is the sense that semiotic systems have causal and biological orders of validation that have little if anything to do with the internal needs of the human process. Signs intersect with other signs because the semiotic conditions are right, not because some mind or proto-mind wishes to impose its own order of meaning onto an allegedly blank canvas. There are no blank canvases within the orders of *nature natured*, even if *nature naturing* remains semiotically blank and radically open to subsequent semiotic scene painting. The potencies of nature make paintable canvases possible in the first place, although they do not do the 'painting' themselves. Their effect can be felt less directly in what is painted by sign systems and interpretants.

Sign systems thus intersect, grow, and die throughout nature. When signs become relevant to the human process they enter into horizons of meaning. The concept of "horizon" is a rich one in the phenomenological and hermeneutic traditions, but it often assumes a role that gives it an isolated status within the world. Horizons wax and wane because of the bodily structures of selves. When the body is ill, the horizon is affected. In some orders it may contract, while in others it may expand in unexpected ways. When the body is healthy (not an unambiguous notion) the horizon may expand in the very areas that were denied to the sick body, while it may be withdrawn from those areas that were pertinent to its earlier state. One of the best literary statements of this process is Thomas Mann's *The Magic Mountain* (1924) in which semiotic systems are directly correlated to the internal path of disease within the bodies of the patients of the sanatorium.

Human horizons are vastly more complex than prehorizonal sign systems. Not only will a horizon 'contain' the semiotic richness of the prehuman orders, it will also send streams of illuminative regard into the heart of sign systems, opening them to their own transfiguring or demonic depths. On the highest level of sophistication, hermeneutic strategies have been developed to move from suspicion to restoration, and everything in between, so that the inertial charge of sign systems can be unfolded in an endless variety of ways. While this process is often confined to the so-called cultural semiotic orders, it can enter into prehuman orders and reek havoc on delicate or attenuated biological semiotic systems that do not have the power to withstand the searing gaze of a human horizon. This is especially ironic where the hermeneutics of suspicion, developed to be a tool of liberation, distorts and wounds a semiotic system that might otherwise have continued to flourish.

Horizons have their own forms of fragility. Not only is a meaning horizon 'forced' to house incompatible sign systems, it must also intersect with alien and often hostile horizons that wish to annihilate it. The concept or metaphor of "horizon" should not be taken in a purely visual or spectatorial sense. A horizon is also a locus of power and force that must secure a semiotic domain against hostile internal and external forces. If hermeneutic traditions often eulogize horizons, as centers of illumination and insight, ecstatic naturalism insists that they are also fitful and often demonic structures of privilege and rage. Horizons 'contain' everything from aesthetic harmonies to genocidal impulses. The curative powers within a horizon are often numbed or dwarfed by forces that may never be overcome or transfigured by the self that must occupy it. All horizons are to some extent broken by the powers that work against the spirit-interpreter. Horizonal intersection may produce an increase in meaning and expand the scope of agape/eros. Yet it may also bring about the total collapse of a horizon and its 'occupant.'

We must be clear that the movement between and among horizons is not always a conscious or even an exclusively human process. Sign systems have lives of their own and can enter into all kinds of alliances outside of the needs and desires of selves. This may seem like a hopelessly anthropomorphic way of speaking. Yet this formulation merely acknowledges the ways in which signs come together through a congruity of some of their interpretants. These conjunctions are not intentional or conscious, but they are efficacious and have effects that continually impinge on human horizons. A clear example of this effective conjunction can be seen in the intersection of material in the unconscious (insofar as the unconscious lies outside of the horizon of meaning). Unknown to the conscious self, there is a recurring linkage of unconscious contents (Jung's "feeling toned complexes") that continue to intrude into the horizon through indirect somatic and ideational means.

Nature's self thus belongs to sign series not of its own making. At the same time it lives out of the eternal rhythms of the ontological difference. On one level this primal difference is manifest in the great divide between *nature naturing* and *nature natured*. This self-fissuring within nature propels orders outward into the realms of signification. Nature's self emerges into its position insofar as it rejects (yet longs for) the hidden potencies of a self-othering nature. On another level, the ontological difference is manifest in the tensions between the unconscious and consciousness. From the standpoint of the self, the unconscious is as alien as the heart of nature. Through the unconscious, which at its depth is transpersonal, the human process gains access to the elusive potencies of *nature naturing*. The self is wounded by the ontological difference and struggles to find the interstices within the attained realm of signs that open to the unconscious of nature itself.

Sign systems surround and permeate the self. They have a hunger to become incarnate in embodied media of transmission. At the same time, these sign systems also hunger for the lost object that lies beyond the reach of the 'sum' of all interpretants. The logic of sign linkage can be disclosed with or without reference to the elusive presence/absence of the lost object. Peirce detailed the many forms of semiosis without any explicit acknowledgement of the powers of origin. Yet he partially opened the door to this deeper insight with his concepts of "ground" and "spirit." Ecstatic naturalism clarifies the unsaid lying at the heart of Peirce's semiotic theory and allows this unsaid to turn backward toward signs and transform them from within. Had Peirce gone further down this road, his semiotic theory would have looked much different, precisely insofar as it opened up betweenness structures.

Signs have their own intrinsic vector directionality. The self is buffeted by these vector forces and must often bend to their momentum. Any talk of a sphere of free "interpretive musement" is premature if it ignores the scope, power, and ferocity of sign systems. The realm of free musement is often won at great cost and represents a momentary escape from the semiotic forces that invade the self. The success of musement, when it does occur, is made possible by the spirit-interpreter that protects the self from premature semiotic closure. Where do we see the marks of the spirit within interpretive life? The answer has been indicated in several ways in the preceding analysis. The spirit emerges in the betweenness structures and spaces that represent the clearings within which signs function. The spirit is not a body of interpretants of attained meanings so much as it is a momentum of opening in which signs can become translucent to each other. If Peirce's concept of "ground" points to the "respects" in which signs signify, the concept of "spirit" points to the grace-filled enabling conditions that appear in the interstices of signification. The spirit does not provide an extra-natural world of signification (whatever that would be) but opens intraworldly semiosis to transfiguring possibilities.

Nature's self is quickened by the spirit that appears in the innumerable betweenness structures of world semiosis. Semiotic theories act as if communication were little more than the process of decoding an encoded transmission along predictable lines. What is continually being ignored is the sense of mystery that lies within all sign systems. The irruption of meaning is itself a mystery, more basic than the mystery of the particular meanings that occur within signification. The spirit operates much like Peirce's infinitesimals which give birth to marked and located units within the world. As we will see, the correlation of the spirit with a transformed conception of the infinitesimals is a crucial aspect of the ecstatic naturalist perspective. Initially, the infinitesimal can be defined as a quantity/reality that is infinitely small yet greater than zero. The transition from *nature naturing* to *nature natured* is made possible by the mysterious self-unfolding of the infinitesimals. The self is as much a gift of the infinitesimals as is any other order within the world. What makes the self distinctive is its ability to probe into the mysteries of the infinitesimals and their relation to the rhythms of the spirit.

In what follows, we will look at nature's self from a variety of perspectives. These approaches are not incompatible, even if they often seem to move at cross purposes. The contour of the self can only emerge from the cumulative phenomenological description of these orders of relevance and relation. The mystery at the heart of the self can never be exhausted. Yet we can gain clarity into the 'how' of the self by examining its products, its sign systems (both 'internal' and 'external'), its unconscious momentums (which point to the lost object), and its innumerable communal involvements. The self is more than the 'sum' of its signs, and richer than the 'sum' of its involvements. As a gift of the ontological difference and the opening power of the infinitesimals, the self is the locus for the most intense semiotic transformations within the pre-divine orders of world semiosis. In describing and evoking this self, with all of its transformations (both demonic and salvific), we also honor the mystery of nature, a mystery that reminds us of the utter ubiquity of that which cannot be captured by any semiotic theory.

Chapter One
Finitude and Embodiment

The perennial curse of the self is to see itself as much larger than it can ever be. From the standpoint of nature, the self is but one curious and fragmented product that crosses the stage of life for a brief moment and then moves on to another vastly different stage. During its brief time among the other manifest orders of the world, the self struggles to stabilize its contour and to magnify the importance of its products. Yet most of these products are merely random ejects from the self's cumulative momentum and they often have little extra-personal significance. The self that would like to write itself large across the face of nature is actually an inscribed and finite product of a world that seems to have little interest in human prospects.

Naturalist perspectives, whatever their metaphysical failings, have been unrelenting in reminding the self of the conditions of finitude and the limitations that come from sheer embodiment. The finitude of the self is not some kind of separate quality or layer of the self so much as a dimension or aspect of all forms of interaction. The finite dimension of the self is not a 'negative' dimension, in contrast to the 'positive' dimensions of transcendence. The concepts of negativity and positivity can only operate *within* each primal dimension and only in specific respects. Certain aspects of finitude may be negative while others may be positive. We must avoid giving a premature moral cast to either inevitable dimension of the human process. Transcendence in not more real or more positive for the self, even if it does transfigure many aspects of finitude.

In saying that the self is much smaller than it thinks it is, we are not saying that it is bereft of possibilities or that it has no transfiguring relation to the spirit. It is to say that the self is bound by conditions of origin and resistance that shape it through time, space, and its products. These conditions of origin provide vectors and momentums that tie the self to antecedent states, even while goading it beyond them. Resistances surround and permeate the self acting as a kind of semiotic friction. While the universe 'contains' an infinite number of signs and sign systems, only some will be pertinent to a given self at a given time. If the self tries to leap out of these conditions of semiosis, it risks a psychic inflation and consequent collapse of meaning that can spell closure and decay.

The human process is thus located in vast powers of origin that both empower and limit it. Both sides must be fully described. The powers of origin empower the self by giving it its unique location and place within the world. On the other hand, the powers of origin also, and at the same time, limit the reach and scope of the self to particular forms of embodiment. Race, class, and gender structures represent fairly clear powers of origin as they operate in both modes. To be gendered is to be 'granted' some possibilities and actualities, while being denied others. Philosophy and theology have often ignored the gender aspects of finitude because of a deeper fear of the powers of origin. When this fear is translated from ontological to psychoanalytic terms, it becomes clear why the ontological aspects of our gendered finitude have been effaced. The root of this fear is in the maternal presence that threatens to swallow autonomy. The history of patriarchy is also, and perhaps more fundamentally, a history of the flight from finite conditions of embodiment, due to this fear of the maternal.

The concept of embodiment also needs to be approached with some care. It is an exceedingly broad category and should not be restricted to one of its form—say, that of matter or materiality. Whatever matter is, it does not exhaust the depths of embodiment, nor does it represent some kind of paradigm toward which all other forms are moving. To be embodied, in the broadest sense, is to be the locus for traits (some of which will be semiotic—or at least virtually semiotic) and to make these traits available for semiotic interaction. The concepts of finitude and embodiment are not strictly equivalent, although they are commensurate, by which is meant that they have strong similarities, resemblances and overlaps occuring between them. In certain orders of description, the concept of finitude is more pertinent, while in other orders, the concept of embodiment is more appropriate for framing the relevant complexes.

The concept of positioning has become increasingly helpful for semiotic anthropology and will function in much of what follows as a primary concept of finitude. Within the genus of positioning are the species of depositioning (made prominent by post-Freudian perspectives) and repositioning (made prominent by pragmaticist perspectives). In probing into the features of finitude and embodiment, the various species of positioning must be delineated and described. Often, perspectives privilege one of the species of positioning as if to illuminate the phenomenon as a whole. This temptation, which comes from a felt sense of moral urgency, must be resisted in a generic level analysis of the human process, in which each form of positioning must be examined in its pertinent order of relevance. Perspectives that privilege depositioning (in the form of the avant-garde) wish to free the self from the strictures of patriarchal codes. While this is certainly an appropriate move, it is not the only, or always most liberating, mode of positioning. Each species of positioning has its role to play in sustaining and transforming the contour of the human process.

A. Positioning and Origins

We must examine the genus in some detail before working through the species variations. This order of procedure might jar on a sensibility used to piecemeal analyses of forms of difference, yet it has its own inner logic and warrant. Categories of greater scope can illuminate categories of lesser scope, especially in the sense that they can provide a clearing within which subaltern structures may appear. This is not to say that the generic analysis takes place in a vacuum, or that it fails to feel the pressure of the subaltern configurations, but that it moves by a different inner logic. In the case of positioning and its forms, there is also a temporal priority for positioning that will emerge from the analysis. The first stage of the human process, reaching back into the heart of the pre-Oedipal drama, is one of initial positioning. The original position marks the self throughout its later transformations of depositioning and repositioning. Thus positioning is prior to its subalterns in two primal senses—namely, that of scope and that of temporal priority.

Often it is necessary to move in the other direction, from more specific orders of relevance to more generic orders. Semiotic ontology needs the flexibility to proceed in either direction as dictated by the matter itself. The contemporary hostility toward the generic clothes itself in the comforting words of moral sensitivity and outrage against the imposition of identity. Yet there lurks a deeper theoretical impoverishment behind the scenes that fails to manifest itself. The move toward the generic is no more imperial than the obsession with innumerable forms of difference (which often actually manifest a deeper narcissistic core). Both the generic and the subaltern can be misused. By the same token, either can be used with care and for the goal of eventual liberation. A perspective that forcefully denies the generic will inevitably contain demonic seeds. The generic will be present (as must be the case for any sign-using organism) but will take on a hidden and destructive logic that will emerge in an unacknowledged way. The choice is never between the generic or the liberating, as if such a simplistic dyad makes sense within the sign systems that surround and permeate us. Rather, the choice is between the emancipatory and the restrictive. Emancipatory structures are both generic and local, but in different respects. The deeper categories here are the demonic and the emancipatory, not the generic and the particular. After all, some differences are destructive, while some generic structures are transformative.

On a deeper level, this rage against the generic manifests a profound confusion about the nature of semiotic life and the role of signs in giving shape to present immediacies. If the generic is understood in terms of principles of connectedness and transformation, then it can serve to enhance our understanding of particularities. If the generic is understood in terms of power and premature identification (as manifestations of semiotic colonialism), then it will be a demonic structure. The test for any generic category is always: How is the particular clarified, both internally and in terms of its innumerable connections and non-connections? In the end, the relation between the generic and its subalterns is a dialectical one. Any given phenomenological description may choose to start with either pole, although one pole will often present itself with a special urgency in a given context.

Our procedure in this case will be to start with the most general and temporally prior forms of positioning, in order to prepare the ground for a delineation of the various forms of depositioning and repositioning. Of course, these later phenomenological descriptions already make themselves felt in the initial descriptions of positioning. In any dialectical structure, the consequent elements are already contained in a muted form in the antecedent structures. Hegel saw this more clearly than anyone before him, even if he erred in overstressing the nature and scope of intelligibility within the internal rhythms of this dialectic.

All objects, signs, and interpretants emerge from antecedent conditions (Corrington 1994). The self cannot be an exception, insofar and especially in that it is constituted by all three elements of this ontological triad. The self is certainly an object in that it has dynamic and immediate aspects that govern semiosis. The term "object" should not be confined to the spatial connotations associated with it. Like the term "phenomenon" in the phenomenological tradition, the term "object" functions in the pragmaticist tradition to cover all modes and forms of the world insofar as they function underneath the manifest signs of interaction.

By the same token, the self is a sign, or better, locus of innumerable sign series. This is not to say, as some semiotic perspectives do, that the self is nothing more than its signs, but that the semiotic dimensions of the self are among the most pervasive and important for self-identity across time and place. Most of these self-signs become or are interpretants insofar as any sign interpreted becomes an interpretant; namely, a new sign that serves to augment or diminish the antecedent sign from which it has come.

Depending on the needs of the analysis, we can see the self as either object, sign series, or interpretant series. Of course, a complete analysis (insofar as such a notion makes sense) will honor and describe all three dimensions of the self. Yet even this pluriform analysis must also acknowledge that the heart of the self contains a presemiotic mystery that can never be exhausted, let alone violated and 'penetrated,' by a full semiotic probe. Consequently, an analysis of positioning must find a place for the ontological triad of sign/object/interpretant, while listening to the depth rhythms of *nature naturing* and the mysteries of the presemiotic potencies.

The self, then, is what it is because of a prior positioning that brings it into the location of other selves and their signs. Heidegger speaks of a kind of primal "thrownness" (*Geworfenheit*) that casts the self out into the world of involvements (Heidegger 1927). Naturalists, like Justus Buchler, speak instead of a kind of "natural debt" that haunts and shapes the self once it enters into the world of other complexes (Buchler 1955). In either case, what is being acknowledged is that the self comes into the world with a powerful relation to antecedent structures and powers that cannot be fully integrated into the living configuration. Insofar as the self is "thrown" into the world of involvements, it has a dynamic and melancholy relation to the conditions of origin that compels it to seek for some kind of transfiguring center that in turn brings it momentary stillness (*Gelassenheit*). Insofar as the self is born in "debt," it will struggle to cancel its dimly felt indebtedness through a variety of barely understood semiotic subterfuges. Whatever the self's prospects, it remains bound by the hidden, yet always operative, conditions of origin that deeply mark it through its subsequent trajectory.

The self is a new object in the world that has been ejected from the prepositioned potencies of *nature naturing*. The elusive and elliptical rhythms of nature are self-othering. The telos of nature is to produce *a* world. We cannot know whether *this* world is directly intended or not (contra Leibniz), but we can know that nature spawns the world out of the recesses of the potencies that are not yet orders of relevance or positioned complexes *within* the world. Put differently, the potencies are what they are by becoming other to themselves. The inner logic of any potency is to become a semiotic order of relevance among the other orders of the world. Yet the shock of the ontological difference remains. We can never fully enter into the deepest logic of nature and come to understand why there are potencies that are self-othering.

At this stage of the analysis, we must confront the *ground* of positioning, even if we have to remain silent about the ultimate whence of the potencies. In confronting this ground we see how the self becomes marked by its basic ontological wound. Heidegger's metaphor of thrownness and Buchler's image of natural debt are replaced by the metaphor of the ontological wound. This wound is the clearest mark we have of the continual presence of the powers of origin that bring the self into its original position. The wound points in two directions. On one side, it points to the stage of integral wholeness before the cut of the ontological difference. On the other side, it points to the fissure of the self as it leaves the realm of "dreaming innocence" (Tillich 1951) for the realm of the world's codes and signs.

The ontological wound emerges when the self is ejected from the maternal ground of the potencies and finds itself amid the signs of public semiosis. Put in other terms, the self moves from the prepositioned rhythms of nature's unconscious toward the positioned orders of the manifest world of *nature natured*. Of course, the self is not conscious of this transition (as it takes place at birth, if not before). The formation of the self in the physical maternal womb is analogous to the momentums of nature in which potencies give birth to orders. The potencies, operating in this case in the physical maternal body, position the materials of the self into a contour that will be compelled to find its finite place among all of the competing orders that surround it. This transition from potencies to orders runs through the self like a grand fissure that appears with more and more clarity as the self matures.

The initial spatial and temporal location of the infant, both before and after the birth process, opens up the cleft between *nature naturing* and *nature natured*. As the self matures, the physical mother assumes the deeply ambiguous role of the ontological difference itself. The mother (who, as noted, can be 'played' by a physical male) becomes the locus for the self-fissuring of nature insofar as she is the origin of the self, *and* the momentum that propels the self outward into the postmaternal orders of semiosis. The birthing process, manifest throughout the organic orders of the world, is perhaps the most dramatic manifestation of the sheer self-othering force of the ontological difference and the prepositioned potencies. In terms of the logic of the analogy between the physical maternal and *natura naturans*, the womb (*chora*) is prepositional rather than a positioned space. Of course, in other respects, such as the social or political, the womb is deeply positioned by sexual codes and powers that may distort or damage the location of the womb in the overall economy of life (Foucault 1975).

There is a tension between the purposive aspects of positioning and the prepurposive (Oliver 1993). The purposive dimension is manifest in the movement of the infant away from the maternal through an eventual affirmation of public semiotic codes. This is the dimension denoted by the concept of matricide. Yet there is a deeper, prepurposive dimension of this momentum that comes from the self-othering power of the maternal. This itself has two subaltern dimensions. The depth dimension is the self-othering of nature as it moves outward from the potencies toward the attained orders of signification. The other dimension is the self-othering of the maternal as its own bodily states propel the child toward the mirror and Oedipal stages. As we will see, the mirror stage involves the discovery of a full self-image as seen in a literal or figurative mirror. Out of this triadic momentum emerges the embodied and sign-using self.

The movement toward the original position of the semiotic self thus has roots that reach down into the heart of the ontological difference. The infant is thrown into the world of involvements and is positioned on both sides of the presemiotic and semiotic. The ontological wound is latent but still present in the earliest stages of life. It is actualized when the infant moves further and further away from the immediacies of the maternal and struggles with the soaring codes of the public order. The transformation of the self is made possible by the internal and external rhythms that open out the ontological wound. Without this wound there could be neither consciousness nor social positioning.

Ambivalence about the prepositional womb of nature remains a perennial part of the human process. Nature's self flees from the conditions of origin by a momentum that is as old as phylogenetic history and drives outward into innumerable interpretants that promise to free it from the haunting presence of the lost maternal. Of course, the frenzy of public semiosis, which ignores the betweenness structures of signification in favor of semiotic plenitude, points to the constant presence/absence of the ontological wound. As noted, the temporality of origin is a complex one. Insofar as the lost object lies in the past it points to a kind of dreaming innocence that lures the self back toward the preconscious (a manifestation of the death drive). Yet the deeper logic of this temporality points to the domain of the not yet in which the lost object returns from out of a transfigured future to bring the self back into the heart of the self-fissuring of the ontological difference. It is as if each interpretant had a penumbra of meaning that casts an indirect light forward/backward toward the lost maternal. Public semiotic codes contain the maternal in a cryptic but discoverable way.

The temporality of the original position remains with the self throughout its trajectory. Chronological time becomes manifest after the mirror stage in which the self finds itself as an isolated totality over and against a world from which the maternal has apparently fled. The sovereignty of linear *chronos* gives way before a dynamic temporality that opens the self to a past and future as both in turn enhance the mobile present. Yet even the existential temporal structures open to deeper momentums. The power of the past returns in the not yet, which lives on the edges of all interpretants. The lost object appears on the edges of both chronological and temporal time. The lost object is pretemporal in that it spawns time for the human process, just as the potencies of nature spawn time for the prehuman orders of the world. Yet the lost object is posttemporal insofar as it lives on the other side of all positioned forms of time.

The same logic holds for space. The newly positioned self (prior to the mirror stage) lives within a rhythmic spatiality that does not yet splinter the object pole into here and there. At this stage space is little more than the possibility for spatial difference. It is the mobile and rhythmic matrix from which positioned orders emerge. We could almost speak of the prespatial here. From this prespatial potential space (Kant's manifold?) comes the manifest and bifurcated domain of positioned orders. The mirror stage represents that cusp or moment of transition/transgression in which the dreaming innocence of the prespatial gives way before the unrelenting power of differentiation. Thus we have the tension between the prespatial and the spatial. Is there a sense in which, by analogy with time, we can speak of a postspatial? This concept makes sense when the material aspect of the maternal/lost object is recognized. The postspatial aspect of space is manifest whenever configured and positioned space opens up to a nonlocating momentum on the other side of the fissures of spatial life. This momentum comes from the potencies of nature, which spawn both time *and* space as they are transfigured through the spirit.

Thus far we have delineating some of the basic ontological features of positioning. The potencies of nature, which 'use' the maternal for their own 'ends,' spawn the prespatial and the pretemporal, which are manifest to the human process in the form of dreaming innocence. This floating domain connects the infant to the maternal presence and makes all subsequent forms of positioning possible. This domain becomes fractured through the mirror stage in which the nascent self is compelled to recognize its finite and located status within the semiotic codes and orders of the world. The powers of chronological time and geometric space surround and position the self so that it becomes but one order among others. It is as this stage that the ontological wound moves from its latent to its manifest form. The self is cast out of the garden of dreaming innocence and feels the innumerable lures of the semiotic orders. The immersion in the maternal gives way before the blinding powers of interpretants. The ontological wound opens itself up like a poison flower that permeates all dimensions of the self.

Consciousness is a deeply ambiguous gift of the ontological difference. Is it a poisoned fruit of *nature naturing* or is it part of a deeper grace-filled momentum that remains veiled from us? The answer to this question can only come at the end of our investigations. At this stage it is at least clear that the directionality of the self is toward a renewed participation in the lost object on the other side of spatial and temporal structures of intelligibility.

The self is both a product and a producer. This, of course, is the case for many orders of the world. What makes the human process unique is that it carries within it profound and recurrent traces of its origin. Post-Freudian perspectives err when they confine the relation to origin to the repetition of the repressed. There *is* a sense in which the powers of origin are repressed and thus charged with a special dynamism on the edges of conscious forms of signification. But there is also a sense in which the powers of origin act 'on their own' to recede from view and to hand the self over to public codes and processes. Are the powers of origin merely waiting in the wings for a new appearance at the end of the play of life or are they present in a different way that can be both demonic and salvific at the same time? The latter possibility is the one that suggests itself to us insofar as we come to acknowledge the breaks and fissures within the robust semiotic codes that belong to the positioned self.

Some perspectives tend to emphasize the demonic aspects of the powers of origin, as if they represented mere opacity and a blind reiteration of the will to power. At the other extreme are those perspectives that eulogize all prepositioned momentums as if they could somehow free us from the encrustations of personal and social inertia. In carefully describing the recurrent presence/absence of origin it is imperative that we avoid either extreme. Origins are in some sense prior to the distinction between good and evil, a distinction that only makes sense within the context of communities of interpretation that can make judgments about manifest powers and meanings. The prepositional momentums of *nature naturing* are without internal or direct moral value. Hence the powers of origin, manifest to the human process in the lost object, are not yet moral. The moral dimensionality only fully emerges in the posttemporal and postspatial aspects of the return of the maternal on the edges of signification.

We noted in the introduction that the Peircean concept of the infinitesimal is actually directly pertinent to the concept of origin in semiotic anthropology. More importantly, Peirce, almost in spite of himself, moved toward the perspective of ecstatic naturalism (Corrington 1993) when he struggled to show how the infinitesimals move outward from a kind of zero state toward the manifest orders of the geometric spatio-temporal world. Our delineation of the structures of finitude and origin cannot proceed further without working through some of this complex material. In his Cambridge Conference Lectures of 1898, delivered under the rubric, "Reasoning and the Logic of Things," Peirce makes some daring connections that point right to the heart of the ontological difference (Peirce 1898: 162–163):

> The *zero* collection is bare, abstract, germinal possibility. The continuum is concrete, developed possibility. The whole universe of true and real possibilities forms a continuum, upon which the Universe of Actual Existence is, by virtue of the essential Secondness of Existence, a discontinuous mark—like a line figure drawn on the area of the blackboard. There is room in the world of possibility for any multitude of such universes of Existence. Even in this transitory life, the only value of all the arbitrary arrangements which mark actuality, whether they were introduced once for all "at the end of the sixth day of creation" or whether as I believe, they spring out on every hand and all the time, as the act of creation goes on, their only value is to be

shaped into a continuous delineation under the creative hand, and at any rate their only use for us is to hold us down to learning one lesson at a time, so that we may make the generalizations of intellect and the more important generalizations of sentiment which make the value of this world.

Peirce applies the concept of the continuum to all of the pre-positioned 'spaces' of the world, but there is a special pertinence in applying it to the powers of origin that animate the semiotic self. The continuum is not so much an actual positioned line or space as it is a potentiality waiting to manifest itself in the realm of "Existence." By "Existence" Peirce means the dyadic and fully positioned realm of finite particulars. This domain of secondness is the place where the infinitesimals have given birth to attained orders of relevance.

How does he connect the concept of the continuum to that of the infinitesimal? Both concepts point to the realm of possibility/potentiality. The infinitesimal is not so much an actual measured point on a line as it is a full "monad" that explodes into actual positioned points. It is as if the infinitesimal is a pregnant potency awaiting a birthing process in which its plenitude can move into the world of orders. The continuum is the prespatial 'space' of possibility that gives the infinitesimal a means for its manifestation. Peirce asks about the point at the end of a line. What is its ontological status? He states, "The end of a line might burst into any discrete multitude of points whatever, and they would all have been one point before the explosion" (Peirce 1898: 160). The momentum from the one to the many is the precise momentum of the ontological difference between *nature naturing* and *nature natured*.

The self-fissuring within the heart of nature's self can be looked at in several ways. Post-Freudian accounts stress the momentum of the pre-Oedipal maternal that both spawns and weans the self in a rhythm that is eternal and highly compulsive. Ecstatic naturalism stresses the movement from the potencies of *nature naturing* to the manifest orders of *nature natured*. Peircean pragmaticism stresses the transition from the infinitesimal to the innumerable points of the spatial order. The continuum of feeling links the infinitesimals together in both spatial and prespatial ways. It is important to note that these three formulations are all commensurate and that each in its own way points to the self-fissuring of the ontological difference. On a deeper level, ecstatic naturalism encompasses the post-Freudian and pragmaticist approaches and moves from one formulation to the other as the context requires.

Peirce advanced our understanding of the semiotic self by showing how the positioned self traffics in sign systems of great scope and power. He combines two arch images in his anthropology; namely, Shakespeare's metaphor of the "glassy essence" and his own simile of the "bottomless lake." Each image contributes something to his overall perspective, although the image of the bottomless lake proves to be the more valuable one. Before proceeding, some attention must be paid to these explicit formulations so that they can be tied back to his understanding of the infinitesimals.

For Peirce, the self is not so much a sovereign self-consciousness as it is a sign-using organism that must negotiate between and among a vast and evolving network of signs. The self is likened to a glassy essence through which the signs of the world pass as they move onward toward more and more generic spread. There is a passive dimension to Peirce's sense of the self. The self lets the plenitude of world semiosis pass through it as it watches the passing scene with detachment. The so-called 'ego' is at best a social construct and at worst, a fiction produced by the misuse of language. Our glassy essence allows us access to the full semiotic universe, but it keeps us from developing a will and from manifesting the higher orders of self-control.

As if to modify this ocular and passive perspective, Peirce developed the much richer image of the bottomless lake. The surface of the lake is the point of interaction where the wealth of the semiotic universe, manifest in sun and rain, can enter into the dark stillness of the lake itself. Beneath the active surface are innumerable life forms and structures of interaction. Peirce modifies associational theory to account for these vast underwater and unconscious associational patterns. He uses the concept of the "skeletal set" to illuminate the momentum of pattern formulation within the lake/self. Any material that comes into the lake from 'above' quickly sinks below the surface and links up with already attained semiotic series that shape the new material along the lines of habit. The newly arrived signs must bend to the forces that lie below the surface of consciousness.

Peirce was fully aware that the semiotic self 'contained' a kind of universal or collective unconscious that has its roots in the evolutionary past. He further insisted that this unconscious is highly active in forming vast gestalts that in turn shape all incoming semiotic material. The dynamic dimension of the self is rooted in its unconscious, since the conscious self is passive and lives through its unconscious perceptual judgments. The image of the glassy essence, while not incorrect, is limited to the surface of the lake (the fragile sphere of consciousness). The image of the bottomless lake, on the other hand, is capacious enough to include both cosmic and personal forms of semiosis and to show how sign systems actively shape and groove the self in time.

Where, then, do the concepts of the infinitesimals and of the continuum come into play? The connecting link lies in the transition from the glassy essence to the bottomless lake. As noted, the infinitesimal is more akin to a potential point than an actual space-time actuality. When it becomes actualized it explodes into the existents of space and gives birth to the many-fold spatial points that collectively constitute the manifest orders of the world. The continuum is the enabling condition that gives the infinitesimal a 'place' to explode. Is the collective unconscious (the depth of the lake) itself a continuum? Peirce would answer: yes, in a sense. It is a continuum in that it is the enabling condition for all subsequent manifest forms of semiosis. It is not yet a continuum in that it is not a conscious self. Peirce's panpsychism compelled him to tie the concept of the continuum too closely to that of consciousness. Had he let go of his panpsychism, he would have understood even more about the correlation between the collective unconscious and continuity.

What of the infinitesimals? The unconscious semiotic material is what it is whether it is manifest or not. In this sense, it is like a prepositioned infinitesimal that contains the possibilities for manifestation. An unconscious sign system may hunger to become manifest. Insofar as it achieves its 'aim' it moves from the domain of potentiality to that of actuality. Like the exploding infinitesimal (end point of a line), the unconscious sign material becomes self-othering and achieves its positioning within the conscious codes and experiences of the self. The ontological difference is thus manifest, as always, in more than one way. The difference between the conscious and unconscious parallels, but is not reducible to, the difference between the positioned sign systems and the infinitesimals that spawn sign systems.

The movement from the infinitesimal or the material maternal toward some kind of positioned code or product is always made possible by the presemiotic rhythms of *nature naturing*. To be in any respect is to be an eject from the infinitesimals, which are themselves the means by and through which the power of the maternal is manifest. Previous investigations have failed to correlate the concept of the point/position spawning infinitesimal with the rhythms of the pre-Oedipal maternal because of an unwillingness to probe into the deeper logic connecting pragmaticist with psychoanalytic perspectives. This failure has made it difficult to show just how origins relate to positions in the personal and social orders.

The infinitesimal and the maternal power speak in and through the ontological difference. They are self-othering origins in that they manifest an eternal restlessness that can only be fulfilled when the prepositional gives birth to positioned orders of relevance. The infinitesimal is like a Plotinian One, ready to emanate into innumerable created orders. However, unlike the neo-Platonic reading of emanation, ecstatic naturalism insists that the transition from the prespatial and pretemporal infinitesimal to the points and times of the world is more akin to an ejective explosion, a miniature apocalypse in which the birthing process repeats itself again and again with great force and power. Peirce shied away from a strict affirmation of the traditional conception of *creatio ex nihilo* precisely because he understood that creation is continually taking place in and through the infinitesimals, which may or may not have a collective integrity.

Thus the self-othering of nature, which works 'literally' through the infinitesimals and 'metaphorically' through the material maternal, positions whatever is in whatever way it is. Each positioned order contains traces of its hidden origin. In the human order, these traces are most clearly present in the melancholy longing that arches back toward the dimly sensed presemiotic potencies that refused to close in on themselves. If Emerson and Nietzsche want to see us as gods in ruin, we must probe more deeply into the spawning/weaning power of origin and come to the point where we see the self as a *foundling* cast into a world with no manifest whence or whither. The plenitude of the whither will become clarified only and when melancholy is transfigured into love.

The infant, then, is cast into the unwanted role of autonomous pilgrim. The original position that is attained in the pre-Oedipal stage sustains the self for a brief period so that it can gain some foothold in the universe of signs and codes. As the internal powers of the archetypes and the genetic codes (both fully semiotic) unfold, the self is gathered into another type of momentum that comes from the power of origin but that is also gathered up into the developmental purposes of all living systems. The self probes into the meaning and scope of its original position and begins to find some shifting outline that can separate its own internal drives from the external powers that continually threaten to undo it. Using semiotic terms, the self moves from the stage of the representamen (original sign) toward the stage of the interpretant in which the original sign takes on a wealth of new semiotic material. Beneath both the representamen and the interpretant is the dynamic object of the self that contains the hidden powers of the archetypes and manifests them in the gestalts that shape the internal and external interpretants.

The so-called "mirror stage" works to give the self its first real glimpse into the shock of semiotic autonomy. The fragmented stage of dreaming innocence gives way to a breach in which the self enters into the eternal fissures of the ontological difference. For the infant to see itself as what it is, namely, as a center of desire and momentum that is not connected to the maternal, is for it to be dramatically opened up to the ontological wound at its core. This shock is a revisiting of the original birth trauma but on a higher semiotic level. Absence becomes the entrance point into the world of signs.

The classic analysis of this breach is found in Freud's description of the *fort-da* game as played by his eighteen month old nephew. The German terms *fort* and *da* mean "gone" and "there" respectively and indicate how the child entered into the breach of the ontological difference through objects, and in turn, through the mirror image that enabled him to become the missing and returning object itself. The following is from Freud's 1920 "Beyond the Pleasure Principle" (Freud 1920: 599):

> This good little boy, however, had an occasional disturbing habit of taking any small objects he could get hold of and throwing them away from him into a corner, under the bed, and so on, so that hunting for his toys and picking them up was often quite a business. As he did this he gave vent to a loud, long-drawn-out "o-o-o-o-", accompanied by an expression of interest and satisfaction. His mother and the writer of the present account were agreed in thinking that this was not a mere interjection but represented the German word *"fort"*. I eventually realized that it was a game and that the only use he made of any of his toys was to play "gone" with them. One day I made an observation which confirmed my view. The child had a wooden reel with a piece of string tied around it. It never occurred to him to pull it along the floor behind him, for instance, and play at its being a carriage. What he did was to hold the reel by the string and very skillfully throw it over the edge of his curtained cot, so that it disappeared into it, at the same time uttering his expressive "o-o-o-o." He then pulled the reel out of the cot again by the string and hailed its reappearance with a joyful *"da."* This, then, was the complete

game—disappearance and return. As a rule one only witnessed its first act, which was repeated untiringly as a game in itself, though there is no doubt that the greater pleasure was attached to the second act.

The spool represents the cunning of the ontological difference. The child is tied to the spool by a line that represents the burgeoning power of signs (as strings of interpretants). The spool thus remains under the control of the self and is never fully in oblivion. Yet the child, operating through the power of the *nature naturing* must throw the spool into an abyss where it disappears and is gone. This loss is a shock and a delight (the first glimmerings of the emerging dialectic of melancholy and love). As the spool is reeled in and returned to the light of the *da* it is truly reborn. The loss of the spool is, of course, a physical and spatio-temporal substitution for the maternal/infinitesimal. The child struggles to retain control of this process by holding onto the string. This semiotic string comes to reside on both sides of the ontological difference.

The manifest string that is still within the child's field of vision is the realm of semiotic codes and interpretants. The hidden part of the string reaches into the presemiotic and insures that the lost object will return into view when bidden by the pull of the hand. The child plays this game into order to enter into the mysterious rhythms of the ontological difference. It still feels in control of this process. Soon this sense of control will take on a different and more demanding configuration when the body is substituted for the object. In a footnote appended to the above passage, Freud shows how the mirror takes over from the string (Freud 1920: 599):

> A further observation subsequently confirmed this interpretation fully. One day the child's mother had been away for several hours and on her return was met with the word "Baby o-o-o-o!" which was at first incomprehensible. It soon turned out, however, that during this long period of solitude the child had found a method of making *himself* disappear. He had discovered his reflection in a full-length mirror which did not quite reach to the ground, so that by crouching down he could make his mirror-image "gone."

The mirror is the clearing within which the ontological difference can become directly pertinent to the life of the child. The absent mother is represented by either the missing spool or the missing child. In each case, the child has the ability to move the maternal power from the present to the absent and back again. The transition from an object in space and time, as a substitute object, to the mirror is a dramatic one. When the child makes itself disappear it takes on the power of the ontological difference. It enters into the hidden dialectic between the originating pulses of the potencies, which spawn orders, and the mysteries of signification in which objects come and go within the world of signs. What does the child 'see' when it makes itself absent by crouching below the mirror? Does it see into the loss that must now overtake it with greater and greater force? Does the startling return of its own image in the mirror signal the return of the maternal in a transfigured way? Put differently, is there a deeper logic connecting the gaze of self in the mirror and the new self that will come to the adult from out of the power of the spirit? While Freud hesitated to probe into the last prospect, the Jungian tradition made this insight central to its reflections.

The entrance of the spirit, in the mode of the spirit-interpreter, must await the transition from positioning to depositioning and repositioning. Yet the spirit is present/absent in a latent way in the original position that resides in the pre-Oedipal connection between the infant and the material maternal. Implied in the above analysis is the sense that there is a developmental teleology guiding the self across and through the frontiers that mark its various stages of transformation. The infant must be weaned, both physically and ontologically. The inner rhythms of the maternal actually push the self into a reluctant autonomy. Behind and within this weaning process lies the spirit that will return in its plenitude on the other side of the movement into the original position. The mirror stage, which need not be taken in a literal fashion, marks the first crucial ontological break in the self (harking back to the birth trauma). The self-fissuring of nature appears obliquely in the break. Nestled within the momentums and shocks of the ontological difference is the spirit.

Freud's *fort-da* game, then, represents the struggle between the propulsion for autonomy, accepted yet resisted by the nascent self, and the longing for the lost object. At this stage, the lost object is still too close to become a dynamic center set over and against the sign-using self. Yet it has a fierce vector directionality that moves the self further away from maternal self-fissuring. As the physical string and the plane of the mirror recede, other structures take their place and insure that the sign-using organism has some chance of negotiating the complex rhythms of the ontological difference. As Jung understood with more clarity than Freud, the propulsion of the self away from the maternal has a teleological structure that points toward a transfiguration in the spirit. This prospect begins to emerge when the original pre-Oedipal position gives way to a seismic shifting of the semiotic terrain.

B. Depositioning and Loss

Mirrors crack and strings break. This harmless truism points to the heart of the ontological difference and its seemingly indifferent yet sovereign presence/absence within the life of the self. The developmental teleological structures of the individual move toward a momentum that can be denoted by the term "selving." The selving process is one that cannot be reduced to origins or to a repetition of antecedent/repressed conditions. The original position of the infant was made possible in a literal way by the maternal. Its ontological depth structures were secured by the self-fissuring of nature—a self-fissuring that enters fully into both the maternal and the child.

The disappearance and reappearance of the integral spatial-temporal self in the mirror opened the door to the power of selving, which 'takes over' as it were from the propulsive rhythms of the maternal. The self now enters into the universe of interpretants and learns to maneuver among vast semiotic chains that often show an astonishing indifference to the needs of the self. Selving quickens and deepens after the mirror stage and initiates the complex repression and denial of the maternal that makes some form of semiotic autonomy possible.

The original position thus gives way to a profound reversal, a depositioning in which ontological and personal values are inverted under the aegis of the ontological difference. Psychoanalytic perspectives often ignore the ontological and natural enabling conditions that make the movement from the presemiotic to full semiosis possible. At the other extreme, pragmaticist perspectives often downplay the inner drama of the self as if moves through the various breaches of positioning/depositioning. Peirce often argued as if the inner life was little more than an arena for cosmic and social forms of semiosis. He remained profoundly insensitive to his own struggles against the maternal and thus failed to illuminate the whence of semiosis (Corrington 1993: 21–24). This in turn weakened his understanding of the whither and the role of the final interpretant. As will emerge later, the return of the maternal in the spirit is correlated to the final interpretant, but in a way that Peirce only grasped through a glass darkly.

Depositioning is a recurrent process. The original position of the pre-mirror stage infant is now splintered into innumerable radii of involvement in which interpretants, both internal and external (a difficult distinction), take over the life of the self. Selving, struggling against the inertia of dreaming innocence, slowly and fitfully transforms the self so that it can become permeable to interpretants that are not directly correlated to the maternal. Theologically, this appears to the self as the movement from grace to wrath in which the acceptance of and by the basic ontological structures gives way to an endless fissuring process in which stable semiotic structures shift and move in ways that confound the nascent self. Its powers and prospects seems hardly up to the challenge of the new wealth of postmaternal signs and their elusive portents.

The cunning of the ontological difference is nowhere as dramatic as it is in the transition from the original position to depositioning. This depositioning emerges in its first guise in the momentum that pulls the self away from the maternal. The maternal now becomes the lost object that will haunt and fascinate the self for the rest of its brief trajectory among the signs of the world. Yet the original shock of depositioning returns again and again on the edges of semiotic life as the fissures of the ontological difference refuse to efface themselves before the codes of the manifest orders of semiosis. Unfortunately some perspectives eulogize the powers of depositioning, in the mode of the avant-garde, as if they were liberating per se. The depth logic is more complex, especially when examined through the dialectic of melancholy/wrath and love/grace. In a striking sense, depositioning is beyond good and evil.

For the Freudian and Jungian traditions, the move toward autonomy is made possible by matricide. This voluntaristic language says far too much about the powers of the nascent self and reads later developments backward onto the selving process. The better term for this transition is "denial" (Corrington 1994) in which the hidden momentums of the ontological difference work on the personal level to pull the self away from the presemiotic womb toward the manifest orders and codes of the public world. The self is gathered up into the momentums of interpretants that compel their own form of denial. The self is not so much a murderer of the maternal, as it is a passive participant in a natural process that results in its denial of the maternal, thus converting it into the lost object. This denial is an ontological event that surrounds and permeates the self and need not be conscious.

Needless to say, denial is not a negative event per se but a necessary structure or potency of selving. It has both negative and positive manifestations and ramifications, but it is as inevitable as the prior state of dreaming innocence. By shifting from psychoanalytic analyses of matricide toward a more pragmaticistic analysis of signification and the role of interpretants, some clarity can be brought to the outer and inner urgency of the post-mirror stage. This in turn puts creative pressure on the ubiquity of the Oedipal theory that would reduce the conflict of interpretants to contra-sexual tensions within the immediate biological family. Ecstatic naturalism insists that the momentum of autonomy is much more complex and layered than any Oedipal structure.

The representamen gives way to the exploding realms of interpretants that radically transform the self. The object remains elusive and lies in the heart of the selving process. The core of the self is wrapped in mystery yet emerges in some contour that can be partially mapped through its semiotic traces, both social and bodily. We can make a series of abductive analyses that read backward from manifest signs to their purported origin in a unique self. This reading is fraught with difficulty, even though the hermeneutics of suspicion has greatly overstated the difficulties of self-knowledge. The dynamic object at the heart of the self only truly emerges out of the not yet of the spirit that awaits the final interpretant. Yet it is continually operative in giving some felt shape to the interpretants that cluster around the human process.

The depositioning of the self is, as noted, more than a once and for all event. The 'purpose' of depositioning is to open the self to the elusive potencies of *nature naturing* that goad all actualities and located possibilities into existence. Hegel gave a dramatic coloring to this perennial process with his image of the death of the various shapes of self-consciousness. Each shape, semiotically dense, must experience a profound reversal of its trajectory so that new interpretants can enter into its growing and receding contour. Unfortunately, Hegel's triumphalist anthropology actually undermined his insights into depositioning, imposing metaphors of resurrection where they were not yet appropriate. The ultimate resurrection for nature's self comes to it out of a radically unpredictable future in which the spirit transfigures the lost object in the light and power of the final interpretant.

Melancholy is the most basic affect and effect of depositioning. As Kristeva notes with some care, the emergence of language is deeply correlated to the sense of loss that comes from the emergence of the self out of the *chora*. Her analysis fails, however, to move beyond a kind of poststructuralist "glottocentrism" in which language is privileged over other forms of signification. This mistake is exacerbated by her binary model of signifier/signified, which ties the drama of signification too closely to internal drives and momentums. Put simply, her perspective fails to understand the role of the interpretant and its embeddedness in nature.

The melancholy self is the post-mirror–stage self that is suddenly and forcefully lifted into the world of interpretants. This world as yet has no collective shape or contour and appears to the self to be an endless infinite with no integral logic or telos. The melancholy actually points in two directions. It clearly points to the sense of loss as the maternal recedes more and more from view. Yet this melancholy also points to the despair that emerges over the manic plenitude of interpretants and their unpredictable and shifting configurations. This second form of melancholy is ameliorated in time but remains a part of the selving process. What is not often noted is that both forms of melancholy reinforce each other and remind the self of its precarious tenure in nature.

One striking advantage of this stage of the selving process is that it has some sense of the betweenness structures and gaps that surround signs. Semiotic theory almost always privileges the role of attained cultural codes and downplays or ignores the empty spaces that make any form of signification possible. The depositioned self has an awareness of the gaps that separate signs and their objects as well as the gaps that keep signs from collapsing into each other. These gaps seem to have no inner logic, and their haunting presence further deepens the process of depositioning. As the self matures, however, these gaps take on a very different meaning and can become loci of the spirit-interpreter who lives among signs as their transforming "ground" relation.

The self is a true foundling among the world of interpretants. Internal and external sign series play across and through the self. Indexical signs actively shape and groove nascent self-awareness as well as give the self its growing sense of spatio-temporal structures of resistance. Without indexical signs, the self would never negotiate the inner logic of causality. Indexicality helps to move the self away from the dreaming innocence of the pre-mirror stage. That the indexical is experienced as wrath rather than love is part of its melancholy dialectic. Yet even this gets transformed in later semiotic stages, when the strange grace of dyadic interaction becomes integrated into the fuller semiotic self.

As the melancholy deepens, the hunger for signification intensifies. The loss of the maternal can be partially compensated for by a rush into the plenitude of interpretants. The grounds for this hunger are evolutionary and prepare the self for its integration into physical and social orders. The pragmatic tradition, in spite of its insensitivity to the inner life, has shown how semiotic habit serves to bring the self into the structures and powers that can insure its survival. What it has failed to recognize is just how these powers can serve to close off the self to its own deeper needs. Depositioning and the emergent betweenness structures open up semiotic possibilities that are often quickly filled by demonic social codes and restrictions.

The irony is that the ubiquity of melancholy cries out for alleviation on almost any terms. The social order is more than willing to dampen the fires produced by the shock of the ontological difference with a promised semiotic plenitude and order that is accepted precisely because it deadens the pain felt over the receding lost object. The explosive infinite of interpretants can be given some manageable shape when the selving process binds itself to semiotic social paradigms that bring a premature closure to the semiotic process. There is a clear correlation between the shock of the ontological difference and the silent cunning of the social order. Were the self a mere sign-processor, there would be no need for social control. The chasm of the ontological difference, which propels the self out of its dreaming innocence, calls for strong semiotic measures so that the self can begin to recover from its profound decentering.

The greater the sense of melancholy loss, the more the lost object must be transformed into a promiscuous unfolding of interpretants. The maternal gets captured in innumerable ersatz substitute objects and signs that only partially still the hunger of the foundling self. This process attains momentary forms of stability through the policing power of the social order—a natural community that is not self-interpretive—and the self is given the ambiguous gift of semiotic stability. Depositioning, while absolutely necessary to the human process, opens it up more fully to the semiotic viruses of the social order that invade and remold the nascent self. Dreaming innocence quickly gives way to a kind of semiotic imprisonment that pushes the maternal into false and demonic social substitutes. The fragile self is more than willing to enter into this Faustian bargain and to accept semiotic closure rather than endure the mystery of betweenness and the loss of Eden.

What is the ontology behind this process? The self has been pushed out of the domain of the maternal and finds itself swimming amid a sea of new and strange interpretants. Its connection to its whence has been broken, and its sense of the whither of the semiotic world is shrouded in mist. We must avoid an analysis that would translate the momentum of depositioning and loss exclusively into the terms of desire and will. These elements are present, but they are not the most basic structures. More primordial than the desire or the drives is the momentum of signification that has its roots in the explosive power of the infinitesimals. The original position, connected directly to the maternal, yet already groaning away from it, was made possible by the self-fissuring of *nature naturing* as it manifested itself in the infinitesimals. Each infinitesimal is a potency, more precisely, a possible point system, that awaits its actualization in the domains of space and time. The self is constituted by innumerable attained 'points' that position it within personal and social space, not to mention cosmic and physical space.

The second phase in the depth rhythm of the infinitesimals takes place when the original position, only a momentary way station, suddenly inverts itself and moves in a new direction. The attained point oscillates between a kind of semiotic centripetal movement, holding it fast to the maternal, and a semiotic centrifugal movement, driving it outward into a vast network of involvements. When the original position gives way, depositioning shakes the point system, making it centrifugal. As the finite semiotic points of the self move outward and lose their original position, the loss of the maternal becomes a thematic background that surrounds the self.

Peirce barely understood this momentum, preferring to ignore the lost maternal by converting it into the domain of firstness and pure feeling. When the self is depositioned it makes firstness thematic *as* firstness. Prior to depositioning, firstness could not assume any shape or texture over and against the self. At this second stage, that of depositioning, firstness now becomes the other, and quickly threatens to become the abject, that is, the denied and the feared. Suddenly the primal qualitative immediacy of firstness/feeling haunts the self and holds it in a melancholy embrace. Peirce, because of his own fear of the maternal, refused to probe into the deeper and darker logic of firstness, preferring instead to cloak it in the comforting garments of evolutionary love and sympathy.

The infinitesimal, never itself a semiotic point or position, thus gives birth to an ever-expanding realm of signs and positions that in turn suffer from a further vector inversion in which all original positions are radically inverted in the face of powerful centrifugal forces. The desires and drives of the self come from the heart of *nature naturing* as it uses the explosive power of the infinitesimals to give birth to configured meaning.

What of the products of the self? In the original position, the self is continuous with the maternal and has not yet learned of the otherness of the world of involvements. Its products are random and without particularity. Cries and waste products are generic features of the human process and have their own semiotic meanings, although these meanings will be minimal and highly predictable in the initial stages. When the selving process quickens its momentum after the mirror stage, the products of the self emerge with greater particularity and begin to assume their own autonomous positions within social and personal codes, which at the same time being shaped by these very codes.

To talk of the finitude of the human process is also to talk of the inertia of the products of the self. The semiotic understanding of the human process has a tendency to over emphasize the conscious or communicative structures of the self's outward involvements. Commensurate with the semiotic analysis is an analysis that sees the self as the locus of innumerable products, each one of which has both semiotic and presemiotic features. It should be understood that the concept "product" is an exceedingly broad one. A yawn is as much a product of the self as is a detailed public artifact that plays a role in social history. The finitude of the self is sharply manifest in the products that emerge from the self and have their own inertia and density.

Part of the tragedy of the self is that many of its products have little or no lasting semiotic force or value. As noted, the self is as much characterized by sheer drift and waste as it is by novel and rich semiotic products. The self is continually productive, even in sleep, and its products radiate out from it like an expanding field, with varying degrees of density or transparency. Some products are especially opaque and exert little or no semiotic momentum for the community of selves. My struggles with and against gravity do not assume a special thematic focus for the community, and pass unnoticed. Yet should I lose a limb, these struggles can suddenly be starkly etched into the consciousness of the community and become the object of intense scrutiny. The earlier products of my complex muscular adjustments to gravity now assume a special poignancy as my new and more demanding struggles remind the community of this ubiquitous background that continually calls forth adjustments.

When we think of the products of the self we tend to think of particular space-time objects that have been shaped by bodily motions and intentions. Heidegger erred in confining the domain of the ready-to-hand (*Zuhandensein*) to these obvious tools and pieces of equipment that shape local structures. But it is equally valid to see our scrambling after slipping on ice as a product, insofar as such scrambling is constituted by a series of bodily productions designed to restabilize the organism in a precarious local environment. We cannot help but be productive in every aspect of our lives. Our dreams are as much products of the finite self as are our public artifacts.

Not all products are semiotic in all respects. Our continual adjustments to gravity need not have semiotic features, although in extreme cases, the latent semiotic features can be forced to emerge. When a comedian slips on a banana peel in a movie, this invokes a kind of primal sense of the momentum of depositioning in which a stable presemiotic background suddenly shifts into an unstable and thematic configuration. Our laughter is a recognition of the continual presence of depositioning in our productive life. The exaggerated gestures of the comedian reinforce our sense that bodily products are less secure than we usually admit.

Any given product may thus live on the cusp between the semiotic and the presemiotic. Insofar as the product is unique and publicly available, it will have obvious semiotic features, even if the community may not yet have an assigned value or meaning for those features. Yet the same product may also reach back to conditions of origin (the maternal and the infinitesimal) that can only be rendered into semiotic terms by great effort. Yet these features can only assume their thematic place after depositioning and loss have overtaken the self.

When an infant yawns, there is no concern with finding a detailed semiotic meaning for this product. Internal bodily states are assumed to be sufficient causal forces in the generation of this common act. But when a student yawns during a lecture or a parishioner yawns during a sermon, it is common social practice to assume that larger semiotic structures and evaluations are at play. The move from the minimally dense yawn of the infant to the coded and significant yawn of the adult can only take place because the shock of depositioning gives all products of the self greater meaning. The presemiotic features of products recede more and more into the background as the more fully semiotic dimensions take up their roles in social space. To be finite is to be condemned to produce more meanings that we can assimilate, and to betray more semiotic codes and values than we wish.

Our products, then, can quickly become alien from us. As products they will 'contain' presemiotic and fully semiotic features. The ratio between these two dimensions will shift, especially insofar as the given product enters into complex webs of public semiosis. The hidden dimension of the product, Peirce's dynamic dimension, will be on the way toward semiosis, but will not fully manifest itself at a given time. The eschatological core of semiosis insists that the fullness of the object/product will be manifest in the final consummation of history. This "would be" hovers over and around the object holding out the promise of the final enriched transparency.

Until the final manifestation of the full semiotic scope and meaning of the product, its dense and taciturn dimensions may assume some priority. Whenever a product becomes detached from its producer it must find its own way in the semiotic universe. If Peirce was willing to replace natural selection with evolutionary love, we must be more reticent and assume that many products do not survive their initial conditions of origin. One of the perennial tragedies of the human process is the continual loss of the efficacy of public products. If even our most cherished products may not outlive us, imagine the sheer loss of semiotic value for the bulk of our products. Idealist perspectives, whether panpsychist or not, can preserve products from loss by elevating their internal semiotic core to some kind of nontemporal mind that can sustain their intrinsic value in perpetuity.

Thus both the self and its products suffer from depositioning and loss. The stigma of finitude lies in its inability to secure the human process and its innumerable products from premature decline and closure. Most of our products are not intentionally produced. Yet even those that are suffer from the sheer inertial drift of a semiotic world that often seems indifferent to the needs and claims of its newest members. If the self is a foundling, the same reality follows for its products.

The correlation between the self and its products is a symmetrical one. Not only does the self relentlessly add new products to the world, it must also enter into the rhythms of its own products as they return to reshape the self that spawned them. The most extreme version of this natural momentum is expressed by Sartre when he envisions the objective order (*en soi*) as a threatening realm that closes in on the decompression in Being known as consciousness (Sartre 1943: 83):

> It is impossible to grasp facticity in its brute nudity, since all that we will find of it is already recovered and freely constructed. The simple *fact* "of being there," at that table, in that chair is already the pure object of a limiting-concept and as such can not be grasped. Yet it is contained in my "consciousness of being-

there," as its full contingency, as the nihilated in-itself on the basis of which the for-itself produces itself as consciousness of being there. The for-itself looking deep into itself as the consciousness of being there will never discover anything in itself but *motivations*; that is, it will be perpetually referred to itself and to its constant freedom.

Our products and the immediate objects (such as the table) in our environment return to compress and harass their producer. Less extreme philosophic perspectives also honor the curious dialectic in which seemingly detached objects return to limit and constrict further productive possibilities in the self. The product is, after all, a momentum of the powers of origin and thus carries a unique vector directionality handed to it by these powers. The self may cast off products naturally, yet they will return in a series of orbits that seem to close in more and more on the originating self.

The products that make their return to the originating source, deposition the origins that made them possible. Marx was one of the most insightful students of this process of productive alienation in which our very issue will dramatically alter our prospects. He clearly saw that no product is innocent of its productive conditions and that once produced it will continue to haunt its producer, mocking future possibilities by the sheer opacity and indifference of its presence.

Finitude is thus far more than the condition of being noninfinite. It entails the momentum of depositioning and constriction in which both internal signs and external products (which are themselves both semiotic and presemiotic) return with their uncanny logic to limit the scope and richness of the self. It is a truism of postmodernism that we are deeply alienated from ourselves. It is equally pertinent to acknowledge the ways in which we are alienated from our products. Freud's image of the "return of the repressed" is relevant in this context, even if its claims to exhaustiveness must be radically denied. The alienated product returns to us like a repressed content that we wish to deny and place under erasure. Our own most intimate products often become abjected from us and quickly speed to the edges of our horizons of meaning. Yet they return from these recesses to haunt us and to remind us of the iron bands of finitude.

The temporality of depositioning is different in kind from that of the original position (which contains both temporal and pretemporal dimensions). The temporality of depositioning and loss is fully temporal and has a kind of oscillating rhythm that moves backward and forward across and through time to bring the self and its products into the dialectic of intimacy and abjection. Once spawned, a product moves toward the edges of the horizon of meaning, where it enters into the density and closure of the past. Yet it returns in the guise of the repressed and fills the present with a kind of inertial drag that slows down the self in its forward momentums. The future is muted in this mode of finitude. This is not to equate the past with the repressed. Other possibilities will emerge in subsequent analyses where transcendence works itself fitfully in and through the self and its products. But even this transforming process is always wedded to finite conditions. The return of the repressed, which involves both inner states and public artifacts, keeps nature's self bound to the conditions of origin and embodiment. Yet this logic of the return of the repressed contains another dimension that works within the limits of finitude to reshape and transform the self. The spatial and temporal image of return is a complex one. There are two dimensions to this phenomenon. We have examined the dimension of return in which the focus is on repressed material. This can be called the return of the same. Yet within this momentum lies the possibility that the same can be transformed and reshaped by conditions both internal and external. Our products and our own inner states can return to us in a new guise and take on richer colors of meaning and signification. The 'return' in this case is enriched by novel or generic conditions of world semiosis that add their own structures and potencies to the original signs and products of the human process. With this next stage, the logic of finitude is completed.

C. Repositioning and Return

The self and its products can be understood in terms of the concept of resistance. Each sign and each product constitutes a sphere of relevance that resists any addition to its semiotic stock. The self is shaped and molded by a mobile network of resistances that actively give the self its inner and outer contours. The phenomenon of depositioning and loss manifests these resistances in terms of inertial drift and the drag of what could be called "semiotic mass." As we probe into the third form of finitude, that of repositioning and return, we see that the shape of resistance becomes altered in its inner logic. What returns to the self in this dimension is not a mere inert sphere of resistance, but a prospect for transformation that moves beyond resistance toward a new configuration. The mechanism shifts from that of secondness to that of thirdness, in which teleological structures work to open up the spheres of resistance to more capacious horizons of meaning.

The sense of loss, and the return of the repressed in the same, now gives way to a different kind of return in which the resistances of inert products and signs transform themselves. The new form of resistance is not a dyadic closure or dense momentum of reiteration, but a goad or lure to deeper possibilities of interaction. In the previous stage, the self was radically shaken out of the original position and thus depositioned. This disorienting momentum moved the self away from the sustaining powers of origin toward a semiotic plenitude that first emerged as a confusing and chaotic "bad infinite." The self was thus caught in a painful oscillation between a desire for a collapse back into dreaming innocence and a movement outward and forward into the blinding realm of public interpretants. Were the self to remain in the domain of depositioning, it would be caught in a closed backward and foreword rhythm that would stunt the selving process.

As the depth logic of finitude moves toward its final dimension, the power of origin takes on yet another guise in the now stabilizing domain of interpretants. At the same time, the innumerable products of the self lose some of their opacity and become loci of deeper and more secure semiotic powers. It must be remembered that the concept of finitude is commensurate with the concept of embodiment. All signs and products are embodied in some respect. Even the most fleeting thought, which seems to be locked in the private space of inner life, has its own form of diffuse embodiment. All signs and products have a primal hunger to locate meaning within their scope. Put metaphorically, it is as if meanings themselves hunger to become incarnate in specific signs and products. When the selving process moves toward repositioning, these meanings emerge with greater force and power.

Thus the sheer and opaque resistance of products is transformed into a forward-moving resistance that goads and coaxes the self toward the final kingdom of meaning. A given product can either restrict and close off the self, or it can move the self into larger orders of relation. The latter prospect is the one that emerges in repositioning. The resistance felt in depositioning is deeply tied to the return of the same. When depositioning becomes transformed into repositioning, the resistance of the same is itself transformed into the lure of the enriched world of meaning. The growth in meaning and freedom held out by repositioning brings about a profound realignment of the self.

Throughout, the concept of the spirit has been invoked as a semiotic momentum that lies just 'beneath' the ontological triad of sign/object/interpretant. With the transition to repositioning, the spirit emerges with greater clarity to show just how semiotic meaning can be secured against the inertia and waste of the human process. The concept of spirit is, of course, an exceedingly rich one in the history of philosophy and theology. The ecstatic naturalist concept of spirit must be sharply distinguished from antecedent concepts if it is to function properly within the current categorial framework.

Initially, it is important to make clear that the spirit is not some kind of consciousness or eternal mind that merely contemplates the world of the self and its innumerable signs and products. The spirit is not an intentional agent that has specific visions and plans that are to be handed over to the human process. Put in fairly stark terms, the spirit is in and of nature as one of nature's most important momentums. But the spirit is not some kind of superorder that lives over and above nature. The spirit is within the other orders of nature or not at all.

Theologically, the spirit is tied to trinitarian reflections in which the power of the Christ is carried into history by the spirit that was also the momentum behind the resurrection. It is customary to distinguish between an immanent and an economic trinity. The immanent trinity is that which obtains in itself, prior to any relation to history or the orders of the world. The economic trinity is held to be the trinity as it actually unfolds within the finite orders of reality. Ecstatic naturalism affirms something analogous to the economic trinity insofar as the spirit must exist within the shifting and fragmented orders of the world. The spirit is thus a complex, but nonconscious, momentum that works itself into many of the orders of the world. A reconstruction of the trinity must await further explorations, but the preliminary sense of an economic trinity can be seen to operate in a muted fashion behind the scenes.

Peirce's own semiotic version of the economic trinity is briefly adumbrated in the last of his 1866 Lowell Lectures, where he attempts to rework the sign/object/ground structure along theological lines. The concept of "Symbol" is held to be pertinent to all three dimensions, but in different respects. Peirce opened up a door onto the grounds of signification that he did not completely walk through, yet his youthful insights moved him toward the direction of ecstatic naturalism (W 1.503):

> Here, therefore, we have a divine trinity of the object, interpretant, and ground. Each fully constitutes the symbol and yet all are essential to it. Nor are they the same thing under different

points of view but three things which attain identity when the symbol attains infinite information. In many respects, this trinity agrees with the Christian trinity; indeed I am not aware that there are any points of disagreement. The interpretant is evidently the Divine *Logos* or word; and if our former guess that a Reference to an interpretant is Paternity be right, this would be also the *Son of God*. The *ground*, being the symbol that partaking of which is requisite to any communication with the Symbol, corresponds in its function to the Holy Spirit.

The symbol, or sign, is built up through three movements that collectively make semiosis possible. The Father is directly correlated to power of reason or the "Divine Logos" that is manifest in public interpretants. Yet, insofar as the interpretant is also the place where meaning is incarnate, it is at the same time, but in a different respect, the Son. The ground relation, which is in some respect prior to semiosis as its enabling condition, is the spirit. Peirce makes a very strong claim here; namely, that infinite meaning is possible when the trinity is manifest in worldly semiosis. Of the three persons of the trinity, the spirit is the most relevant to "any communication with the Symbol." I take this to mean that the spirit is not *an* interpretant, but the ultimate enabling condition for any and all meaning within the world. When our intraworldly semiotic triad participates in the economic trinity it becomes the locus of infinite meaning.

When dealing with the human order, the spirit is best understood to be the spirit-interpreter (Royce 1913), who acts within the self to bring about a deepening of semiotic meaning. The selving process is deeply wedded to the spirit, even if it is rarely conscious of this connection. The full scope of the spirit's work can only be detailed when we examine the momentums of transcendence, yet some aspects are pertinent in the dimension of finitude. The spirit is present throughout the movement from dreaming innocence to repositioning and the return of enhanced meaning on the edges of signification.

As noted, the spirit lies 'beneath' the ontological triad of sign/object/interpretant. This is to say that the spirit is neither a sign, nor an object, nor an interpretant. As Peirce sensed, the spirit lies in the betweenness structures that make any form of signification possible. Thus the spirit is an enabling condition that keeps the ontological triad open to its own possibilities and to various forms of semiotic intersection. The spirit-interpreter in the human order lives between and among signs, objects, and interpretants keeping each domain supple and translucent. Without the continual movements of the spirit, meanings would quickly return to the repetition of the same. With the presence of the spirit, meanings can unfold in a manner that enhances and enriches the human process.

The resistance of the spirit is the resistance of the open future. If the powers of origin are dyadically present in the return of the repressed, and thus resist in the temporal modes of the past and present, the powers of origin are triadically present in the return of enriched meaning that comes from the momentum of the spirit. This return is triadic in that it always creates a space for a new and more encompassing meaning (a third) that gathers up the opaque dyad of the same and moves it into the future of the new. The spirit is eschatological, even if it must always work with antecedent structures and powers. Yet the transition from dyadic opacity toward triadic transparency is only possible through the often hidden enabling presence of the spirit that lives out of an open future.

Psychoanalytic perspectives have failed to see the curative powers of the spirit as it groans toward a transfigured future. Pragmaticist perspectives, on the other hand, are deeply tied to an open future and await the healing third that will overcome the dyadic closure of the return of the repressed. Peirce's spirit, as the enabling ground, must move toward a transfigured future in which infinite meaning "would be" present to the sign-using self. If the concept of spirit is located in the depths and interstices of semiosis, rather than in some kind of separate transcendent realm, than it can begin to assume its proper place in a theory of the self.

The spirit, then, moves between and among signs in the form of relational communication that keeps semiosis moving toward convergence in the future. This convergence is not a static type of identity, nor a mere mask for semiotic colonialism, but a deep rhythm of mediation that seeks to incarnate the healing power of developmental thirdness into the broken dyads of semiosis. Finite structures are quickened and transformed under the power of the spirit. However, these structures never cease to be fully finite. The transfiguration promised by the spirit is always deeply tied to the limits and confines of finite forms of embodiment. Spirit belongs to both nature and history as the presemiotic momentum of semiotic transparency. Nature is thus the genus of which both history and the spirit are species. Put differently, nature, in the dimension of *nature naturing* is the enabling potency for the located orders of history and the ever elusive spirit.

Behind all of the transformations of nature's self is the inner power of selving that propels the self out of and away from the domain of dreaming innocence. The rejection of the material maternal, and the simultaneous affirmation of the codes of the father, can only take place because of a far deeper evolutionary momentum toward individuation and autonomy. Tillich (1912) has correlated autonomy with guilt consciousness, showing that guilt is the inevitable product of the movement away from the potencies. In the radical inversion of depositioning, in which the lost object becomes sensed *as* lost for the first time, guilt enters into the rhythms of the self as it begins to negotiate among the exploding interpretants of public life. In the countermovement of repositioning, the explosions of public signs become muted and transformed into centers of stable semiosis. At the same time, the guilt of autonomy begins to assume new forms as the grace of the spirit secures the sign using self against the rages of the bad infinite.

Thus, the repositioned self has negotiated through two perilous passages. On one side, it has felt the wrath of the receding lost object and has found numerous substitute objects within the outer and inner worlds. On the other side, it has learned to find some stable contours among the infinite and expanding codes and sign systems of public space, thus securing its own evolutionary survival in a vast and often indifferent universe of signs. Inner life, which is in many respects an introjection of inscribed public space, begins to shape itself around projected models of self-identity that have a cumulative and directional momentum. As the loss of the maternal becomes transfigured under the thirdness of the spirit, the images of inner life take on a grace-filled clarity that can provide a momentary haven from the unrelenting explosive power of public interpretants. This in turn provides a means for stilling the chaos of the outer world. Needless to say, the movement from internal to external models is a dialectical process in which each dimension helps to co-constitute the other.

The momentum of selving works itself out through both inner and outer models and brings them into closer configuration. This is not to say that there are not deep pockets of semiotic chaos and sheer opacity within the self. Indeed, it is an exceedingly difficult task to bring semiotic transparency to each aspect of inner and outer life. The proud delusion of psychoanalytic perspectives is that such transparency can be attained without extra-human means. Ecstatic naturalism insists that the self cannot attain any lasting self-understanding without the presence and power of the spirit, which moves against the structures of resistance and opacity that haunt the self. Put differently, semiotic anthropology receives its measure and validity from semiotic eschatology, in which the spirit moves out of the future to illuminate the world of interpretants, both inner and outer.

The time structures of the self of repositioning and return differs from the previous stage in two respects. Depositioning works out of the temporal past and present to tie the self to the lost object in the past and the return of the same/repressed in the present. The self of repositioning moves toward the future by allowing the spirit-interpreter to shape its relation to interpretants. On a deeper level, the self becomes permeable to what can be best termed the posttemporal. If the domain of dreaming innocence is pretemporal, that is, obtains prior to the full manifestation of temporality, then the domain of the return of the spirit is one that can only take place after and because of the flowering of temporality. The self of repositioning is opened to its private and its public future. But this momentum points toward a deeper religious transformation in which even the future gives way to the posttemporal. An analysis of the posttemporal must await the delineation of the structures and powers of transcendence, yet certain traces are available at this stage.

The posttemporal dimension of finite existence is manifest on the extreme edges of the interpretants that permeate inner and outer life. Each given interpretant will have its own mobile order of meaning. This meaning will be intrinsic to the sign, but will also contain relational structures that link the interpretant to its pertinent sign series. Any given interpretant may be located where several discrete sign series intersect, thus taking on a radical increase in semiotic scope and power. Yet the given interpretant also participates in the depth rhythms of nature and the spirit. Neither nature nor the spirit are signs or interpretants. Pansemioticism often ignores the abyss created by the ontological difference between *nature naturing* and *nature natured*. The nether side of the difference, that of the potencies of *nature naturing*, can not captured in semiotic terms, precisely as it is presemiotic. A given interpretant participates in the ontological difference and carries dark and elusive traces of *nature naturing* within its horizon of meaning. These traces of the spawning ground of signification are usually effaced by the sheer semiotic charisma of the interpretant which exists by drawing attention to itself.

Beneath the shining surface of the interpretant, then, lie traces that link it back to the maternal/infinitesimal. These traces are not part of any public code. In fact, codes could not function at all if they provided equal space for the receding infinitesimal. Whenever an interpretant enters into a public or private code, it leaves the spawning ground behind. How then, can these lost traces emerge again for the sign-using self? Here we see how the movement of selving serves the deeper cunning of nature.

The traces of the maternal return whenever the self moves into the inner heart of semiotic codes and sees their unthought and unsensed rhythms. This transition is made possible by the spirit-interpreter who is not part of the code-filled universe of signs. In a sense, the spirit is concerned with finding the open spaces within all codes so that they can founder on their own illusory plenitude. There is a depth dialectic, dimly sensed by Peirce, between semiotic plenitude and semiotic emptiness. The codes of public space manifest semiotic plenitude, whereas the traces of the maternal (latent within all codes) manifest the presemiotic emptiness of nature in its naturing. The sign-using self spends most of its life ignoring and repressing the abjected domain of the presemiotic. Only something greater than the self can coax it back toward the lost object that leaves its traces between and among interpretants and codes.

The spirit is thus the power that underlies the selving process, bringing the depositioned self back around toward the lost object by showing how all interpretants are actually servants of the darker rhythms of *nature naturing*. In the return of the spirit that takes place in repositioning, the wrath of depositioning gives way to the love that comes from the spirit-interpreter, a love that is itself rooted in the grace of the ontological difference.

The melancholy of the depositioned self opens into the love of the repositioned self of the spirit. Of course, this is not a simple linear process that takes place once and for all, but a dialectic that reshapes itself over and over again, sometimes moving forward, and sometimes moving backward into a frozen and repressed state. There is no providential guarantee that this process will succeed in any given case, or that, once obtained, it will maintain itself against semiotic decay and entropy. There is only the hope of the spirit that opacity will give way to grace-filled transparency on the edges of signification.

The public expression of the dimension of the transition from the wrath of the bad infinite to the love of stable yet growing interpretants is found in the products of the self as they assume greater degrees of transparency toward ultimate meaning. The self is the locus for innumerable codes, yet it is also, and as important, the locus for a growing network of products. Insofar as the self remains trapped in depositioning and loss, these products merely return to the conditions of origin. When the self allows the spirit-interpreter to transform its positions, then the products of the self enter into the clearing provided by the spirit. This clearing is the locus for all of those meanings that transcend the instrumental.

Consider an actor who must build up a complex character through external gestures. By working from external gestures inward, the actor can introject public signs and make them into deeply resonating products of the self. These gestures have a cumulative momentum that can be shaped and modified as the process of internalization matures. Stance and eye gestures can show how a multilayered character such as Shakespeare's Richard the Third can make his vaulting ambition manifest to his peers. The products of the actor's craft enter into public space and convey something of the complexities of the inner life of the character. The low cunning and public fawning of Richard suddenly break open to a new layer of meaning when his character betrays his deeper intent. This process can only be manifest through specific public gestures. The outward thrust of a hand, tilted downward to signal kingly power and the demand of obedience, conveys a vast semiotic network of internal interpretants. How can the actor enter into the clearing of deeper meaning?

The external products of the actor's craft shape an inner and outer contour of meaning. Richard now bursts forth from the recesses of his own self-masking to assume demonic and frightening proportions. The limp and the stoop of the hunched back add force to the transition from warped plotter to king. The products of the actor, namely, the sum of all gestures, inflections, and positions, creates an inner life out of the raw material of space, time, and semiosis. The power of the portrayal is measured by the scope of the public products and by their pertinence to the inner life of the character. Insofar as the cumulative gestures follow stock patterns, the characterization will fall flat. Yet, when the gestures emerge out of a deeper openness to the inner logic of the character, they enter into the drama of repositioning and return.

A great actor, then, enters into the rhythms of the spirit-interpreter who holds open a space within which public products can be probed and fashioned to create a powerful characterization. The gestures now enter into social space, embodied in the history of the genre, and become available for detailed scrutiny and appraisal. After an Olivier presents a portrayal of Richard the Third, the genre is permanently augmented and enriched. Subsequent portrayals will be compelled to feel the echoes of the antecedent triumph.

It must be remembered that products need not be space-time particulars. A sneeze is as much a product as a book or a piece of equipment. The gestures of an important actor can have as much effect on public space as an important physical artifact. The pertinent question always is: How does the given product enhance possibilities and actualities within an evolving social horizon of meaning? Can the product continue to goad creators into novel and life-transforming prospects and forms of contrivance? At the heart of any compelling product of the self is the spirit-interpreter, who fills each product with some sense of ultimate import and value. The closure of mere repetition is overcome by the repositioning, which allows ultimate import to return in a new guise.

The products of the repositioning self enter into the power of the future and the posttemporal. The future is manifest in the opened space of possibility that now hovers around the product. The posttemporal is manifest in the hints of ultimate import that empower and quicken the product. The product remains the finite product that it is, condemned to occupy specific and shifting conditions, yet it does leap forward into anticipatory structures that promise deeper prospects for the sign-using self. While finitude can never be overcome, it can be quickened and deepened by the spirit-interpreter, who speaks through codes and products.

The lost object is never fully lost. In this third stage of finite life, that in which the future and the posttemporal emerge to reposition the self, the lost object returns with a transfigured guise. The maternal, operating through the momentum of the infinitesimals, moves from the pretemporal to the posttemporal through the power of the spirit. The wrath of the abjected lost object, which gets covered over by the bad infinite of blinding and chaotic interpretants, is transfigured into the love of the returning object on the edges of signification. The maternal enters into the hidden rhythms of the spirit and supports the repositioning process. The best metaphor of this transfigured maternal is the "encompassing" (Jaspers 1935) as the enveloping and supporting power of ultimate meaning. From the standpoint of the finite human process, the spirit-interpreter becomes the encompassing maternal that provides the clearing within which lasting meanings may be secured against semiotic closure and entropy. New semiotic and productive groupings emerge to turn chaos into the growth of meaning in time. The lost object of the *fort-da* game returns in the full light of the "there" to bring nature's self back to the sphere of ultimate meaning. Finitude becomes open to its depths and provides a space and time for transcendence.

Chapter Two
Fitful Transcendence

Transcendence is neither free-floating nor eternal. It emerges fitfully from the innumerable shifting conditions found on both sides of the ontological difference. From the side of *nature naturing*, transcendence is manifest in the seemingly opaque forward movements of the potencies as they emerge from their heterogeneous state to open up prospects of and for the spirit. From the side of *nature natured* transcendence is manifest whenever signs and products open out novel and transformative prospects for further semiotic interaction and integration. In both senses, transcendence is in and of a self-transforming nature and therefore cannot lift the self outside of the potencies and orders that collectively constitute nature.

The movements of transcendence can be traced through a three-fold momentum, each moment of which is correlated with aspects of finitude in an internal dialectic. However, the explication of transcendence must take the reverse order from that found in the description of finitude and embodiment. While the description of positioning, depositioning, and repositioning starts with the original pre-Oedipal state, the explication of transcendence moves from the realms of attained semiotic codes and public products 'backward' to the lost object, which becomes transfigured as it moves forward into the spirit.

The momentums of transcendence are thus both forward and backward looking. They look forward insofar as they groan toward a realization of the lost object in the posttemporal dimension of the spirit. They look backward insofar as they long for a return of the pretemporal maternal precisely in the embrace of the posttemporal spirit. When the rhythms of transcendence join goal and origin, melancholy gives way to the ecstatic power of love, known to us as eros/agape.

Our analysis will thus move through three stages. The first dimension will involve a delineation of the powers of transcendence within the orders of *nature natured*. This entails an analysis of public forms of semiosis and their correlation with the world of the self's products. This dimension corresponds to the dimension of repositioning as it works to reshape finite conditions of embodiment. The second dimension will involve a detailed description of the developmental teleology found in the unconscious as it relates both to 'itself' and to the compensatory dimension of consciousness. This dimension correlates with that of depositioning, although, as the analysis will show, it also points directly toward repositioning and makes it possible as an integral movement of the centered self. The unconscious represents the bond for us between *nature natured* and *nature naturing*. The third dimension will involve the unifying power of the spirit-interpreter as it brings the public self into intersection with the unconscious. This dimension correlates with that of the original position, with the important difference being that it also links the dimensions of depositioning and repositioning together. The spirit-interpreter, while not itself a "third," is that which makes thirdness (concrete reasonableness) possible in the fullest sense.

A. PUBLIC INTERSECTIONS

Nature's self is fully embedded in vast social and natural structures that locate it and give it the inner power of the domain of origins. At the same time, these very powers are self-othering and evocative of distinct prospects for transformation. It is important that both the assimilative and the manipulative dimensions of this form of transcendence be clarified. There is a strong sense in which the self is transfigured simply by participating in the momentum of interpretants with which it is in intersection. The self thus assimilates new and augmented meanings insofar as it has any semiotic life at all. Within the large momentum of assimilation lies the other prospect of manipulation in which the self is able, often by relying on collective social strategies, to compel signs and products to move in directions desirable to the community and its members.

Within the external structures of world semiosis are innumerable sign systems that move outward as incarnated interpretants, each with its own density and scope. Signs are best seen as spheres of power rather than as discrete meaningpackets that somehow need to be pried open. Any given interpretant is already open in innumerable ways, even if human methodic activity can accelerate a natural process and bring it into a preferred level of transparency. Nature's self lives within the already grace-filled domain of meaning held open by innumerable interpretants. Put in stronger terms, the world is exploding with far more meaning than can ever be assimilated by finite processes, and this "more" brings the self into the edges of its own horizons of meaning and intelligibility. In a striking sense, the self often needs to do little more than to become slightly more permeable to the expanding universe of interpretants. This is a process that does not require will or the drives.

Meanings desire to be assimilated. This may sound like an anthropomorphic projection until it is recognized that meanings, by definition, become augmented whenever one interpretant collides with another. While something may be lost in the intersection, more is gained (at least in the dimension of transcendence). In this sense, any given interpretant 'desires' to add to its scope and density and to become more inclusive of the surrounding semiotic features of its immediate world. Interpretants transcend themselves whenever they find themselves involved with another interpretant. These interpretants need not be part of a human self in process any more than they need to be conscious centers in their own right.

There is a surplus discharge of ecstasy whenever one interpretant enters into the orbit of another. The term "ecstasy" does not here denote or connote joy or bliss, but refers to the momentum of self-transcendence in which an antecedent state welcomes an internal transfiguration in which its plenitude is enhanced. This sudden increase of scope and density is ecstatic insofar as new energies are released that can sustain and integrate the new semiotic material. An ecstatic interpretant, if this formulation is not too jarring, is one that suddenly bursts beyond its current configuration to gather in the semiotic richness and diversity of another interpretant. Unlike the melancholy that corresponds to the loss of meaning, ecstasy moves forward into the power of the not yet. At the heart of the not yet, which is manifest to the human process as hope, is the power of love.

Interpretants never exist alone. They come from a dimly lit past and point toward an equally dim future. They belong to at least one sign series, and usually to many at the same 'time.' Openness is built into the interpretant, and any augmentation of the openness is ecstatic and self-transforming. Insofar as these openings occur, more semiotic light is created that enhances the retrospective and prospective reach of the given interpretant. The interpretant is thus an arena in which semiotic light and darkness play across meanings attained and point toward meanings hoped for or to come.

A sign series itself is ecstatic whenever it opens itself to another series that can augment its meaning. Whenever such series intersect with the human self, they play across and through the internal and external signs of the human process and exert their opening power. For example, whenever the self finds a new and powerful self-interpretation, say that emerging from a psychotherapeutic situation, it becomes radially opened to new prospects that can only be disclosed insofar as the new sign system is allowed to do its work on the self. This new system is assimilated by the self in process and becomes part of its internal framework for negotiating through and among the blinding wealth of introspective signs and interpretants.

Before detailing the momentums of inner life, which is constituted by introjected signs and vast inherited phylogenetic structures, it is important to show how the life of public signs lives on its own terms and fully participates in the elusive rhythms of transcendence. Signs and their series are busy, constantly intersecting with internal configurations and with larger orders of relevance both within and without the immediate semiotic area. If the ontological difference gives nature a primal restlessness, the life of signs on the side of *nature natured* has its own unique form of dynamism in which given meanings elide forward and backward seeking to enter into other vectors and dynamic centers of power and meaning.

Communal space is the most active of all because of the sheer density and richness of the sign systems involved. Earlier attempts to freeze this activity into the more static terminology of codes and their inner forms of encoding and decoding failed to show just how protean signs are in their movement toward the state of the final interpretant. On a deeper level, the analysis in terms of codes failed utterly to show how the underlying ground relation opened up the rich betweenness structures that in their own way add to the restlessness of signs. After all, restlessness makes no sense, in the human sphere and elsewhere, unless it is goaded by prospects that hover around the edges of attained structures of meaning and interaction. For a sign or its series to be restless is for it to feel the subtle opening created by larger prospects of intersection. Betweenness hovers around signs 'reminding' them of their current limitations. This seemingly negative presence is actually the depth structure of serial intersection.

Looking more closely at human communal space we see that it is constituted by horizons of meaning within which an infinite number of sign series play out their drama in which meanings become incarnated and presented to finite interpreters. More subjectively driven philosophies stress the role of the human agent in transforming sign material into a kind of plastic realm of sheer possibility. The actual situation is much more complex. Signs do not simply wait in the wings hoping that a human agent will somehow elevate them to a momentary starring role so that they can work out their inner destiny. Rather, it is as if signs and their series enact their own drama in which we are invited to participate. In any event, our participation is inevitable and can take several forms. Insofar as a sign is especially numinous or powerful we will be compelled to participate in it no matter what our intentional acts seem to dictate. Insofar as a sign is less dramatic, but nonetheless valuable in its own right, we will be coaxed into some kind of participation and response to its penumbra of meaning.

Semiotic participation may or may not be a conscious process. Even where the process is conscious, we may have fewer interpretive options than we might like to think. Each sign or series is a dynamic momentum that has a vector directionality that will intersect with the self in process. The image is that of a swimmer moving across a vast expanse of water in which each wave or ripple represents a sign series that washes over the swimmer and shapes the forward or backward movement. It would be absurd to think that we create any but the most immediate waves, and even here, the motion of the legs and arms change vast antecedent conditions that only allow themselves to be augmented or spoiled in specific ways.

This image is meant to remind us that whatever transcendence is, it is not a kind of overwhelming power that can lift us out of the waters of semiosis. Transcendence occurs within a context that already limits its possibilities. However, the situation is not as hopeless as it might seem. If transcendence were merely a human phenomenon it would indeed have little power in a universe that seems to mock human aspiration. But if it is understood that transcendence comes from the heart of nature itself, then it becomes clear that the human process can participate in healing energies that are not human products alone.

Two foci of our current analysis have emerged. The first is that of the self-transcending possibilities within horizons themselves, while the second is the momentum of sign series as they feel the gentle agitation of betweenness that opens them to new prospects.

We will speak of these processes as if they worked on their own terms. This will prepare the way for an analysis of how they work directly into the heart of the human process and make transcendence within nature actual.

Can we ever confront the edges of a horizon of meaning directly? It seems clear that this is impossible in principle. As Hegel noted with some insight, every attempt to map the edges of a horizon (shape of self-consciousness) entails that we somehow transgress the immediately attained boundary. However, the dialectical logic is less transparent than Hegel assumed. We learn about the edges of a given horizon when we go beyond it, but we are, by definition, already in a new horizon, which itself has elusive boundaries. Consequently, it follows that no horizon, as horizon, can ever become the object of a thematic gaze. Such a gaze both falls too short and reaches too far, but in different respects. The gaze falls too short because it can only deal with one aspect of the horizon at a time. The gaze goes too far because it thematizes a real or alleged boundary from a point just outside of it and hence changes the rules of the game.

If we were to personify horizons we could say that they recede from view just as we get close to their outer edges. There seems to be a kind of self-effacing quality to horizons such that they are reluctant to become intentional objects or delimited sign series. In this primal sense, horizons give and grant space for meaning but they are not themselves a 'product' of their internal signs. That is, a horizon is far more than the 'sum' of its signs and moves silently on the other side of all available meanings that occur 'within' it. Horizons transcend their internal life and always live as a mobile field of future prospects.

Horizons transcend what is within them. This basic phenomenological insight needs to be strengthened so that the power of transcendence within and around the human process can be more sharply drawn. In a clear sense, I am rarely aware that I am actually *in* a horizon of meaning. I live in the center of a meaning-granting clearing that is itself hidden from view. The horizon radically transcends its human occupant. It is only when the horizon suffers some kind of shipwreck or encounters the pressure of an alien horizon that the self can become aware of its sovereign presence/absence. When the breach occurs, the self suddenly discovers that its meaning-clearing is actually a finite and delimited space within which some configurations and not others can become manifest. This is analogous to the fall out of dreaming innocence, although it moves from the opposite direction—namely, from the 'top' of the world of *nature natured* and its attained semiotic forms toward a less stable state. Instead of falling out of the womb, this fall represents a swift descent from a great height.

Within the heart of this process of semiotic and horizonal shipwreck lies the genuine possibility of transcendence. Consider what happens when an individual is confronted with his or her own powerful shadow projection. In Jungian terms, a shadow projection takes place whenever an inferior and denied aspect of the self is unconsciously projected onto an external object. The object, which may or may not be 'innocent' on its own terms, becomes the locus for a powerful semiotic momentum that holds the projecting self in its grip. In this sense, the shadow projection is itself a horizon, albeit of more limited scope than the total human horizon of the agent. The horizon moves unconsciously and directly to contaminate the object so that it is forced to carry on its immediate surface certain demonic features. If the object is another human subject, it is easy to see the danger involved in failing to withdraw the projection.

The object may resist being the subject of this shadow projection, but the peculiar tragedy of this situation is that the object often fails to exert its counter claims against the imperial and unconscious power of the projection. How does the shadow learn of its very existence so that it can withdraw its projection from its victim? To answer this question, it is necessary to enter into the deeper rhythms of horizonal intersection. At the edge of each horizon of meaning is a penumbra that both hides and grants light. In a striking sense, this penumbra has its own sensitivity to alien semiotic material and responds with a kind of seismic tremor whenever alien material crosses its path. It is as if shadowy light waves are subject to new gravitational attractions that shift the patterns of meaning and interaction. The shift occurs whenever new sign systems make their presence felt.

Altering our terms slightly, the penumbra around the meaning horizon is an unconscious semiotic system that is especially sensitive to surrounding sign material. While in one dimension, horizons remain opaque to alternative horizons, in another and more sensitive dimension, they are open to the influx of alien or even abjected material. This openness becomes the hidden gateway for the necessary transformation of the horizon that can appear either in a gentle augmentation of meaning or in a powerful shipwreck that breaks open the horizon so that its inner content is spilled out. In either extreme case, the horizon is compelled to incorporate new semiotic material that may force it to realign its own internal structures.

An important historical example of this momentum can be seen in the political and personal tactic of fasting. It is often thought that fasting is simply a power move that will shame the opponent into granting certain denied rights and privileges. While this dimension is certainly present, it is not the sole, or even primary dimension of fasting. As Gandhi knew with great clarity, fasting is a very powerful strategy for opening out the demonic depths of one's own horizon of meaning. Horizons are extensions of felt bodily space. The body moves with its own inner rhythms which are directly manifest in the 'outer' horizon of meaning that surrounds this bodily space. Fasting inverts and transforms the dialectic between inner and outer. Insofar as the agent refuses to take in external material, he or she puts the outer horizon into a kind of hovering state in which its forward momentums are temporarily thwarted. The stasis of the body forces its horizon to become a still presence that can be thematically examined.

What happens in the seemingly simple act of giving up food? The most dramatic occurrence is the sudden appearance of the body/horizon dialectic, in which the horizon is shown to represent an important aspect of the outer involvements of the body. By cutting off the most primal of these outer involvements, the taking in of nourishment, the horizon becomes implicated in the shrinking and lessening of the body. The omnivorous quality of the meaning horizon is dramatically stilled, while the internal logic and rhythm of the horizon begins to come into some kind of thematic focus. Where does transcendence enter into this process?

The horizon becomes open to its own fissures and breaks. The loss of physical nourishment quickly reminds the body that it is indeed a finite and inscripted product that is deeply embedded in social space, a space that is much richer and more complex than that of so-called intersubjectivity. At the same time, the self, feeling the diminution of its body, becomes aware of the ways in which its horizon of meaning may contain the very seeds that it found in its shadow projection onto outer horizons and objects. It is as if the energy that once went to sustain a powerful and unconscious projection is slowly withdrawn so that the projection begins to break apart through a kind of quasi-physical entropy. The self can no longer sustain the raging power of the projection, which demonized its object, and must withdraw the shadow back into its own horizon. In this process, the agent's horizon begins to unveil its own demonic depths, depths from which the original shadow projection came.

This is not to say that the outer object is somehow freed of its own demonic features. Rather, it is to show that the body-horizon of the faster is implicated in the movement of the social shadow and that it must confront it as an internal structure before it can accurately gage its outer force. But here the plot thickens. The person or group responsible for invoking the fast is suddenly confronted with the inner power of the subjugated selves that have chosen to fast. They are witness to the uncanny power that comes from doing absolutely nothing; namely, from refusing to let the power of the outer social horizon enter into the self in the form of food. The symbol of food is one of the most powerful ones in the cultural history of the human process. To reject its power, and all of its economic and social connections, is to go right to the heart of the power structures that shape and inscribe the self in process.

The witnesses to the fast are thus brought into a sphere of power and meaning that had hitherto been hidden to them. This is not to say, of course, that the inner connections are always drawn, but it is to say that the horizon of power that had previously existed has now been illuminated in a key way. The faster and the witness are brought together in the depths of their horizonal intersection. This is precisely where the momentum of transcendence is manifest. Insofar as the faster becomes aware of the demonic shadow within his or her own horizon of meaning, there now appears the possibility of radical transfiguration in which the creative power of the shadow can be released for new purposes. By the same token, the witness can confront his or her own reverse shadow projection and see just how destructive and uncanny is its logic. In both cases, the meaning horizon is opened to new and expanded possibilities of meaning. From the 'negative' space of fasting comes the positive space of renewed understanding.

The possibility of transcendence opens up within public space whenever the inner rhythms of any central horizon become thematized in some basic respect. This is never to say that the horizon suddenly becomes illuminated in its full nature, or that the horizon is now encompassed fully and seen in its plenitude. Transcendence is always more modest in scope and power. Within the finite and broken power of the competing horizons, certain transfiguring possibilities are opened that can have their own life history. Needless to say, these transfiguring prospects may be short lived, as the forces of blindness and social and semiotic inertia move to cover over the open spaces created by the withdrawal of the shadow projections. But it must never be forgotten that even in the heart of the most demonic projections, other possibilities may slumber that can be quickened by the right kind of bodily and horizonal action.

There are innumerable, and less dramatic, ways in which transcendence can occur in public space. What has often been called the "moral imagination" is itself a force for transcendence that enables one horizon to come into rich contact with another. When Schopenhauer regrounded Kant's categorical imperative in the deeper logic of sympathy, he showed how the moral sense can enter into the inner rhythms of a suffering horizon and move to alleviate some of its inner stress. This process is a direct form of transcendence and does not require anything like a generic sense of duty for its semiotic dynamism. What is required is a deep awareness of the connecting threads of social signs and their manifest forms of inscription.

From the other side, a given horizon can experience transcendence when its own inner resources are evoked and transformed in a new way. The analogy with shipwreck applies best to those horizons that need to experience a lessening of their imperial claims. But what of those horizons that need to move in the opposite direction, namely, toward a power and security that has been denied by either the social order or by internal mechanisms? Here the better image is that of birthing, in which repressed or denied semiotic material can assume a new role in the strengthening of the horizon. This is the obverse side of the tactic of fasting. In the previous description the focus was on the movement to find and dissolve the shadow projection that demonized the outside object. But for an inscripted and broken horizon, this is only one half of the story. Of even greater import is the counter move to find a center of power and meaning that can rebuild the horizon so that it gains some of the stolen strength that belongs to the horizon of the oppressor. The depth dialectic is that between shipwreck and birthing. Perspectives that ignore shipwreck because of a desire to stress empowerment run the profound risk of generating a new demonic self-inflation. Yet, perspectives that ignore the difference between broken and already empowered horizons run the risk of dissolving social reconstruction into a kind of private therapy that can cleanse the self of demons, but that utterly fails to create the conditions of justice.

Hence, the movement of transcendence can be traced in either direction. Insofar as a horizon suffers shipwreck or unfolds outward through the moral imagination, it transcends it conditions of origin. Insofar as a horizon transforms its own inner material and gives it greater scope and validity within social space, it transcends social and personal demons that have blocked positive expansion and the movement into shared semiotic space. Without some initial sense of power, horizonal humility is just another way in which the powers can shrink the semiotic space of given groups or individuals.

Transcendence moves on the edges of horizons whenever they change their basic configuration. The 'matter' of horizons is semiotic. This material is concresced into innumerable sign series that have their own vector directionalities. Commensurate with an analysis that focuses on horizons is one that focuses on sign series. Horizons are nothing unless they are fully incarnated and located within and by signs. While the horizon is a clearing *within* which meanings occur, it is also the 'sum' of current and possible sign series that move within its light and power. Any given sign series is a subaltern horizon in its own right. Obviously the larger horizon can contain incompatible and competing subaltern horizons. Moral life consists in the constant struggle, which may be looked at in aesthetic terms, between and among sign series that have different vector forces and 'hungers.'

Since sign series are open at both ends, the mist-shrouded point of origin and the open region of the not yet, they are always available for an augmentation of meaning. As noted in the previous chapter, sign series can be spoiled or partially destroyed by the conditions of finitude. Our focus in this chapter is on the ways in which sign series can enter into the complex rhythms of transcendence and move closer toward a kind of semiotic lucidity that seems just beyond reach. In the human order, unconscious momentums and powers also directly affect the scope of sign series. Before detailing this aspect in the next section, the focus must be on the series themselves as they undergo an alteration of their shapes.

What does it mean to say that sign series are vector forces in their own right? It means that no sign series is totally free floating or unlocated. Any given series will move in some semiotic directions and not others, while denying or affirming alternative possibilities along the way. It helps to see such series as moving organisms that take in and exclude surrounding structures as they move fitfully toward some dim future in which internal and external semiosis will become transparent. Of course, this quasi-eschatological momentum is not one with built-in guarantees, but one that must negotiate through difficult terrain in which other sign series may serve to blunt any forward momentum. Yet forward momentum does exist, and this represents one aspect of transcendence.

A sign series moves forward whenever its own 'internal' interpretants feel the distant pull of other subaltern horizons of meaning. Serial intersection is basic to the life of signs, whether in the human order or not. Where does this 'pull' come from? Here Peirce's distinction between the dynamic and immediate objects becomes pertinent. The restlessness of sign series comes from their lack of correspondence to the dynamic momentum of the objects lying just 'beneath' them. The vector directionality of a sign series comes from two sources. The first source is the momentum of the interpretants themselves, since each given interpretant is a sphere of power and meaning, as is the series itself. The second source is the ever elusive and moving dynamic object that lies at the heart of the sign series. A sign series becomes self-transcending whenever it becomes open to unshaped prospects within the object itself. The dynamic object lives in and out of the not yet (nature's own eschatological heart). This momentum is handed over to the parallel sign series that feels the incompletion of its attained incarnate body of meaning. The sign series struggles to keep up with a moving dynamic object that lies just beyond its own horizon of meaning.

A sign series moves to overcome its antecedent position through its 'sensitivity' to the dynamic object and to its own moving interpretants. Were the world of *nature natured* an inert body of configured positions, such self-transcendence would be impossible. Sign series are granted a dynamism from the partially hidden object and from their own configurations that move outward toward new interpretants.

Yet sign series also transcend themselves whenever they confront alien subaltern horizons that represent an immediate challenge to their sovereignty. And, were the world simply one monolithic series of series, a la Leibniz or Royce, such possibilities would not prevail. Since the world is broken into innumerable competing series, it follows that any given series must transcend its own limitations if it is to enhance its scope within a potentially hostile semiotic environment. Hence a competing series is a different kind of dynamic object that must somehow be assimilated or changed as it comes into the orbit of the original sign series. It is like a dynamic object insofar as it contains hidden powers and rhythms that stand outside of the immediate assimilative powers of the given sign series. It is slightly different from a true dynamic object because of its attained semiotic density.

Vector directionality is dynamic and hungry for more semiotic prospects. By entering into the depth rhythms of the dynamic object, the series can realize its own internal prospects. At the same time, by entering into the momentums of external series, which appear like a hidden dynamic object, the series can transcend not only the conditions of its own semiotic origin, but the limitations of its own dynamic object. This burst beyond the given is an ecstatic transfiguration that births new meanings and brings new dynamic objects into the sphere of the sign series. This logic is part of the inner logic of horizons as they move into new configurations. No horizon could expand its meaning unless its own subaltern horizons (sign series) were themselves undergoing the same process. In this sense, incarnated interpretants and their series represents the self-transcending body of the horizon.

Horizons expand and contract as they confront internal and external subaltern configurations. The 'matter' of horizons; namely, their internal sign systems, have their own hunger for increased serial intersection. It is rarely recognized that sign systems are 'guilty' of a kind of concupiscence, that is, of a desire to encompass and contain an indefinite amount of semiotic material. Semiotic density is measured by the combination of depth and scope of signs in a series. Given signs increase their depth when they add rich and powerful interpretants to their orbit. Signs increase their scope when they make alliances with surrounding sign material. Above, we spoke of the power of a shadow projection to contaminate and clothe the object toward which it is directed. Looking at complexes in general, we can see that any given complex, as a center of feeling and power, will continue to add to its density and scope whenever new semiotic material comes into its orbit. Interpretive life rides fitfully on the back of these hidden and mobile unconscious determinants and struggles to find its way among the dark powers of the unconscious.

For the human process, sign systems negotiate their way between the limited powers of consciousness and the unlimited powers of the unconscious. If consciousness becomes inert and seems to close off novel semiotic possibilities, the unconscious moves quickly, through a compensatory momentum, to augment the conscious sign series so that they are compelled to add to their semiotic stock. On the most basic level, the unconscious of nature moves in and through the human process to augment meanings had so that they open themselves to the potencies that are pre-semiotic. This rhythm is beyond the control of the conscious self in process.

B. Developmental Teleology and the Unconscious

The repositioning manifest in the realm of public intersections, gives way to a dynamic depositioning as the powers of the unconscious become more and more efficacious after the loss of the pre-Oedipal stage of dreaming innocence. The public sign systems, each with their own hunger for expansion, move the self into the shifting domains of *nature natured*. The social life of the human process is supported by vast sign systems that leave strong traces within the heart of the self. However, underneath this robust and public process are the momentums that serve to give the self its link to the lost domain of *nature naturing*. Melancholy haunts the self in its social existence, and this melancholy is intensified in the initial encounters with the autonomous and abjected unconscious. The flight from the unconscious is exacerbated by the lure of public interpretants. This lure would continue indefinitely but for the developmental powers of the unconscious.

Initially, the unconscious confronts the self in process as an alien and dangerous force that seems to have only one semiotic function—namely, that of disrupting and inverting the secure and time-tested interpretants of public semiosis. The expansion of scope and depth in the social sign world is matched by a darker counter-logic that appears to undermine the security of the public self. From the simplest irruptions of language in Freudian slips, to the rage of demons in personal relations, the unconscious announces its counter-logic by depositioning and challenging meaning-granting interpretants. Hence the fear of the unconscious is warranted by a self that has shifting and unstable social contours. Our attitude of abjection toward the unconscious represents a valid recognition of its dangerous power.

While not using the language of the "unconscious," Heidegger came close to understanding its uncanny dark allure when he described the force of social curiosity in the inauthentic life of the self. We flee to the realm of the "they" (*das Mann*) because we cannot face into the counter-draft of the depth dimension of the self (Heidegger 1927: 222):

> The supposition of the "they" that one is leading and sustaining a full and genuine 'life,' brings Dasein [the self] a *tranquility*, for which everything is 'in the best order' and all doors are open. Falling Being-in-the-world, which tempts itself, is at the same time *tranquillizing* (*beruhigend*).
>
> However, this tranquillity in inauthentic Being does not seduce one into stagnation and inactivity, but drives one into uninhibited 'hustle' ("*Betriebs*"). Being-fallen into the 'world' does not now somehow come to rest. The tempting tranquillization *aggravates* the falling.

In the manifest semiotic world of *nature natured* we are caught in a kind of vortex that pulls us more and more away from our authentic possibilities of transcendence. Heidegger failed to probe into the inner rhythms of the unconscious, even though his categorial structure points toward a hidden semiotic dimension that has its roots in *nature naturing*. It must be repeated that the movement of falling is a dynamic one that masks itself precisely in the success and power of the public realm of semiosis. The "hustle" of the public realm intensifies as the lure of social semiosis closes off the unconscious and its uncanny counter logic.

In what sense is the struggle between public semiosis and the unconscious purposive? On the surface it appears as if the counter force of the unconscious, which depositions the secure codes of the "they," has no positive teleological momentum. Rather, it seems to be an alien and demonic force serving to undermine those structures that are of positive and enduring value. The initial encounter with the unconscious lacks all hermeneutic transparency. Consequently, the flight into the "they" is read as a positive move away from the irrational and nonsemiotic domain that denies and even thwarts human purpose.

The purposive dimension of this struggle begins to emerge when the self in process comes to see just how precarious its repositioned public codes are. This insight comes from a variety of internal and external sources. We have noted how horizons of meaning suffer shipwreck whenever they are compelled to recognize their limitations in the face of competing or alien horizons. Yet many semiotic perspectives assume that this shipwreck is a fully conscious event and that the self has merely come to augment its meanings because of a hunger for greater scope. Where does this hunger come from? The hunger for greater scope and hermeneutic insight comes from the compensatory unconscious that 'recognizes' the limitations built into the realm of the "they." Heidegger speaks of the voice of "conscience" as the call of "care" to the inauthentic self from the deeper authentic self. While this analysis is not incorrect, it does not go far enough into probing the uncanny teleology of the unconscious.

How does the unconscious, then, 'call' the self away from the hurried frenzy of public semiosis? As noted, the first announcement of the unconscious in the post-Oedipal stage is through a destructive irruption that frustrates the smooth functioning of sign systems and their encompassing horizons. Is this disruption merely a demonic force that rages against infinite semiosis, or is it a teleological momentum that seeks to open sign systems to a compensatory shadow horizon that can enrich personal and social life? Here the concept of "shadow" takes on a more positive connotation insofar as the shadow side of an attained and public horizon is meaning filled and purposive for the sign using self.

Consciousness is, by definition, perspectival and finite. It grants light while casting its own internal and external shadow. It is important to stress that the positive shadow cast by consciousness is not some kind of random semiotic noise whose sole purpose is to drown positive semiotic signals, but a one-to-one compensatory structure that carries forward precisely what is missing from the light of consciousness. Any given perspective maintained or endured by consciousness has its exact compensatory corollary in the unconscious. This corollary is fully semiotic and filled with meaning structures that are of immediate value to the human process. The initial abjection that results from felt depositioning hides the positive shadow side of meaning that can, when the conditions are right, overcome abjection and move the self toward a more encompassing perspective. Without the developmental teleology of the unconscious, the self could not participate in the deeper aspects of transcendence.

Developmental teleology is, quite obviously, a unique form of teleology. Unlike a kind of built-in entelechy that will unfold according to encoded and antecedent principles, developmental teleological structures are deeply responsive to current shifts in surrounding conditions. Any given purpose is subject to 'self' correction as its field of operation is modified. Put in more technical terms, a developmental purpose is one that contains both actualities and possibilities within its structure so that given internal actualities can be modified by internal and external actualities and purposes. If an external actuality perishes and a new possibility enters into the semiotic field, itself concresced into an actuality with scope and power, the inner purpose of the sign-using organism may respond to the shift and send out a different momentum that can enter into semiotic intersection with the new structure. For example, if the self has moved forward according to a life plan that involves public musical performance, but a permanent injury makes such activity impossible, a new configuration may emerge that works around the damaged organ so that a deeper aspect of the inner teleology may unfold. In this example, a life of public performance may become transformed into a life of teaching and composition. One actuality dies to give birth to a different, but commensurate, field of possibilities. The sign-using self probes into new fields for purposive unfolding and finds the means to transform a destructive situation into one with renewed prospects for enhancement.

Any given purpose, then, will be located and shaped by surrounding and precarious structures of interaction that are unrelenting in their efficacy. Yet the hermeneutic power of the unconscious is nowhere more clearly manifest then when a given purpose suffers shipwreck in the face of a changed personal and social environment. The counter-logic of the unconscious, which always shadows and compensates the conscious attitudes and purposes of the self, sends out new prospects that are announced to the self through a variety of direct and indirect means. It is important to stress that the unconscious is not some kind of self-censuring mechanism bent on hiding its meanings and semiotic contents. Rather, as our link to the innumerable potencies of *natura naturing*, the unconscious is a dynamic and forward momentum of self-disclosure that 'wishes' that its contents become assimilated by the self in process.

As noted above, dream material is one of the most semiotically dense and profound manifestations of the unique developmental teleology of the unconscious. A given dream is an uncontaminated product of the personal and, perhaps, collective unconscious. In calling such a semiotic product "uncontaminated," we are affirming that it represents a fairly clear internal semiotic map of a hidden terrain that shadows the conscious dimensions of semiosis. Freud erred in assuming that the dream itself is a masked wish that must hide its semiotic charge from the dreamer, whose primary concern is with remaining in an unconscious state during sleep. The insistence and inner vector force of dreams, manifest especially in cases where they wake the dreamer and provide an initial hermeneutic key, make it clear that the dream wants to enter into the orbit of conscious deliberation so that the self can enrich its hermeneutic field. Put in even stronger terms, the dream serves a deep evolutionary purpose by compelling the self to recognize its cut-off and abject semiotic dimensions. Evolutionary competence, in both natural and social space, can be measured by the self's willingness and ability to allow the inner vector force of dreams to shape conscious purpose.

The Jungian tradition has long been aware that dreams are direct products of nature and that they have a force that is much greater than many of our conscious images and perceptions. Recent studies have made this much clearer (Whitmont & Perera 1989: 6):

> As expressions of prerational, 'altered' states of consciousness, dreams are as variable as nature itself. Indeed they are a *lusus naturae*, a play of nature, that can never be fitted into rigid systems.

Rather, our rational thought capacity has to learn to adapt itself to the Protean variability of the life processes which dreams represent. Rational or 'secondary' thought must learn to adapt itself to the feeling tones and images of the dream, to reflect in reverie and to play intuitively, as seriously as a musician does with a sonata, until meanings emerge.

It must be stressed that the "play of nature" is the true teleological ground of dream material. This is not to say that *nature naturing* has some kind of overarching teleology, but that it does work in and through the human unconscious to provide a clearing for compensatory developmental teleology. This distinction between some kind of metapurpose and finite developmental purposes is crucial. Nature does not give us a magic key to ultimate meaning in our dream material, but does show us past our current one sided attitudes that thwart the health of the organism. Transcendence comes out of this play of nature whenever we allow the vector force of dream material to deposition and reposition our conscious trajectory.

The hermeneutic question is often raised as to whether or not a given conscious hermeneutic perspective can contaminate the production and assimilation of dream material. Put in colloquial terms, do Freudians dream Freudian dreams while Jungians dream of archetypes? For many, this question is deeply vexing, precisely because of a contemporary over emphasis on the power of conscious forms of semiosis in shaping meaning. Yet this skepticism about the ability of the organism to enter into the play of *nature naturing* betrays a profound misunderstanding of the true counter-logic of the unconscious. It has long been noted that dream series are not inert or passive products that merely throw themselves into the waiting arms of the prejudiced hermeneutic agent. One of the most striking features of dream series, that is, a sequence of dreams taking place over many months or even years, is that the series can adjust to inadequate hermeneutic moves and actually invert a misguided interpretation. If the self persists in misreading the dream material, a given content will continue to appear in stronger and stronger configurations until a more genuine confrontation is forced from the self. No misreading will be allowed to stand for too long.

When Freudians speak of the "return of the repressed" in both behavior and dream material, they show their lack of understanding for the deeper hermeneutic impulses of the self in process. Certain dream material will indeed return again and again, seeming to mock the helpless and complex ridden self. Yet this return is never the last word. Failed hermeneutic strategies, tied to the notion that dreams represent unconscious and denied wishes, make it impossible to break free from the endless return of the same. However, when the hermeneutic strategy shifts to an understanding of developmental teleology, it can open a door to the dream assimilation so that the play of *nature naturing* is once again given some scope. We often lock the door to the future assimilation of meaning. The dream material provides us the way out insofar as we become receptive to the uncanny and prospective rhythms of the unconscious.

There is a direct parallel between the repositioning of social signs through the domain of *nature naturing* and the depositioning of the conscious self in and through the unconscious. Horizonal and semiotic intersection are rooted in the deeper rhythms of the unconscious as it struggles to find greater forms of expression for the potencies of nature. My lack of satisfaction with a given horizon of meaning has its source in my dream material, which continually announces to me that I live in a one-dimensional semiotic universe. Even when we do not consciously remember dreams, we do assimilate some aspect of their message, no matter how tenuous the signal may be in a given case. The sign-using self lives in and out of a counter-logic that appears to it on a nightly basis, insuring that semiotic closure will not have the last word.

The unconscious has a different dimensionality from consciousness. It is not in the same kind of tri-dimensional public grid that shapes public forms of semiosis. The temporality of the unconscious is such that it seems to move into and out of public time as measured and lived by sign-using selves. Equally, the unconscious is not in public space, but enters into rhythms and structures that are prespatial. For example, in intense transference situations the dream material of analyst and analysand enter into what is called a "dream field" in which the unconscious structures of both persons are linked. This semiotic connection does not take place through public media of transmission. There are no direct causal links between the dreams of each individual linking meaningful images. Whether or not telepathy exists as a specific form of semiotic encoding, transmission, and decoding, there are other aspects of the dream field that do not correlate to a telepathic causal relation.

The parallel dream series of the transference/countertransference relation come from a common source that is hidden from view. One analogy is to the cosmic dark matter that makes up between 90 and 99 percent of the physical universe. Many candidates have been proposed for this nonradiating matter, although each has so far been dethroned in turn. The key point in the analogy is that while we are not yet in a position to decode the inner nature of this matter, we can see its gravitational effects on galaxies and clusters. By the same token, the unconscious activated in the crosspersonal dream field exerts a tremendous 'gravitational' effect on the observed dream material. The parallel dream series point to a hidden origin around which they orbit, even if that origin is presemiotic for the sign interpreters themselves.

This striking parallelism, in which analyst and analysand dream their way into each others internal dream series, has caused theorists to reinvoke Leibniz's psychophysical parallelism, as if to say that the confused perceptions lying in each monad (consciousness) have a common source in a preestablished harmony that lies just beyond our reach. Each consciousness is thus monadlike in that it does not seem to have obvious windows on another self, but can enter into the inner workings of that self through some third mechanism that lies beyond attained public signs. This third mechanism is the unconscious, which reaches down into the mysteries of *nature naturing*.

The evocative parallels within the dream field point to a connecting link that compels consciousness to attend to powers of origin within nature. Here the compensatory relation, tied to developmental teleological structures, comes to the fore. The dreams of the analysand wrestle with issues invoked in the transference. The countertransferences of the analyst move in their own way to unlock the depth meaning of the transference dreams. It is as if each parallel dream series has its own inner trajectory while working on another level to interpret the other series that is somehow involved with it. Leibniz gives us some clues to this unique process, although he generalized his concept too broadly to cover all semiotic relations, when he argues that monads not only mirror each other, but mirror each other mirroring each other. His perspectivalism, undergirded by his belief in the preestablished harmony of all monads, makes it possible to correlate the finite perspectival field of consciousness with the richer semiotic and presemiotic fields of the unconscious.

The developmental structures displayed here thus work on two levels. Initially, we noted that the unconscious is minimally purposive in that it compensates for a one-sided conscious attitude by providing the sign-using self with a more encompassing semiotic field within which to situate its internal and external interpretants. This compensation is purposive in that it serves to bring the sign-using self into deeper meaning structures that enhance the psychic field. On a deeper level, these developmental teleological structures enter into the lives of other selves by entering into (coming out of) prespatial and pretemporal meaning horizons that enter into finite and particular spatial and temporal horizons. The mutually activated dream field, where analyst and analysand dream each other's dreams (mirroring of the mirroring), serves to compensate consciousness on a deeper level. From the minimal purpose of enriching a given conscious attitude, the unconscious moves to compensate the very world of space/time by pointing to (participating in) a kind of self-giving of *nature naturing* that is never itself a position within the complex fields of public space/time.

Jung developed the concept of "synchronicity" to denote this second form of developmental teleology, in which a larger hermeneutic purpose emerges to transform the very concept of the human process. Whatever the future of his particular concept, which also invokes Leibniz's parallelism, the phenomena of the dream field point toward the unique self-othering fissions of *nature naturing*. The semiotic phenomena of *nature natured* are all within the complex fields of space/time and thus partake of local and delimited fields of public meaning. But when the deeper rhythms of the unconscious emerge to shape the interpersonal field, spatio-temporal structures are bent, or even broken, to reveal the potencies that are not part of any given space/time field. This process is much more dramatic than the analogy between dark matter and the unconscious indicates. It is as if what we mean by semiotic gravity is transformed into something that lies on the nether side of all attained gravitational fields of meaning. Hence the depth rhythm of the unconscious is not a mere gravitational field whose causal agent remains unspecified, but is a momentum that transforms the very concept of semiotic gravity.

The depositioning of the unconscious thus works through developmental teleological structures to enhance the scope and depth of meaning of the sign-using self. Public space is reshaped to correspond to the prespatial and pretemporal dimensions of the unconscious. While there is no grand teleological purpose in this process, contra Leibniz, there are innumerable purposes that cumulatively serve to enhance the human process. Whenever a given dream enables the self to transcend antecedent forms of self-understanding, semiotic life becomes more purposive. On the deeper level, whenever a dream field activates archetypal structures that come from a prespatial and pretemporal dimension, two or more lives are enhanced in the resultant play of meanings that participate in the mysteries of *nature naturing*.

Semiotic closure takes place in a finite system that is bent in on itself. Semiotic entropy increases whenever a sign-using self refuses to augment its meanings by allowing outside semiotic structures and energies to enter into its unfolding. The semiotic self is anti-entropic whenever it enters into extra-conscious powers that can reconfigure its internal forms of self-organization. The most powerful forms of anti-entropic semiotic energy come from the pulsations that have their hidden roots in the unconscious of nature.

Even with the developmental momentum of dream material, we must not downplay the abject quality of depositioning that results when the unconscious invades conscious material. The unconscious is an infinite field of semiotic meanings and structures that has its roots in the phylogenetic history of the species. Personal complexes often intersect with this phylogenetic structure, thus taking on even greater power and autonomy within the psyche as a whole. The sign-using self is one that is also used by internal and external signs. The uncanny counter-logic of the unconscious rightly causes the conscious self to fear its irruptions and to develop the neurotic compensatory strategy of fleeing into the alleged safety of the "they." Few things in the life of the individual are as demoralizing and as frightening as the sudden irruption of an autonomous complex that radically and mysteriously depositions the public interpretants that stabilize and inscript the self in process.

This is not to say that public semiotic codes are somehow morally neutral, or even positive in force, but that the self sees itself caught between two powers, only one of which it recognizes. A given complex is autonomous in the sense that it is not integrated into the conscious strategies of the self. It emerges from the penumbra outside of public interpretants and carries an uncanny force that can be felt throughout the newly affected sign systems. It is as if a large meteorite suddenly burst into the living sign systems of the self, causing the antecedent semiotic structures to bend and explode under the impact. The self is often helpless in the face of this invasion, an invasion that inverts conscious values and choices. Insofar as the conscious attitude is excessively one-sided, the presence of the complex will be that much the more dramatic and destructive.

Depositioning is, on one level, beyond good and evil. Yet, from the standpoint of the sign-using self, it is often experienced as a personal tragedy. Consider the presence of something like a mother complex. Consider further that this very complex has a demonic aspect, a maternal presence that is destructive of the child, represented by the conscious attitude. The sudden emergence of this complex can tear the fabric of a hard-won semiotic stability and compel the individual into a form of self-destructive behavior. From the ego's standpoint, this behavior is deeply problematic and mysterious. It does not fit into any known economy of the conscious self. Yet, the appearance of the destructive complex has its own underground economy that must exchange its semiotic values with the conscious attitude. The self oscillates rapidly between two worlds and struggles to find some kind of momentary stability that can insure continuity.

Needless to say, this deposition by the demonic complex can only be greeted with fear, and with a conscious attempt to push the complex away and condemn it to the realm of the abject. Of course, it is just this predictable strategy that is equally condemned to fail. It is in dramatic cases like this, felt by all sign users, that the developmental structures of the conscious/unconscious dialectic become clarified. The complex has its own warrant and its own inner logic. It is not a random surd merely floating within the seas of semiosis, but a purposive structure that has its own history and, should the conditions be right, its own transforming future. Unfortunately, in the situation of the repetition of the repressed, this complex has no inner momentum, either internally or in terms of the dialectic between consciousness and the unconscious. It merely returns to mock the sovereignty of the sign-using self and to remind it of the dark powers of untransformed origin.

However, insofar as the conscious self can begin to name the complex and to provide a more capacious space for its appearance within the economy of the psyche, it can start on its journey toward a less demonic life. Naming is itself a liturgical act. It brings a complex into a sphere of pertinence and efficacy that was previously blocked off. The complex begins to remold itself around the consciously selected name. This process is not as arbitrary as it might seem. As with dream material, incorrect naming will be overturned by a negative response from the unconscious contents. If the name is incomplete, or even misguided, the complex will fail to gather up its energies in a transfiguring momentum. The fury of the complex will remain, returning again and again until the naming moves closer to its hidden core.

By naming the complex properly, a new power relation begins to emerge. The conscious self has begun to tame and integrate the demon by showing that it has mastery over its inner logic. This is not to say that consciousness can drain the unconscious of its complexes, an absurd notion at best, but that it can bring the hidden complex into the light of awareness through the naming. It is then as if the complex, in being nominated into liturgical semiotic space, becomes open to an exploration of its actualities and possibilities. As Heidegger has shown with great care, the process of naming is one that touches the inner rhythms of the being-thing, bringing it into the clearing of Being itself. In the language of ecstatic naturalism, this naming reaches into the uncanny counter-logic of the abjected unconscious and helps to bridge the abyss between *nature naturing* and *nature natured*. The complex, which reaches down into the unconscious of nature itself, at least now has the possibility of entering more fully, and less destructively, into the public codes that surround and inscript the self in process.

Retaining our example, the destructive mother complex has now been named and has been brought by the conscious self into its own public semiotic space. What was a mere meaningless and feared irruption, now becomes a known quantity that at least begins to assume some recognizable shape within the dialectic of the psyche. The shape still retains its demonic and abject qualities, but it has at least been recognized as having *some* parameters. This does not mean that the mother complex can be domesticated and tamed, but that it now occupies a finite space over against other finite spaces with which it must contend. What was a terrifying infinity is now a slightly less frightening finite power with a recognizable history. Mapping the life history of complexes is itself a teleological act, precisely because such mapping shows an inner logic and meaning to what had heretofore been without meaning.

It is always possible that the self will be permanently disrupted by the complex (or complexes) of the unconscious. There are no guarantees that the power of developmental teleology will always ameliorate the ferocity of autonomous complexes. Put in stark terms, some organisms have greater assimilative and transformative powers than others. This is not, and should not be, a moral evaluation, but a recognition that all sign-using selves are caught in vast phylogenetic and unconscious powers that may be too strong for the counter-powers of the conscious self. As we will see in the next section, the individual self must rely on powers greater than its own if it is to negotiate its way between and among the complexes.

The autonomous complex, in being named, is at least open to transformation in which its powers can be used to enhance the growth of meaning for the self. Complexes have such a disruptive power that they seem to emerge from the heart of nature itself. This sense of the uncanny and deep momentum of the complex is a valid one. In no sense is the complex a product of the conscious self, any more than it is a mere random mutation that somehow found its way into the self. It is a natural growth that has direct ties to semiotic events within the life history of the individual. Yet, the sheer power and supremacy of the complex must be traced to deeper roots within nature itself. The complex, and its archetypal core, stem from elusive potencies within the surging rhythms of *nature naturing*. It is to these rhythms that consciousness must turn if it is to find its wholeness amid the powers of the world.

C. THE SPIRIT-INTERPRETER

The unconscious is the locus within the self where *nature naturing* and *nature natured* intersect. The public codes that position the self collide with the depositioning power of the unconscious that has its own roots in the primal rhythms of *nature naturing*. At this stage the process is a dyadic one; namely, one in which repositioning and depositioning interact to locate the self in both its finite and transcendent dimensions. Public codes move the self out of its original position and reposition it within social semiotic space. This primal form of repositioning concresces into a more stable form of positioning in which the self is inscripted again and again by codes not of its own making. The counter-logic of the unconscious depositions the repositioned/positioned interpretants that guide the self in process. Were there no third momentum in this dialectic, the self would remain caught in a to-and-fro movement that would have no positive outcome. The third momentum comes from a power outside of the self and makes it possible to correlate the conditions of origin with the movement of transcendence.

As the self leaves the pre-Oedipal stage of dreaming innocence, quickened by the liberating powers of the mirror stage, it retains traces of its origin. These traces of the original position haunt the self as it negotiates its way among public interpretants. The irruption of the unconscious, whose developmental teleological structures frustrate all attempts to render it fully denied and abject, moves the self forward by depositioning the codes of the "they" that surround and support it. In this dramatic depositioning, the traces of lost origin become intensified and struggle to exert their legitimate claims. These claims can only be met when the self enters into the rhythms of a new positioning/repositioning in which the lost origin can return out of the not yet.

The means by and through which this transformation takes place is the spirit-interpreter that hovers in and around signs and sign users. The post-Lacanian psychoanalytic tradition of Kristeva remains trapped in a dyadic momentum in which the healing power of the spirit remains in eclipse. It is also blind to developmental teleological structures within the unconscious, and to the enriching and encompassing power of the spirit-interpreter that reawakens the original position in a new and deeper form.

Needless to say, we cannot go back to the domain of dreaming innocence. The propulsive rhythms of *nature naturing* drive the self outward into the domain of interpretants and close off any possibility of a direct return. Otherwise the self would be vulnerable to a kind of semiotic autism in which the public sphere would fade away only to give way to a kind of inert form of psychic envelopment and closure. Consequently, the return to the original position must honor the powers of repositioning and depositioning that have their own logic and grace. The original position can return, but in the transfigured guise of the not yet in which the maternal is reborn out of the heart of the spirit.

Why do we speak of a "spirit-interpreter" rather than solely of the "spirit?" In certain contexts, it is appropriate to speak of the spirit as the healing extra-personal power within semiosis. In much that follows, this language will be used. However, the spirit is most clearly present to sign users in its movement between and among signs. This movement is not purposive in a straightforward sense, but is so indirectly in that it works to enhance the richness and scope of meaning rather than to create some kind of extra-natural meaning. Meanings are always in and of a self-transforming nature. Consequently, the work of the spirit-interpreter is always in and of natural meanings that already obtain. The momentum of the spirit is forward looking in the sense that it moves signs and sign series into the encompassing and healing power of the not yet. The not yet is not some kind of already delineated kingdom of meaning so much as an opening presence/absence that keeps meanings from premature death and closure.

What, then, is the spirit-interpreter? Can we apply personal predicates to it or its is nonpersonal? By now, the answer to this question should have suggested itself. The spirit-interpreter is not a person, but it is deeply connected to structures that are personal. It lives to enhance personal centers of power and meaning by opening them to the depth correlation between the original position, repositioning, and depositioning. As 'friendly' to personal structures, the spirit must have some connection to those orders that are conscious and intentional. It does not follow, however, that the spirit-interpreter must be a superperson or a center or field of consciousness.

It makes the most sense to see the spirit-interpreter as a clearing that is postpersonal. It enters into the scene where persons are present and transforms the conditions of personal and interpersonal life. The spirit-interpreter gathers up the domains of selfhood and time and moves them into a new dimensionality that is only hinted at in the previous stages. Both consciousness and the unconscious can house the spirit-interpreter, but do so in different respects.

Consciousness houses the spirit through specific religious acts or practices that welcome its healing configuration into public interpretants. It should be noted that the term "religious" is being used in an exceedingly broad sense. Any act that invokes and or welcomes the spirit-interpreter is a religious act, no matter where or how it takes place within the so-called "secular" orders of interaction.

The unconscious houses the spirit-interpreter whenever it feels the momentum of thirdness (generality and meaning-filled connection) operating between and among complexes. The spirit-interpreter neither creates nor destroys complexes. What it can do is to bring these autonomous powers into play with each other so that their competing claims become ameliorated and transformed. The spirit-interpreter breaths healing life into the dark unconscious by connecting the pulsations that have their roots in *nature naturing* with the moving interpretants of *nature natured*.

As noted, the unconscious itself serves as the connecting link between *nature naturing* and *nature natured.* Yet it does not have the power to transform this link into a healing third in which the two domains actually become open and transparent to each other. The spirit-interpreter works in and through the unconscious to bring the fissure of the ontological difference into the domain of meaning. This meaning is not a mere product of antecedent states, but returns to the self from the posttemporal clearing of the not yet.

The spirit-interpreter goes beyond the developmental teleology of the unconscious into the liberating eschatology of the posttemporal. The term "posttemporal" is meant to connote a domain that has lived in and through time, but has gathered up the products of time into a new qualitatively rich integrity that is not part of the mere reiteration of time's flow. Put differently, the spirit-interpreter overcomes the return of the repressed that remains trapped in the flow of chronological time. By taking this return of the same and transfiguring it in the space of eschatological time, the spirit-interpreter delivers the unconscious of its own darkness.

The posttemporal spirit-interpreter lives on the 'other side' of time. This means that the spirit must gather up and preserve time's products as it gently moves them into the transfiguring power of the not yet. This relation is not causal, but involves a momentum that opens up prospects for the attained orders of meaning of *nature natured*. As noted, the spirit-interpreter is not thirdness per se, but lives and moves in such a way as to enhance and strengthen the amount of thirdness in the world of signs. The spirit works against the brute and preintelligible dyads of secondness, while honoring the return of firstness in a new guise.

Peirce was oblivious to the deeper logic of his own category of firstness. His abject denial of its future prospects drove him to privilege thirdness as the teleological outcome of personal and cosmic evolution. What he failed to see is that firstness has a deep restlessness that can only be stilled when it moves into the posttemporal domain of the spirit. Firstness, correlated to the maternal, is not only self-othering and heterogenous momentum (akin to Kristeva's *chora*), but lives out of the not yet when it returns to the self in the form of the liberating spirit-interpreter.

Put in different but commensurate terms, the lost object of the maternal is not merely a possibility now closed off in the past, but lives out of the not yet so that it can return in a transcendent guise. In this third form of transcendence, the sign-using self becomes open to the deeper correlations between the original position of the lost object, mediated now through the depositioning of the unconscious, and consummated in the repositioning of codes and sign series. How, then, does the lost object make its way into the not yet so that it can empower the self to transcend repetition and the static grid of the codes?

The lost object has an intrinsic hunger for self-othering. As deeply wedded to the spawning powers of *nature naturing*, it moves beyond itself whenever it forces any positioned self into autonomy and guilt consciousness. From the standpoint of the post-Oedipal self, the lost object is an indifferent and even hostile point of origin that no longer enters into the complex trajectory of the self as it moves among interpretants. The lost object seems truly lost in the darkness of the ever-receding origin. Yet this very restlessness, this strong momentum of self-othering, contains seeds of another type of relationality that emerges whenever the lost object is reawakened by the spirit.

The lost object contains possibilities and actualities, like any other order of relevance. The possibilities seem to be exhausted when the lost object casts its issue adrift amid the interpretant sea. Tragically, for many sign-using selves, this condition remains the permanent one, marking the self with a profound melancholy that has no ameliorating prospect. Yet this stasis is always open to another possibility that can emerge when the conditions are made right. It is here, on the edge of melancholy, that the spirit-interpreter makes its appearance.

The spirit can awaken a deeper rhythm within the lost object by unleashing its uncanny energies in a new direction. The lost object is in some sense pretemporal. It gives birth to selves that enter fully into chronological time, while seeming to lie outside of all temporal fields itself. Yet it too must feel the presence of temporality as it supports from afar the semiotic structures that have emerged from its cleft. It has at least a derivative sense of the ferocity and unrelenting sweep of the arrow of time, an arrow that moves in only one direction, namely, from the attained past to the partially open future.

How does the pretemporal lost object find its correlation with the posttemporal spirit-interpreter? And how does this linkage relate to the 'between' world of full temporality? Time itself, as an order of relevance, contains both possibilities and actualities. These are not infinite in extent however. Chronological time cannot march backward, nor can the pretemporal suddenly explode into a full temporal spread. What we are seeking are the connections among these three distinct forms of time, such that their intersection does not destroy their unique integrities. The pretemporal must exist in the form of self-othering momentum that spawns temporal orders from a point of origin just outside of chronological unfolding. The posttemporal must hover around chronological time without being fully caught in its one-directional network. We have used two distinct images here: that of spawning and that of hovering. The spawning power of the pretemporal seems radically different from the hovering momentum of the posttemporal. The one-directional network of chronological time seems to be neither spawning nor hovering, but unfolding.

These real differences among the three modes of time should not paralyze our phenomenological investigations. Connections, hard to see while we confine ourselves within the middle realm of temporality, do obtain and can be delineated through careful observations of their forms of intersection. In this context, the pertinent connection is between the hovering and clearing momentum of the spirit-interpreter in the posttemporal and the spawning and self-othering pulsations of the lost object in the pretemporal. As sign users we live most fully in the between world of chronological time. We stand at the point of intersection in which time's three possibilities come into fullness.

The pretemporal domain of the lost object does not exhaust itself in giving birth to temporality. Nor does the posttemporal domain of the spirit-interpreter confine itself to gathering up the children of temporality. There is a kind of arching back momentum in which the spirit moves past and through temporality to its spawning ground so that it can carry that ground forward in a new way. Put in metaphorical terms, time has its own restlessness that is most clearly manifest in the hunger of the pretemporal and the posttemporal for each other. The pretemporal hungers to escape from its endless repetitive spawning in which its own issue fly away from the point of origin and only look back in melancholy longing. The posttemporal hungers to overcome its own empty hovering so that it can become incarnate in the hidden origin that lies in the recesses of the no longer.

The spirit-interpreter cannot remain satisfied with an endless hovering. The bringing forth of thirdness, out of the dyadic collisions of preintelligible orders of relevance, is itself incarnational insofar as it wants generals to find a home in semiotic media of expression. Each third must find its purchase in the world of interpretants. Yet the incarnational hunger of the spirit moves past and through temporally shaped interpretants toward the pretemporal firstness that is itself preincarnational. As Peirce noted, firstness is not yet actual, that is, is not yet an efficacious sphere of interaction within the world of *nature natured*. Yet Peirce erred in assuming that firstness remained behind the scenes as a mere soup of possibility. Firstness 'desires' to become incarnate in the interpretants that mark its outer body.

The metaphorical connections now beginning to emerge prepare the way for a deeper categorial analysis. The spawning power of the pretemporal hungers to find its body in the world of interpretants. The posttemporal hovering of the spirit-interpreter moves toward the body of signs and toward the no longer of the lost object. The linking image is that of the incarnation. The embodied signs of the world incarnate thirdness. The spawning ground of the maternal incarnates firstness in an incomplete stage of unfolding. The spirit-interpreter incarnates meaning through its movement among the signs of the world. In each direction there is a hunger for deeper incarnational presence. Signs hunger for their lost object, while the lost object hungers to return to signs through the intervention of the spirit. The interpretant itself becomes the clearest locus for the gathering momentum of the pre- and posttemporal.

In examining the role of the interpretant in bridging the transcending powers of the pretemporal, temporal, and posttemporal, we move from a metaphorical evocation of structure to a categorial analysis that shows how the three modes of time must interact to make the fullness of meaning possible. The interpretant occupies a unique position in semiosis because it moves beyond the original position of the representamen while remaining permeable to the spirit. Peirce did not fully grasp the depth logic of the interpretant even though he made some minimal progress toward an understanding of the three modes of time.

The realm of temporality, that is, the realm confined to the orders of *nature natured*, is asymmetrical. Time can only move from the past to the future in a nonreversible flow. Put in other terms, a sign interpreted is a sign forever transformed. Each interpretant gathers up the semiotic wealth of its antecedent interpretant and augments or transforms it in certain respects. Even where there is a spoilage of meaning, the new interpretant represents a transformation of past actualities and possibilities. Consequently, like the flow of intra-worldly temporality, the movement of interpretants is asymmetrical. Every so-called 'backward' move is by definition a type of forward move. Past interpretants can be augmented, but they cannot cease to be past.

If the temporality of *nature natured* is asymmetrical, the domains of the pre- and posttemporal are symmetrical, but in different respects. The domain of the lost object moves outward from the pretemporal into the temporality of the original sign. In one sense, the now positioned sign, captured in the domain of temporality, cannot return to its source. But this is an illusion, deepened by the corrosive power of melancholy that seems to block off the no longer. In fact, the pulsations of the lost object can regather the offspring of temporality by entering into the returning rhythms of the spirit. The interpretant retains traces of the lost object as it moves into intersection with other interpretants. These traces may remain locked in the return of the repressed, or they may suddenly become transfigured into a promise of eschatological consummation out of the not yet.

The momentum of the pretemporal is symmetrical in that it allows for a movement backward and forward in which its own inner structures can become transformed. It is as if time can indeed flow backward from the posttemporal to the pretemporal. To get clearer on this form of symmetry, it is helpful to trace the actual unfolding of time within the interpretant.

A given interpretant is, as noted, fully caught in the asymmetrical momentum of temporality. It cannot erase its own history.

Yet, it also contains the traces of the birthing ground of the pretemporal that 'remind' it of its elusive conditions of origin. It can return to the hidden origin of these traces insofar as it becomes permeable to the spirit-interpreter that reawakens the lost object by welcoming it into the not yet of a transfiguring future. It is important to note that this momentum is not equivalent to Peirce's naive conception of the infinite long run or the counterfactual imposition of the "would be," but is deeply eschatological. There is a profound qualitative transformation within the heart of time itself as the posttemporal gathers up the pulsations of the pretemporal.

The symmetry operating here is complex. The pretemporal seems to have a one-way relation to the signs that have entered into the original position. It cannot swallow them back into the abyss of the no longer. From the standpoint of conscious sign users, there may be no sense of the future prospects of the hidden origin. What is past is locked in its own preintelligible momentum. The lost object cannot 'return' on its own account. It is here that the concept of the symmetry of time becomes crucial. The posttemporal has the unique power of moving past and through the temporal realm of interpretants to their inner traces. As the spirit-interpreter awakens the traces of the lost object, these traces become activated in a new way. They take on a unique semiotic charge that hovers around the interpretant, pointing it toward the posttemporal. The pretemporal traces of the lost object move backward and forward by a simultaneous dialectic that lives within the heart of the fully temporal interpretant.

The backward movement, made possible because of the symmetry of the pretemporal, actually serves to bring the lost object forward. Yet, as pretemporal, the lost object cannot be brought forward as it is, but must enter into the liberating presence of the posttemporal spirit. The symmetry of the posttemporal also has its own backward and forward dialectic. The momentum of the spirit is toward interpretants, that is, toward what is already prevalent within the orders of *nature natured*. It moves from the posttemporal into the temporal. When it moves into the temporal it 'finds' the pretemporal within the heart of the interpretant. It enters into the pretemporal in order to coax it outward into the liberating power of the not yet. By 'allowing' itself to move into the not yet, the pretemporal becomes wedded to the posttemporal. In this process it becomes transfigured in its inner being.

Returning to more metaphorical terms, the material maternal (pretemporal) enters more fully into temporality when it is opened to the spirit that gives it new possibilities. The maternal returns, not in the guise of the repressed or abjected ground, but in the form of the eschatological spirit that makes the maternal actual in the deepest sense. The maternal becomes more than a hidden birthing or spawning ground. It returns to the world of signs out of the erotic momentum of the spirit that heals the great wound left by the self-fissuring of the ontological difference. Eros is the bond that links the post- and pretemporal momentums of time to the asymmetrical unfolding of temporal orders. This erotic gathering of the modes of time is also agapastic in that it comes out of the grace-filled presence of the spirit-interpreter.

For sign-using selves, the drama of the wedding of the three modes of time is a profound form of transcendence. The conditions of finitude are quickened and opened to the rhythms of symmetrical and asymmetrical time, as the repetition of the repressed gives way to the opening of the not yet. Repressed complexes and demonic powers are transformed by the spirit-interpreter as it elevates the lost object into the not yet. The lost maternal, which remained a mere finite and abjected presence, enters into the moving infinity of the not yet. Conditions of origin are never simply negated, but can be brought into the dialectic of the not yet, where they become conditions of hope.

It is one thing to talk of the relationship between a given interpretant and the three modes of time, it is another to show how the sign-using self negotiates the treacherous terrain between the temporal and the pre- and posttemporal. Not surprisingly, however, this relationship mirrors, on a larger level, the momentum of any fully actualized interpretant. The sign-using self is, among other things, a series of intersecting interpretants, some of which live as public products. The self must enter into the dialectic of transcendence as it plays itself out in and through interpretants and products.

Looking backward, the self seems caught in the melancholy longing for what feels like a demonic origin that abandoned it to the fissures of *nature natured*. The pulsations of *nature naturing* remain dark and taciturn, bereft of any healing or forward-looking momentum. There is an abyss separating the fulsome plenitude of manifest interpretants from the 'empty' origin that forever recedes from view. Yet it is at this precise nexus, where hope seems to be in total eclipse, that the spirit-interpreter enters into the play of interpretants to open them to a transfigured sense of the rhythms of *nature naturing*. The sign-using self begins to feel the unfolding dialectic between the no longer and the not yet. Its interpretants, not all of them conscious or clearly demarcated, start to vibrate with a quickening that opens the traces of the lost object to an origin that emerges out of the future.

As the self looks backward by looking forward, the origin that seemed so indifferent or even demonic takes on a healing guise in the form of the spirit that opens possibilities and clarifies horizons of meaning. The maternal spawning ground that cast it adrift is not indifferent to its issue, but contains the seeds of a radically transformed relation to the child of time. The maternal struggles against its own closure so that it can welcome the self from within the heart of the spirit. Put in more direct terms, the maternal comes to greet the lost self from the future in which the ontological wound of birth is healed by the embrace of the erotic spirit. Eros is the bond that serves to hold the self-fissuring of the ontological difference into an encompassing embrace. This embrace is not a quasi-geometric imposition of structure or place, but a momentum that allows the ontological difference to continue its necessary unfolding, while protecting it from a total rupture that would foreclose meaning and abandon interpretants to utter semiotic darkness.

The unconscious is the locus where the two dimensions of nature emerge in their dialectic. The spirit-interpreter is the momentum that works down into the heart of the unconscious to bring *nature naturing* and *nature natured* into a healing dialectic that can be felt in the unconscious and in the subaltern dialectic between the unconscious and consciousness. The self no longer feels victimized by the sheer otherness of the unconscious, but can enter into the spirit as it opens the unconscious in a new way. The developmental teleology of the unconscious 'needs' the touch of the spirit if it is to fulfill its own entelechy. That is, the unconscious cannot bring the full depth of meaning to consciousness unless the spirit-interpreter provides a hermeneutic bridge that actualizes the fierce pulsations of *nature naturing* by bringing them into the clarity of the not yet.

The dominant interpretants of the sign-using self all participate in this dialectic between the no longer and the not yet. Signs of the return of the maternal from out of the posttemporal can be read in the living body of interpretants that give the self its contour. By the same token, the products of the self can take on new configurations of power and meaning when the spirit-interpreter lifts them past the confines of finitude. It must never be forgotten, of course, that finitude and its structures can never be overcome. What can take place is the quickening of finite structures so that they birth transcendent possibilities within nature and its orders.

Any given product will open itself to transcendence when it becomes the locus for the not yet. A public product, such as a work of art, will certainly contain innumerable marks of its finite origin and its finite embeddedness. When the posttemporal power of the spirit enters into the product, it sends out radii of involvement into other selves and other semiotic configurations. By becoming open to its own semiotic depths, the product also becomes permeable to its own vibratory presence in the not yet of the eschatological spirit. Even in the most culturally inscripted environment, marked by destructive patriarchal controls, the product may enter into the dialectic that can hold it in the great between where the no longer and the not yet embrace within the world of temporality. The product can hold its origin forward into the spirit and overcome the closure of its past.

This is not to say, of course, that products of the self are conscious agents, but that they are loci where the no longer and the not yet play out their erotic drama within the limitations of temporality. In no sense, however, are the fruits of this dialectic eternal or safe from the constraints that encompass all orders. What can enter into the not yet can also sink back again into the closure of hidden origin. The fruits of time can wither and die, thus ending their participation in the dialectic of transcendence. While we can hope that the divine mind will retain an eternal memory of each self and each product, not to mention each and every interpretant, we cannot assume that this memory, if it exists at all, will enter in a meaningful way into the life history of sign users.

The self, then, comes into its fullest self-understanding when it allows the dialectic of the no longer and the not yet, the whence and the whither, to shape its brief trajectory among the orders of time. The whence can never be fully brought into the light of semiosis, just as the whither will never devolve into a clear and distinct life plan. Yet the whence and the whither can open up many of their secrets and can envelop the self in the healing powers of eros and agape. The ontological structures making this personal transfiguration possible come from the inner momentum of nature itself. On an even deeper level of analysis we encounter the potencies and their 'agents' the infinitesimals. The infinitesimals live in the heart of the ontological difference and make all semiosis possible.

Chapter Three
Potencies and Infinitesimals

Like any other process in nature, the human process is buoyed by the ejective powers of the potencies, while remaining ensnared yet curiously illuminated by the mobile interpretants of the orders of the world. The great fissure at the heart of nature is not a once and for all event, but a continual presence/absence that can be felt in any complex of the world, insofar as that complex is compelled to reveal its presemiotic traces, as these traces point to the dark cleft from which all things, even God, come. Metaphors of darkness and light capture only part of the story. In order to render the potencies at least partially intelligible, a number of augmenting metaphors and concepts must be either deployed or evoked so that the mystery of the self-fissuring of *nature naturing* can come to the fore.

The momentum of the potencies is best seen in terms of a self-diremption within nature. The prefix "self" is meant to denote that it is nature doing the splitting, not some force outside of nature. The eternal fissure between *nature naturing* and *nature natured* is not a gift of the divine, but the clearing within which the divine finds its own measure. It is a comfort to many to assume that there is some kind of inner telos to the process by which the whither of the world is connected to the whence of the potencies. Ecstatic naturalism provides little comfort for those who wish to import intelligibility into the heart of this fissure. The transition from *nature naturing* to *nature natured* is without any telos that could be decoded semiotically. By the same token, although on a different level of generality, we can find no direct teleological link between a given potency (the term "given" is used quite loosely here) and an order of relevance in the domain of the world. In what follows, these limitations will form the horizon of our inquiry, especially as these limits impinge on the selving process and the movement from the lost object to the spirit and back again. Yet, some striking headway can be made about the elliptical and indirect presence/absence of the potencies and their manifestation through the infinitesimals.

Our primary concern in this chapter is with looking into the great abyss of nature and with gaining some insight into how the self negotiates with and against the primal fissure of the world. We have long been accustomed to understanding time in relativistic terms, that is, as pertaining to the momentum of a particular system of observation. When we probe into the potencies, we will see how temporality is birthed out of the pretemporal and given its own relativized locus within the orders of the world. Process perspectives err in driving their notion of epochal time too deeply into nature. More importantly, they utterly fail to see how the temporal emerges out of the unconscious of nature, and how this unconscious and pretemporal domain still interacts with the human process through the personal and collective unconscious.

One of the most compelling features of intra-worldly time is its deep tie to entropy. All ordered systems will become increasingly less ordered (and colder) through time. The flow of time in any finite system is asymmetrical in that there cannot be a return to previous levels of order, i.e., the system cannot return to a past state. However, insofar as a system can draw ordered energy from outside of itself, it may increase the amount of order that it has. Yet, in the long run, time and entropy will be unrelenting in moving the system toward a state of dissolution. However, when a system encounters the power of the pretemporal, there is the possibility that the entropic arrow of time will be slightly altered so that the system will attain a momentary kind of stasis. This process is especially pertinent to the human order. The pretemporal potency is not so much a new system of order as it is a reshaping of the very meaning of order within a system. The law of entropy is not violated but is transformed through the power of the lost object or the ever returning/receeding potency. The temporal and the pretemporal are both reconfigured in the encounter.

A. SELF-OTHERING

Both potencies and infinitesimals are self-othering. This entails that they have some kind of proto-'self' that can become open to otherness, both internally and externally. A potency is an unconscious momentum within the heart of *nature naturing* that moves outward into the world of orders by ejecting some kind of orderly sign or system from its hidden depths. An infinitesimal, as a number that is infinitely small but greater than zero, is self-othering in that it 'wishes' to become a point, line, or surface that is finite and in space-time. The relation between the potency and the infinitesimal is that of parent to child. The potency births the infinitesimal, which in turn births the manifest points of the world. It is as if each infinitesimal is a singularity that allows space and time to unfold from itself when it becomes self-othering. Strictly, a singularity is a point of near infinite density that has such a strong gravitational field that it pulls space back within itself. The infinitesimal, as understood in the *metaphorical* sense of ecstatic naturalism, is a possible point, tied to Peirce's category of firstness, that can birth particular space-time realities from its movement outward. Hence it is more like a possible space than a point that curves space backward.

Both the singularity and the infinitesimal are outside of space, but in different respects. The singularity pulls all matter into itself and, in effect, swallows space. The infinitesimal moves in the other direction by taking its own emptiness and letting the fullness of space come out of it as it becomes a point. Yet the 'emptiness' of the infinitesimal is a unique kind of emptiness. The potency empowers the infinitesimal to find some kind of delimited content so that it can become a representamen (first or 'pure' sign) with specific features.

Part of the 'how' of the self-othering of the potency is to turn its own churning, yet unconscious, momentum into an infinitesimal that becomes a vessel for specific spatial content. Yet this process is not a conscious one, in which the potency somehow picks from among options and hands over a semiotic content to the carrier (infinitesimal). The connection between parent (potency) and infinitesimal (child) is mysterious and lies outside of more direct semiotic forms of intelligibility. We can never know how a given potency hands over a specific content to the clearing of the prespatial infinitesimal, but we do know that some movement from the potency to the infinitesimal does take place. Let us look at this dual process of self-othering in more detail.

It is impossible to 'sum' the potencies, not only because nature is indefinitely extended, but because we can never actually find a delimited potency in its pure form. We know that potencies exist because of their continual effect on the orders of the world. We know that infinitesimals exist because of the logical connection between the prespatial and the spatial. Yet it is impossible to find either a pure potency or a pure infinitesimal. They are known through their consequences rather than through some kind of unambiguous presence.

We work backward, then, from effect to presumed cause in order to find the 'how' of the potency and the infinitesimal, not to mention their connection. The concept of "self-othering" is an important one in that it shows how something can engage in what could be called a "phase transition." The classic example of a phase transition is that of water when it goes from a liquid state to either a frozen or gaseous state, or back again. The transition is sharp and dramatic, even though water remains what it is in each state. The movement of a potency into self-othering can be likened to a phase transition in which a dark unconscious momentum suddenly becomes housed in a particular infinitesimal. The potency becomes other to itself by going from churning firstness to at least potential secondness in the heart of the infinitesimal. Were the potency to remain fully self-contained, it would never have any efficacy in the world of signs and complexes.

We do not know why potencies are self-othering, nor do we know exactly how an indefinite and unconscious power moves toward a delimited state by giving itself over to the seeming emptiness of the infinitesimal. Potencies are pretemporal, yet seem to hunger to have temporal children. The surging potencies move beyond their own self-encapsulated locus and pour some of their proto-semiotic energy into the possible points that await the potencies on the cusp between *nature naturing* and *nature natured*. A potency can never cross over this fissure on its own, but must find a vessel than can live in the pretemporal and prespatial, on the one hand, and the temporal and spatial, on the other. Peirce's unique understanding of the infinitesimals has given us the needed clue for understanding the form that the vessel must take.

In a letter of March 16, 1900, to the editor of the journal *Science*, Peirce clarifies his understanding of the nature of infinitesimals and how they relate to finite and actualized lines in space. He reinforces his notion that it is impossible to exhaust the possibilities of division of a given spatial unit (CP 3.568):

> We must, therefore, conceive that there are only so many points on the line as have been marked, or otherwise determined, upon it. These do form a collection; but ever a greater collection remains determinable upon the line. *All* the determinable points cannot form a collection, since, by the postulate, if they did, the multitude of that collection would not be less than another multitude. The explanation of their not forming a collection is that all the determinable points are not individuals, distinct, each from all the rest. For individuals can only be distinct from one another in three ways: First, by acts of reaction, immediate or mediate, upon one another; second by having *per se* different qualities; and third, by being in one-to-one correspondence to individuals

that are distinct from one another in one of the first two ways. Now the points on a line not yet actually determined are mere potentialities, and, as such, cannot react upon one another actually; and *per se*, they are all exactly alike; and they cannot be in one-to-one correspondence to any collection, since the multitude of that collection would require to be a maximum multitude.

Infinitesimals do not form a collection that can be compared with another collection, with its given magnitude. Any given line, or spatial unit, can always be further and further divided to reveal more breaks within the continuum. The transition from the possible or potential point (potentiality) to a given point is the transition from a possible universe that has no individuals to one that does. Peirce is quite clear about the nature of genuine individuality: A point can only be actual if it interacts with and against another. By the same token, a point has "different qualities" from its neighbors, and thereby partakes of individuality. The concept of individuality does not apply to the infinitesimals, which are preindividual, and hence bereft of specifying qualities.

Radicalizing Peirce's model, we can say that the self-othering of the potency finds its true home in the preindividual infinitesimal that is itself 'restless' in its movement to spawn space and time. Sharpening our earlier discussion of singularities vis-à-vis infinitesimals, we can say that the singularity swallows space and time and renders them impotent, while the infinitesimal moves in the exact opposite direction to make space and time actual out of the prespatial and pretemporal matrix of the potencies. The infinitesimal is an infinitely small 'clearing' from which space-time structures emerge. It is as if the world of infinitesimals is the locus of continual creation, not out of nothingness, but out of the mysterious and unconscious surgings of the potencies.

We have seen how the potencies are self-othering. They move from a chaotic and indeterminate state toward a particularization in which they hand over their power to the infinitesimals. We certainly cannot count the number of potencies nor the number of infinitesimals involved in this transition. Peirce rules out in principle the idea of finding anything like a given maximum magnitude for the infinitesimals and reminds us that counting entails secondness, that is, individuals in reaction to each other *in* a given continuum.

The infinitesimal is self-othering in that it takes the 'content' from the potency and filters it through its own infinitely small universe so that it can suddenly expand into the world of space-time. Put in strongly metaphorical terms, it is as if the infinitesimal is its own Big Bang that takes primal content and expands it from the infinitely small to the indefinitely large. The process is not something that happens only once, but continues over and over again throughout time, as new infinitesimals come and go.

Of course, the potencies can withdraw through their own inner logic, not to mention through the counter-logic of the manifest orders of the world. The aging process, for example, is one in which the potencies and the infinitesimals both become less and less efficacious in sustaining the manifest orders of the organism. Insofar as the self continues in its trajectory, the infinitesimals continue to present and preserve the power of their underlying potencies. Insofar as the organism wanes in its power, it must acknowledge that the powers of continual creation have become muted.

We have denied that there is a teleological structure connecting the potencies of *nature naturing* with the orders of the world. Yet there is a curious sense in which the potencies and the infinitesimals 'need' each other if they are to become fully actualized in their respective and pertinent senses. The potency can continue to churn in the darkness of the unconscious of nature, or it can manifest itself, albeit indirectly, in the orders of the world. By the same token, the infinitesimal can continue to remain a possible point, or it can burst forth into space-time and become part of a genuine continuum of realized points. Neither the potency nor the infinitesimal can become what they most fully are without each other.

Hence there is something akin to a kind of proto-teleology connecting potencies and infinitesimals. This proto-teleology is not a full blown teleology insofar as it does not represent some kind of plan with a delimited content. Potencies interact with infinitesimals in semiotic darkness. The mutual participation is an erotic coupling without guile or awareness. We must be especially careful of importing gendered language here. It would be a mistake to see the potencies as somehow analogous to male sexual power and the infinitesimals as being analogous to female generative fecundity. For one thing, the concepts of "power" and "fecundity" are extremely ambiguous and can be used to denote either gender's sexuality. For another, the potencies are in some sense, as tied to the material maternal power of *nature naturing*, analogous to female sexuality, while the infinitesimals, as ejective of space-time could be seen as masculine in their operations.

It is more judicious to use such gendered terms in a fuller way to refer to both masculine and feminine features of the potencies and the infinitesimals. Potencies are self-othering and creative, and, of course, creativity can be both feminine and masculine, as can the movement of self-othering. They have both egg like and sperm like features. The infinitesimals are also self-othering and provide the locus for fertilization and growth. The erotic embrace connecting potency to infinitesimal is ecstatic in its release of energy and meaning for further growth. The transition from potency to space-time actuality, via the infinitesimal, represents a continual renewal of the prospects of the world, even though entropy is one of those prospects.

The erotic embrace is one that moves from a less to a more encompassing and actualized state. A space-time point is more encompassing than an infinitely small infinitesimal that, qua infinitesimal, merely hungers to become spatial. An unconscious potency is less encompassing than the sign, qua representamen, that eventually emerges from its encounter with the infinitesimal. The proto-teleology of the potency/infinitesimal embrace is most clearly signaled in the erotic growth of meaning as the pretemporal empties itself into the temporal and thereby becomes efficacious. How, then, does this structure of self-othering relate to the human process and its own drive for encompassment?

The self is a product of the self-othering of the infinitesimals. Deep within the heart of the body and the psyche are the moments of creation in which the prespatial bursts forth into the spatial. At the same 'time' the pretemporal births the fully temporal. We have long become accustomed to speaking of space-time as a unity and have come to see that the emergence of space-time structures is a singular act. In logical and mathematical terms, the human process is constituted by a series of intersecting space-time continua that collectively generate and sustain the self as it negotiates its way between and among the signs of the world. Needless to say, this is not the only way to understand the form and dynamism of the self, but it is a way that brings us closer to the mysteries of the ontological difference.

It is obvious that we cannot 'see' the infinitesimals by an introspective turn. Peirce decisively showed that introspection is a deeply precarious act that involves the introjection of external signs in such a way that neither semiotic origin nor goal can be isolated for special phenomenological treatment. What we in fact see are sign series that have floated into the self-process and have taken residency within the psychic economy of the person. These series are already on the nether side of the self-dirempting infinitesimals. Any given representamen or interpretant is the product of one or more infinitesimals (we can never say how many) and represents the emergence of attained space-time reality.

The self must approach its own internal infinitesimals through more indirect means. Metaphors or similes of vision must give way to structures of feeling, in which transitional structures are brought starkly into view. For it is in the movement from one affective state to another that something like the phase transition marking the self-othering of infinitesimals takes place. Infinitesimals birth space-time realities through a kind of apocalyptic self-expulsion in which the infinitely small becomes the finitely actual. It is not that the infinitesimal is merely getting bigger (a misguided notion), but that it is moving from the prespatial and pretemporal to something that finally has the very possibility of measurement. This ultimate form of a phase transition leaves indirect traces in the self in the form of feeling and a transfigured understanding *of* space-time.

Feelings are clearings within which the structures of worldhood become manifest. As a given feeling moves into its intensified fulfillment, it may suddenly elide away to provide room for another feeling. In between feeling "A" and feeling "B" will be a sudden phase transition in which the antecedent reality will be relocated on a specific plane of feeling, while the consequent feeling will emerge on a different, and in some respects discrete, plane of feeling. Feeling "A" illuminates a complex in a particular way, while feeling "B" will illuminate the same or a different complex in a different way. Put in other terms, two distinct clearings emerge in which an order (or orders) of the world is disclosed to the human process. What is of particular concern is the space 'between' "A" and "B" that is not on a commensurate plane of feeling.

One place where we can gain some help in understanding this dramatic transitional process is in catastrophe theory. While the future of this theory remains problematic in biological studies of morphogenesis, it retains some value for semiotic theory precisely where it points to the leap from one plane or structure of reality to another. The theory is most pertinent when applied to the structures of feeling as they in turn provide clearings on the world of signs. We begin with a definition of the nature and scope of catastrophe theory itself (Woodcock & Davis 1978: 42):

> A catastrophe, in the very broad sense [René] Thom gives to the word, is any discontinuous transition that occurs when a system can have more than one stable state, or can follow more than one stable pathway of change. The catastrophe is the 'jump' from one state or pathway to another. In the landscape imagined by [C.H.] Waddington [British animal geneticist], it could be represented

as a passage of an object from one basin to another, or as a flow of water from one channel into another. The transition here is discontinuous not because there are no intervening states or pathways, but because none of them is stable: the passage from the initial state or pathway to the final one is likely to be brief in comparison to the time spent in the stable states.

In a system that has some form of disequilibrium there is likely to be a phase transition from one partially ordered state to another partially ordered state, such that there seems to be a fold in the fabric of the system. It is as if a plane surface curls under itself for a brief moment so that one part of the surface leaps down to another through the fold, which represents a discontinuity within the plane. A great deal of energy has been invested in showing that there are several such folds, or cuts, within the fabric of an organism or structure, and that there is a catastrophic leap from one state to another when the disequilibrium reaches a certain level of intensity.

Peirce emphasized how feelings flow into each other along a continuum, a continuum that is itself constituted by feeling-toned interpretants. The current perspective takes issue with this simplistic understanding of feeling, not to mention its supporting metaphysics, by stressing the catastrophic nature of the phase transition from one feeling to another, such that the 'between' state is represented as a fold or cut along the so-called continuum. The term "catastrophic" does not here denote anything negative, but merely points to the fact that there is often a profound leap or plunge from one state to another that cannot be predicted from the antecedent material alone. When this theoretical framework is applied to human emotion, it shows just how the transition is unpredictable and radical in manifestation.

The theory argues that there are three types of attractors awaiting any transition, serving as points toward which a system is moving. A fixed-point attractor remains in place and governs the way a simple system works, e.g., as seen in the arrested motion of a pendulum in a so-called zero state. A periodic attractor works in a system that returns to a cycle after existing in a steady state, e.g., in a moving pendulum that swings back after briefly resting in the extreme of its arc, or in a manic-depressive individual who moves cyclically from one extreme to another, with a longer-term stable state in the middle. A strange attractor is less easy to define, even if well exemplified in nature. It involves unstable periodic orbits that seem to repel each other, an example being a bowl of spaghetti with sauce in which each strand of spaghetti is entwined around some others in a seemingly random way (Casti 1994: 29). The movement from one state to another, as governed by the logic of the three types of attractor, is a leap or phase transition involving the transition from stability, to seeming instability, to a new stability, which may or may not be like the first stability.

Returning to the domain of human feeling, we can see that there is a kind of leap from state "A" to state "B" that may involve any one of the attractor types. The simplest type of feeling transition involves a simple attractor that reinstates the same feeling after a brief hiatus. A periodic (limit cycle) transition moves between two or more states that always return to the point of origin, with, of course, intervening states. The strange attractor emerges in a kind of randomness that points toward a form of developmental teleology in which the attractor itself is subject to evolution and transformation in time.

A significant number of feeling transitions are of the periodic variety, with a cusp of transition that opens up a kind of back door allowing a catastrophic leap from antecedent to consequent and back again. The unstable system must make a leap to a new form of stability (Casti 1994: 55):

> So to summarize, catastrophe theory deals with the fixed points of the families of functions. The catastrophes occur when, as we move in a continuous way through the family—usually by smoothly changing parameters describing the system—a stable fixed point of the family looses its stability. This change of stability forces the system to move abruptly to the region of a new stable fixed point.

Thus we jump from one fixed-point attractor to another when the first attractor becomes unstable. Peirce was insensitive to this notion of abrupt change because (if we may be be permitted a psychoanalytic observation), as a manic depressive (Brent 1993), he abjected and denied the intense emotional life that engulfed him, leaving him stunned and demoralized. He therefore priviliged continuity as a compensation. By moving from his continuum theory toward a reconfigured catastrophe theory, it is possible to show how affective states actually function between unstable attractors. In order to tie catastrophe theory to the ecstatic naturalist understanding of infinitesimals, it is necessary to focus on the fringes of affect, where the instability of the emotion matches the growing instability of the attractor.

POTENCIES AND INFINITESIMALS 107

As noted, an emotion is a clearing onto fundamental structures of worldhood and the subaltern domains of specific orders. Peirce was certainly right in tying feeling to firstness, and hence locating it at the heart of the human process. But he did not probe into the transitional structures that emerge when the feeling and its illuminated world become unstable on the edge of a kind of phase transition. Peirce, in a move against Descartes, insisted that feelings and thoughts were fully, if differently, spatial. The edge of a feeling is the point of intersection where the feeling encounters the new irruptions of the infinitesimals. Put in stark terms, the feeling is compelled into a catastrophic leap when its penumbra vibrates with the sudden emergence of self-othering infinitesimals that come to alter the mobile contour of the feeling. How does this happen?

We are dealing with a dialectic in which the given feeling is in search of its attractor, whether fixed, periodic, or strange. The feeling seeks equilibrium in a system that may itself be in flux, and this larger systemic order impinges on the movement of the attractor. For example, consider an emotional encounter with a new person, such that prospects of transformation emerge as a kind of semiotic and emotional lure. The emotional connection vacillates between a form of erotic participation in the new nexus and a kind of otherness in which the encountered person seems strange and deeply alien. The new person, self "B," emerges as a strange attractor, with innumerable folds and cuts that do not fit into preestablished patterns. Person "A" seeks to transform the strange attractor into either a fixed or periodic attractor thereby insuring some kind of higher equilibrium. The emotional states of both "A" and "B" are dialectically tied to this movement between attractor types. Instability marks the initial phase of this encounter, while prospects for a restabilization remain tantalizingly close. The dialectical dance between participation and otherness mirrors the dialectic between emotion and attractor type.

From the standpoint of ecstatic naturalism, the most pertinent aspects of this encounter take place on the edges of the emotional field, where there are shifts between one attractor and another. It does not matter whether the shift is from one attractor of the same type to another of the same type, of from one type to another kind. In either case, there is a strong agitation on the edge of the emotional field that is correlated to an instability in the attractor. This agitation comes, as noted, from the unexpected irruption of the infinitesimals that reshape the contour of the field and its attractor. It is as if the emotional field represents a kind of form, albeit highly mobile, and the infinitesimals represent a kind of dynamics. The dynamic emergence of the infinitesimals on the edges of the field and its attractor destabilizes the internal/external structure so that a dramatic phase transition is necessary. However, there is no telic process dictating just how this transition is to occur. There is a movement in which both attractor and emotive field are dramatically reconfigured so that new structures, however tenuous, may emerge.

Suppose that persons "A" and "B" move from a state of semiotic probing and psycho-sexual bantering into a fierce merging in which the emotive fields become deeply entwined around two fixed-point attractors. Otherness recedes from view for the moment while the depth dialectic of erotic participation envelopes the two semiotic fields. There is an isomorphism between the two attractors, running the risk of a narcissistic mirroring in which the integrity of each self is sacrificed for the new convergent field. The emotive isomorphism is also a mirror of the attractor isomorphism. In some cases, this merging process remains in place throughout the life histories of the two selves. From the standpoint of human community, such a sustained merging is a form of pathology.

Where do the infinitesimals appear in such a process? It is precisely here, where otherness has been totally eclipsed by a form of almost demonic co-participation, that the link between catastrophe theory and the infinitesimals becomes most sharply clarified. The merged selves can only return to a more balanced form of equilibrium by going through a phase transition inaugurated by the nontelic self-othering of the infinitesimals. The emotional fields have become too entwined and too indistinct to sustain healthy autonomy. It is on the edges of each field where the process of otherness emerges for selves "A" and "B." The prerational infinitesimals, as tied to the firstness of feeling, can burst forth where the emotional fields have their boundaries, remembering that for Peirce, the infinitesimals come into their own on the edges of all measured and measurable spaces. The sudden unfolding of new feeling prospects on the edges of attained feeling, destabilizes the larger field and tips it toward a phase transition.

The fixed-point attractor is also destabilized by the irruption of the infinitesimals and becomes less securely embedded in its corollary emotional field. Both the emotional field and its attractor become unstable and must move to regain the lost contours that shaped and secured them. This is where the infinitesimals do the crucial work of establishing the force of otherness within the bonded selves, moving each of them away from their demonic co-participation toward a deeper dialectic of participation and distance. This logic also works for the periodic or limit-cycle attractor, where we have something akin to Freud's return of the repressed in which emotional fields, and their attractors, cycle through again and again without any healing forward momentum.

Thus the self participates in vast and mobile affective fields that move catastrophically from one type of stability, via instability, to another. The attractor can be seen as the whither, guiding the emotion to a new configuration in which the self/world correlation is illuminated differently. In pathological forms of catastrophic change, there is a mere reiteration of previous affective fields, with little or no forward momentum. In healthy forms of catastrophic change, strange attractors can move the self forward through a mobile developmental teleology that can both integrate past affective states and evoke new and more encompassing fields.

Strange attractors involve some form of chaos and randomness and live a more precarious existence in nature than the fixed or periodic types in that they do not form part of a strictly determined system. The selving process involves a complex series of negotiations among the three attractor types (the existential whither) such that the self can provide increasing room for the emergence of strange attractors. The most valuable aspect of the strange attractor is that it opens a space for novelty and semiotic growth in the self in process. It also preserves the dialectic between participation and otherness such that neither side collapses into the other. The psychic fusion described above is overcome when the two selves involved find the appropriate strange attractors that can coax or lure them into new configurations of interaction.

As noted, the movement of self-othering of the potencies and their 'agents,' the infinitesimals, makes it possible for the self to have a new relation to time. The thermodynamic or entropic arrow of time (Hawking 1988) governs the trajectory of nature's self as it moves from a state of high order toward a state of disorder. Yet there are curious irruptions within this process that subtly transform entropic time such that the self, and its emotional fields, can experience a kind of pretemporal reality that is itself a foretaste of the posttemporal domain of the spirit. This split within the heart of time flickers around the edges of the human process and makes genuine transcendence possible under the conditions of embodied finitude.

The infinitesimal births space-time. In a sense, emotional fields are spatial (as argued by Peirce), even while, of course, participating in time. We have focused on the spatial dimensions of feeling whereby feeling "A" is catastrophically transformed into feeling "B." Our current concern is with probing into the reality of time as it is assimilated by the self in process. Needless to say, it is impossible to pry time loose from space, and vice versa, yet a phenomenological analysis can highlight temporal features for special treatment. In particular, it can show how the three primal divisions within time, namely, the pretemporal, temporal, and posttemporal, correlate within the self. Entropy applies to only one dimension of time, the temporal in *its* three modes. This is not to say that the pre- and posttemporal are somehow anti-entropic, but that the concept of entropy simply does not apply to these dimensions of time.

The self is caught in the vast tridimensionality of temporality and feels the pull toward the future. The past can be remembered, but the future cannot (Hawking 1988). The present becomes increasingly determined as the future indeterminacy becomes concresced in the present (Hartshorne 1948). Temporality is thus asymmetrical and modally distinct. The past is determined, the present is becoming determined, and the future is at least partially indeterminate. The arrow of temporality has only one direction. Yet within this unrelenting logic are the irruptions of the pre- and posttemporal, giving the self a renewal of time that defies the logic of temporality.

The logic of this process is clear. The potency, as pretemporal, hands over part of its momentum to the infinitesimal which is itself pretemporal but moving toward time. This is why the infinitesimal is so crucial for its role on the cusp between *nature naturing* and *nature natured*. It is both pretemporal and potentially temporal (unlike the potency which remains pretemporal). As the infinitesimal goes through its *own* catastrophic phase transition it births temporality for the self, while also presenting traces of the pretemporal. Like the representamen, the infinitesimal participates in the two primal dimensions of nature. Its whence links it to the pretemporal, while its whither links it to the time that emerges for the sign-using self. If there is something akin to the Christian notion of the Fall in ecstatic naturalism it is the estrangement that is experienced by the self when it becomes embedded in temporality while ignoring the pretemporal that is also a gift of the infinitesimal.

The self-othering of the infinitesimals surrounds and sustains the self, even while providing goads to catastrophic changes within emotional and temporal life. When the self allows the presence of the whence into its experience of time, it returns to the pretemporal powers that are also embodied in the infinitesimal. The arrow of temporality is momentarily stilled in its flight as the pretemporal enters into the economy of the psyche. This is a kind of reverse catastrophe, enabling the self to find an originating power that is not part of attained and ordered sign series. It is as if the self leaps out of the time plane altogether and finds a pretemporal self-othering that sustains it in a much deeper way than the entropic momenta of temporality.

The posttemporal emerges in a different way in the spirit that is also resident on the cusp between *nature naturing* and *nature natured*. If the pretemporal brings us to a nonentropic whence, the spirit brings us to a nonentropic whither in which signs become gathered up in the erotic embrace of fulfilled time and meaning. The self is most fully part of the selving process when it lives within the richness of the three primal dimensions of time. The pretemporal grounds it in the mysterious potencies. The temporal carries it forward toward states of decreasing order and meaning. The posttemporal gathers it into the kingdom of meaning in which the ravages of temporality are healed. The tradition has referred to this consummatory phase as an "eternal now" in which time is transfigured, even while remaining a temporal process within the world.

The eternal now of the posttemporal, a gift of the spirit, quickens the selving process and brings nature's self to the heart of the mystery of the three primal dimensions of time. It might jar on our philosophical sensibilities to see the spirit as a strange attractor, but there is some warrant for combining these two discrete language games in this fashion. The spirit serves to preserve chaos and complexity for the sign-using self, while also providing a space within which developmental teleological structures can unfold. The spirit is not some kind of unified superorder of meaning, but lives as a goad for the enhancement of complex meanings in time and on the edges of temporality. It is neither fixed nor periodic in its presence/absence, but has a deep complexity that continues to inspire wonder. To say that the spirit "blows where it will" is to say that it attracts catastrophic systems toward a different kind of stability/instability along lines that cannot be predicted or anticipated in advance.

Nature's self moves in and out of the three primal modes of time. The thermodynamic sweep of temporality is the most obvious and pervasive form of time for the self. Its marks are found on all aspects of the world. Tillich coined the phrase "stigma of finitude" (Tillich 1951) to evoke our sense of the entropic and death centered dimension of all intra-worldly complexes. For many, this is the only form of time that seems to prevail for the human process and the world within which it is embedded. Yet the pre- and posttemporal dimensions of time enter into our lives whenever catastrophic phase transitions show us a nonlinear aspect of time in its complex unfolding. The pretemporal richness of the hidden potencies comes to us through the self-othering of the infinitesimals, while the lure of the posttemporal stands before us in the invitation of the spirit. The selving process can never reach final completion, but it can move toward wholeness when it becomes open to the distinctive ways in which time gives itself to the human process.

B. Fissuring

Commensurate with the image of self-othering is that of fissuring, in which the primal realities of time, the self, and nature, are *unfolded* through a breaking of the fabric of space-time and its issue. If the analysis of self-othering evokes images of birthing, the concept of fissuring points to forms of shattering and unveiling that provide us with a different, but parallel, understanding of how nature's self can find its measure within nature and its innumerable orders, both semiotic and nonsemiotic. We are in effect looking at the same phenomenon from different angles. From one angle, the manifest reality is that of self-othering, while from another angle, the same reality manifests a deep fissioning process. These two 'hows' of nature in its diremption are dialectically joined.

By probing into the reality of fissuring, in which the fundamental clefts and wounds of the self and its world continue to appear, we can gain access to the power of the personal and collective unconscious. As is often appropriate in this domain, our strategy is to begin with a specific dream that has strong archetypal components, and which makes the primacy of fissuring central to its semiotic message.

In the dream under study, the dream ego is walking along a narrow passage toward a large building that is currently housing a conference of lawyers and medical doctors. The building is of a plain almost neo-fascist style with large concrete facades. The conference participants ignore the dream ego, sending the implied message that he does not belong with such an august group, even though he is a professor and a writer. On the left of the narrow path is a bottomless abyss that drops off at an almost vertical angle. The path and the edge of the abyss are gravel. As the dream ego walks closer to the building, he sees a man in a plain dark grey suit who is standing in front of a small bare tree. Curled on the branches of the tree is a coral snake, one of the deadliest species in North America. The snake is brightly colored, with red, black, and yellow bands. The man reaches out to capture the snake, but makes the mistake of grabbing it in the middle of its body. The snake proceeds to bite the man again and again. Here the dream ends.

In the Jungian approach to such complex material, it is customary to start with the dream ego, and then to work, via a process of amplification rather than reduction, toward the other images that permeate the dream field. The dream itself is best seen as a complex semiotic web that reaches in and through the dream ego to the structures that connect the self to the archetypes that are also products of the potency/infinitesimal matrix. Often, the fuller meaning of such a dream can only be disclosed through further dream material that carries key themes forward into different horizons of meaning. Later dreams may even serve to confirm or disconfirm current interpretations. With this larger meta-horizon in mind, we can proceed with some cautious observations.

The dream ego feels profoundly displaced in a setting in which the turn leftward, toward the deep cleft of the unconscious of nature, is as dangerous as the movement forward toward the tree, where the knowledge of good and evil can bring seeming ruin. The dream ego is not welcome at the conference of professionals, who represent a kind of judging super ego. The healers and the litigants are not interested in either the abyss or the tree. They are consumed with their own lesser horizons of meaning. For if they do not see the abyss literally at their feet, they are not in a position to understand the vision of the dream ego, who must honor numinous powers that fall outside of the super ego and its worldly successes.

This feeling of alienation drives the dream ego to examine the strange figure in the grey suit, who is neither a doctor nor a lawyer. In his grey suit he is a shadow figure who is removed from the world of the super ego. It is not clear that the super ego even sees him. Yet the dream ego is deeply drawn to the shadow who does not show his face. The tree is barren, reminding the dream ego of the biblical fig tree that is seared by Jesus for its lack of fecundity. Yet on its bare branches is an image of extreme beauty. The coral snake entices the shadow figure, who must possess it. The dream ego watches in horror as the snake starts biting the hand of the shadow figure. The man does not drop dead, but continues to hold the snake, obviously fascinated by its power and beauty.

Thus far, we have seen that the dream ego feels profoundly alienated, perhaps even rejected, by the professionals who represent the judging super ego. Yet he has seen a vision that they have not, and has been transformed by the experience. The abyss is terrifying and must be avoided by very careful steps along its edge. The tree of death, where the dream ego watches in horror/fascination as the shadow figure is poisoned by the snake, stands before the entrance to the great hall, reminding all who truly see it of the deeper powers that dwell here.

At this point, once the inner experiences of the dream ego have been expressed, a process of mythic and semiotic amplification begins. The particular amplifications must ring true to the conscious dreamer, rather than be imposed by an analyst or book of dream codes. Using William James' wonderful image, any proposed amplification must "tingle" with the dreamer's conscious mind if it is to be allowed into the growing hermeneutic circle. Needless to say, this is a delicate process that must proceed slowly.

We immediately see two extreme forms of fissuring in the manifest dream. On the left of the dream ego, the side of the unconscious, is the bottomless abyss that threatens death should the self fall into it. The abyss must be taken seriously and only negotiated with care once the dream ego has achieved the necessary strength and power for the journey. This abyss is a great fissure that opens up beneath the feet of anyone who has the wisdom to see it. On the other side, next to the building that represents professional power and worldly judgment, is the tree where death can be dispensed to the unwary individual. Yet, here, some deep ambiguity enters. The shadow figure is not immediately killed by the snake. It is as if the shadow, that side of the self that is abjected by the ego because of its fearful or unpleasant qualities, has a kind of immunity to the deadly poison. The shadow must take on the task of receiving the venom that comes with wisdom. He is not killed by the snake, and his survival shows the dream ego that the pain of awareness can be integrated into the larger Self.

The snake, as the point of beauty/death, is itself a symbol of the fissuring of the world. In many ancient religions, the snake represents death and renewal. It also lives on the cusp between time and eternity (what we have called the posttemporal). In this sense, the snake is a symbol of the spirit and lives as a strange attractor. In the obvious literal sense, the snake attracts both the dream ego and the shadow. It does not attract the doctors and lawyers, who ignore its presence. Yet it is a strange attractor in that it points toward a developmental teleology that can quicken the selving process. The richness of the snake symbol is that it starts as a cyclic or periodic attractor, because of its return to itself in shedding its skin, while on a deeper level living as a strange attractor, pointing the self toward the spirit.

This is not to say that the fissures represented by the abyss and by the snake do not remain dangerous. Their power must be honored by the dream ego if it is not to be devoured. What is clearly presented is the power of fissuring to reposition the self along a new axis of understanding. The abyss continues to remind the self that nature is a great divide that cannot be overleaped by conscious strategies. The snake reminds the self that the powers of wisdom come at a great price. Suffering is inescapable in the selving process. One can always succumb to the venom that comes with insight. By breaking the skin, and by entering into the body and the blood of the self, the snake shows the fissuring at the heart of the world. The self cannot inoculate itself against the invasion of archetypal material, any more than it can live in dreaming innocence in its original positions.

The fissuring process is thus manifest to the self in its struggles with the depths of the personal and collective unconscious. The dream has personal referents that do not concern us here. On a deeper level, it has archetypal referents that point to the fissure that separates the conscious self from the collective unconscious. Within the dream are several archetypal elements that come from the unconscious of *nature naturing*. The tree image appears in most mythic systems as a symbol of wisdom and power. Whether it be the tree in the Garden of Eden, or the tree that bears the Golden Fleece, it represents the fissure where mere conscious wisdom must be shattered by the deeper wisdom of nature. The abyss is an archetypal representation of the depths of the God of meaning, who cannot be confined in any particular image. The shadow figure represents a kind of courage of being, as well as a foolishness of being, that still lies outside of the prospects of the dream ego. The neo-fascist building represents the power of the social persona to deny the deeper realities that surround it. The snake, as noted, represents the power of the spirit to move an artificially stable system toward one that has a higher form of stability, while allowing for novelty and growth around the strange attractor.

The snake obviously resonates with other archetypal images. In alchemy, the snake is tied to the power of Mercurius, i.e., Hermes Trismegistus, who is the patriarch of alchemical experimentation with the primal elements of the individuation process (Jung 1950: 311). As such the snake represents the possibility of new growth and transformation around the fissuring process associated with the change of the physical elements into the philosopher's stone. The medical association is clear in that the snake also entwines itself around the staff of healing, in the caduceus, which is the most universal symbol of the healing arts. The curious lack of interest in the healing serpent by the medical establishment in the dream only reinforces the depth from which the snake speaks.

There is another archetypal association for the snake as it speaks to the male psyche. The snake is deeply tied to the anima, that is, to the image of the feminine that resides in the biological male. It is difficult to separate out patriarchal elements from the anima projection, especially since Jung himself was often unable to do so. Yet some sense can be made of anima imagery in a post-patriarchal perspective if care is taken to show how such imagery is not a mere projection of male forms of abjection and control. It is in dealing with the contra-sexual archetypes that the greatest caution must be exercised. With these precautions in mind, some conclusions may be suggested.

The snake represents the power of the feminine to both destroy and renew the male psyche as it struggles with its shadow. The shadow is willing to engage the power of the anima in order to be freed from the dreaming innocence that haunts it. Jung gives a brilliant evocation of the anima in a passage that, in spite of its lingering patriarchal projections, shows the numinous power of the snake image (Jung 1934/1954: 28):

> With the archetype of the anima we enter the realm of the gods, or rather, the realm that metaphysics has reserved for itself. Everything the anima touches becomes numinous—unconditional dangerous, taboo, magical. She is the serpent in the paradise of the harmless man with good resolutions and still better intentions. She affords the most convincing reasons for not prying into the unconscious, an occupation that would break down our moral inhibitions and unleash forces that had better been left unconscious and undisturbed. As usual, there is something in what the anima says: for life in itself is not good only, it is also bad. Because the anima wants life, she wants both good and bad. These categories do not exist in the elfin realm. Bodily life as well as psychic life have the impudence to get along much better without conventional morality, and they often remain the healthier for it.

A patriarchal reading of this passage would stress the role of the snake/anima in destroying the 'innocence' of the male psyche. A post-patriarchal reading would understand the anima as the life force that shatters conventional morality by demanding that the self move into the depths of nature, where good and evil are not yet differentiated. What is especially pertinent about this passage is that it points to the irrelevance of the lawyers ("conventional morality") in the dream material. The legal profession lives outside of the self-fissuring of nature and the great unconscious, and thus lives in a truncated and life-denying dualism that sets up false standards of life.

The snake, then, represents the power of life on the edge of the fissure within the heart of nature. The collective unconscious, pointing to *its* source in the divide between *nature naturing* and *nature natured*, compels the dream ego to acknowledge that its own powers are feeble and bereft of life if it denies the importance of the snake. The healing profession uses the snake imagery without understanding its depth logic. Hence, neither the lawyers nor the doctors have seen the vision that has been granted to the dream ego. The shadow side of the self, the part of the self that is beyond good and evil, must embrace the power of life itself, even if that means risking a deadly poison.

Thus the snake imagery is ambiguous and multilayered. As a symbol of the anima it is beyond good and evil. Yet it also points to the power of healing and renewal that has been articulated in the ancient alchemical tradition as well as in modern medicine. Its beauty belies its power over life and death. Does this mean that the dream ego must simply embrace the snake/anima imagery and move toward a fuller life? No, for the possibilities of destruction are as great as the possibilities of healing. The dream ego must become ever more alert to the inner prospects of the dream material, and its archetypal content, if the self is to endure the mysteries of a nature that has little concern for our ethical systems.

Such archetypal dreams are prospective. They describe the situation that the dreamer is currently living, while pointing to the transformed reality that *may* await the dreamer should the complex archetypal terrain be traversed with courage and wisdom. If the great fissure separating the conscious mind from the collective unconscious is ignored, growth possibilities are destroyed. Further, the dreamer runs the risk of dying from the poison of higher wisdom if the demands of the collective unconscious are not met. Thus dreams, as the most powerful link between the conscious mind and the unconscious, both describe the semiotic configuration of the present and demand a strenuous response so that the realities underlying the ego can find their proper measure within the psychic economy.

The self-fissuring of the ontological difference is most forcefully given to us in the dialectic of participation/otherness that we undergo when we confront the personal and collective unconscious. In working through dream material we soon find that many of the key elements in the individual dream, or in a dream series, turn away from us if we presume to have a clear and distinct idea of their meaning. This is not to say that dreams wish to hide their contents, but that they do not reveal their treasures without an appropriate response on the part of the conscious self. The chief obstacle to understanding the depth structures of dreams is the myth that we control the contents of the unconscious. While few would be so bold as to assert that they control the psyche, most of us act as if we do. With this attitude in place, the dialectic between the conscious and unconscious dimensions of the psyche falters.

The mystery found in archetypal dream material points to the fissuring in the heart of nature. Jung is right when he reminds us that dreams do not replace one form of dreaming innocence with another, but move us into an often shattering vision in which the absolute indifference of *nature naturing* to our human needs compels us to let go of our sense of ego power. Put in other terms, archetypal dreams can radically deposition and reposition us along a postethical axis that forces us to enter into the powers of the potencies and their frightening force. It is up to the ego to reweave this powerful material into a matrix than can stabilize psychic existence. But, as Jung also knew so well, our glimpse into the shattering abyss of nature is also a glimpse into the God beyond God that can ultimately provide a new contour for the self in process.

Kierkegaard was right in his analysis of the relative status of the ethical and the religious. Inverting Kant's pervious inversion of these two dimensions of life, Kierkegaard pointed to the paradoxical mystery inherent in the religious reality that lies beyond good and evil. It is a perennial human need to pull the fearful power of the religious back into the calculations and norms of the ethical. Yet the psyche has a greater wisdom than the collective because it sees, often through a glass darkly, that the ethical cannot withstand the force of the numinous. This force is directly rooted in the fissures broken open by *nature naturing* as it continually holds open the ontological difference. As we will see in the next chapter, the ethical can only return to its proper measure once it has been shriven of its illusory power by the dark unconscious of nature.

This is not to say that the human process is a captive of the fissuring of nature, such that it must remain outside of the ethical circle. It is to say that no ethical framework is of value if it has not already passed through the crucible of nature's eternal abyss. The abyss of an indifferent nature remolds all that enters into it. Put in different terms, ethics must die as ethics in order to be reborn as an ethics beyond ethics. The true postethical enters fully into the rhythms of the spirit and lives in awareness of the eternal abyss lying just beneath it. Ecstatic naturalism as a perspective on nature's self has no place for ethics as traditionally understood. No imperative, and no consequentialist analysis can long withstand the devouring power of *nature naturing*.

The cumulative momentum of dream material, especially insofar as it contains archetypal contents, is to undermine ethical frameworks that have as their chief goal the destruction or denial of the deeper forces of life and nature. This is never to say that we are called to be unethical, but that the horizon within which ethics lives is far too small to encompass or illuminate the great divide within nature. If nature is beyond good and evil, and absolutely indifferent to human prospects, then we must honor the archetypal powers that come to meet us from the collective unconscious. The ethical reemerges when we touch the posttemporal domain of the spirit. Yet even here, confining ethical frameworks are shattered in the terrible grace of new life on the edges of communal and personal horizons.

There is a striking sense in which knowledge of good and evil, as expressed in the tree/snake image, moves us beyond all human conceptions of good and evil. The snake that kills and heals at the same time is a symbol of the fissuring that comes from the abyss of *nature naturing*. The snake that kills is the snake of the fissure itself. The snake that heals is the snake of the sheer providingness of nature (to be discussed in the next section). Both dimensions are fully a part of the 'how' of nature in its self-diremption. Insofar as ethical systems live out of a dyadic structure that is hostile to the paradoxical joining of opposites, they remain blind to the powers that support and often terrify the human process.

As noted, this analysis of the fissuring of nature runs parallel to the analysis of the correlation of the potencies and the infinitesimals. The potencies are beyond good and evil, or, more precisely, prior to their differentiation in the orders of *nature natured*. The infinitesimals are possible points that lie just 'beneath' the space-time realities to which they give birth. It would be absurd to assign some kind of moral value to the vehicles of the potencies, especially insofar as they can give birth to any kind of order whatsoever. What would it mean to talk of a "good infinitesimal" as opposed to a "bad infinitesimal?" Such language clearly violates the nature of the ontological structures involved. Nature's self-othering is neither ethical nor nonethical. By the same token, self-othering, as the 'positive' movement outward into sustained realities, is no more nor less ethical than the fissuring that opens realities to the abyss that represents the unconscious of nature. The ethical dimension opens up when attained orders, as encountered by the community of interpreters, become permeable to the spirit which moves them toward nondemonic realities.

Returning to the tree/snake imagery once again, we can see how the snake is not only a manifestation of the great fissure within nature, but also stands as a symbol of the self-othering power of the potencies. The snake is a power in its own right that points back to the receding whence of the potencies. The shadow figure of the dream feels the full power of the potency as the venom enters into his bloodstream. There is a depth dialectic combining the power that is manifest prior to the split between good and evil, and the fissure that shows the finite ego that it stands over an abyss that cannot be filled in with conscious semiotic content.

In the Gospel of Mark we see a profound example of this curious dialectic of self-othering and fissuring in the above mentioned encounter between Jesus and the fig tree (NRSV Mark 11:12–14 and 11:20):

> On the following day, when they came from Bethany, he was hungry. Seeing in the distance a fig tree in leaf, he went to see whether perhaps he would find anything on it. When he came to it, he found nothing but leaves, for it was not the season for figs. He said to it, "May no one ever eat the fruit from you again." And his disciples heard it. In the morning as they passed by, they saw the fig tree withered away to its roots.

This passage is remarkable for its lack of natural justice. Jesus condemns the fig tree for doing precisely what natural law calls for in this particular season. His judgment is one that violates any sane principle of ethics, and his punishment lies beyond human conceptions of the good. The tree itself, as a product of the infinitesimals, has its own internal/external rhythm that cannot be violated. Its roots are its metaphorical link to the whence of the potencies, and its fruits are its link to the whither of full growth and power. The 'innocence' of the tree is manifest to the disciples who do not understand this irrational judgment of Jesus.

What is the upshot of this archetypal story? Jesus represents the power of being that lies beyond the good and evil norms of the human community. His power, both to heal and to destroy, comes from a source that is both pre- and posthuman. It is a prehuman power in that it comes from the heart of the ontological difference between *nature naturing* and *nature natured*. It is a posthuman power in that it also comes from the spirit that empowers all radical depositioning and repositioning. The fig tree, as an order within creation, has its own powers, but these powers are not of the same order as those of Jesus. His destruction of the future fecundity of the fig tree represents his message that even the powers of *nature natured* are of a secondary order compared to the power that points to, and participates in, the kingdom of meaning.

On a 'lesser' level, the fig tree can also symbolize the powers of the money changers in the temple (discussed in the same passages), who also make the mistake of confusing the powers of the world with those of nature itself. The withered fig tree, then, symbolizes the fissure that opens up beneath all attained realities. At the same time, it symbolizes the importance of retaining the connection between the living realm and the hidden realm of the potencies. It is almost as if Jesus is showing the tree, which he addresses directly as if it were a person, that it is not enough to live out of the rhythms of *nature natured*, but that deeper fecundity is found if one's roots reach down into the potencies and their continual self-othering.

The self-fissuring of nature appears to us in the shattering power of that which is beyond good and evil. The story of Jesus and the fig tree has long been a stumbling block to exegesis and to a rendering of Jesus in humanistic and ethical terms. Yet when this story is rotated through the ontological difference, it finds its proper measure and interpretation as an invocation of the abyss that underlies all natural and human realities. No order in *nature natured* is safe from the sudden emergence of the abyss of *nature naturing*. If ecstatic naturalism has a Christology, it is of a Jesus who participates in the fissuring of the ontological difference and manifests that fissure to the human community. His death on the cross of *nature natured* unveils the supremacy of *nature naturing* in the cosmic scheme. The resurrection from the bonds of *nature natured* is the return of the potency of *nature naturing* in the form of the spirit that combines power and meaning.

It is only through the tearing of the fabric of space-time in the domain of *nature natured* that the depth of nature can be unveiled.

The cross lives on the nexus of the ontological difference and reaches into the pretemporal and points to the posttemporal, while fully gathering up the demonic powers of the temporal. A 'softer' understanding of nature, that is, one that fails to understand the ontological difference, would utterly fail to see the depth structures of the cross, the snake, and the tree of life and death. Current efforts to rewrite our understanding of nature along quasi-theological lines that stress unity and stewardship show an astonishing lack of insight into the demonic and self-othering powers that flicker on the edges of all things within the world.

We have seen the correlation of the self-othering of nature and the fissuring of the ontological difference. The momentum of self-othering makes it possible for any order to emerge in the first place. The potencies deposit a small 'part' of their power and structure into the infinitesimal, which in turn births some small dimension of space-time. Once an order emerges into its own measure, it must compete with others for its own place within the domain of *nature natured*. This process is never complete, and must undergo continual depositioning and repositioning. The self-othering of the potencies thus forms space-time particulars that 'collectively' constitute the orders of creation.

Attained orders remain secure against the whence until the power of fissuring is manifest. The human process has special access to the fissuring of nature through archetypal dream material that shows how attained spheres of meaning are often overshadowed, or even overwhelmed, by an abyss that has no contour that can be fathomed. It is as if dreams represent one of the most direct ways in which nature can direct us toward its secrets, the primary secret being the ontological difference. The shattering of our normal horizon of intelligibility prepares us for the unveiling of nature's depths so that we can enter into the healing power of the spirit. The spirit is fully as much a part of nature as is any other order, although it has unique features that allow it to move where it will between and among orders that are themselves more delimited and static in their relation to place and time.

Thus we see that the self-othering of nature through the potencies and into the infinitesimals, is part of a depth dialectic that also involves the fissuring of the ontological difference as a shattering of attained place. The presence of the abyss can only be announced through archetypal images and paradoxes that put pressure on our analogical bridges. The snake in the tree of life/death and the withered fig tree both point to a frightening reality that lies before the bifurcation between good and evil. The human process, in its estrangement from the depth of nature, often refuses to look into the bottomless divide that lies just beneath its secure meaning horizons. Is there a way past this place where nature's self is asked to open its very heart to a cosmic tear that seems to betray all that is most deeply felt to be supportive of life?

C. PROVIDINGNESS

Nature is inexhaustible in scope, power, and meaning. There is a sense in which the very word "nature" should not be used in a philosophical, theological, or semiotic perspective, because it cannot denote anything in particular. Nature is not some kind of genus within which it is possible to find species. It is best seen as the inexhaustible source for whatever can be talked about, and much that cannot be talked about. We have been clear that none of the traditional theological predicates can be applied to nature. Thus we cannot say that nature has an origin outside of itself, or that it has a teleological or providential plan within its own forms of unfolding. Justus Buchler, who brought descriptive naturalism to its own edges, thereby preparing for its transformation into ecstatic naturalism, uses the image of "providingness" to show the 'how' of nature's unfolding (Buchler 1989: 3):

> Nature in the barest sense is the presence and availability of complexes. It is the provision and determination of traits—providingness, if we must strengthen the emphasis, but not providence, not providentness.

This reconfiguration is especially pertinent when the traditional God of theology becomes rehoused within the heart of ecstatic naturalism and is brought closer to the actual 'how' of an indefinitely ramified nature. In the present context, the important point is that nature makes all orders possible, while not itself being an order in any sense. Nature provides for selves, galaxies, photons, conflicts, death, resurrection, colors, betrayal, meanings, signs, losses, transformations, the unconscious, and everything whatsoever, whether known by the human process or not. It does not birth a specific providential plan that can gather up the foundlings of *nature natured* and bring them to an ultimate consummation. Yet in its continual providings, it makes all actualities and all possibilities. It also cancels many actualities and many possibilities, even while 'replacing' them with others.

Every attempt to romanticize this process is doomed to failure when the true indifference of providingness is made starkly clear to the self. We do not know why nature provides what it does, nor do we know if and when providingness will cease. Regardless of whether we have an eternally expanding, or a steady-state, or a cyclical universe (combining expansion and eventual contraction), the mystery of providingness and its 'term' will be with us. That there are providings at all is a mystery that should never be covered over by a triumphalist God or an imported providential plan. To talk providentially about nature is to exhibit a profound lack of courage in the face of an abyss that ever recedes from view. Heidegger argued persuasively that theology should be willing to put much of its categorial structure 'on hold' until the full mystery of the ontological difference had entered into the rhythm of thought. Ecstatic naturalism equally insists that the depth structure of the divine can only be articulated, in however tentative a fashion, *after* the sheer providingness of *nature naturing* has entered into *every* horizon of meaning. To simply equate providingness with God, unless there are some very careful categorial refinements, is to violate the most pertinent insights of the ecstatic naturalist perspective.

Nature provides for all orders, including the divine. It is in the depth understanding of providingness that we come closest to understanding the ubiquity of the whence that enters into the self in process. The convergence of self-othering and fissuring within the image of providingness, brings us to an awareness of how the selving process, with all of its precarious movements, becomes open to the domain of natural grace. As will quickly emerge, natural grace, as opposed to religion-specific saving grace, underlies all that we do, feel, shape, say, and undergo. It is the quiet presence that makes it possible for us to enter into the seeming terrors of the abyss. Indeed, without natural grace, the self could not enter into any of the depth rhythms of nature. Not only does natural grace support the meaning-granting structures of life, it also sustains the worldhood of the world.

The innumerable providings of nature do not add up to a collective 'provided' in the sense that there is an ultimate plan with a knowable contour. Each order of the world will interact with some but not with all other orders. There are spheres of profound discontinuity as well as spheres of fragmented continuity. Natural grace is found at the place where each order is sustained by its antecedent conditions in the infinitesimals. Nature sustains what it produces, even if its own entropic momentum will ultimately annihilate each and every manifest order. Providingness is not some kind of cosmic force that guarantees immortality. It is the 'how' of nature in its continual generation of orders and signs. During the life history of any order, whether semiotic or not, there is a natural grace that keeps it from falling back into the unconscious of nature. For the human process, this natural grace is often very hard to see and to understand.

For the selving process, moving fitfully between and among complexes, natural grace appears on the edges of psychic life as a kind of sustaining field of meaning that has no delimited content. The self has a background awareness of this presence but is too enamored of the semiotic noise that is continually streaming through it. Peirce has his own, perhaps truncated, understanding of this surrounding field when he speaks of the spiritual consciousness that we only come to see fully at the moment of death (CP 7.577):

> In the same manner, when the carnal consciousness passes away in death, we shall at once perceive that we have had all along a lively spiritual consciousness which we have been confusing with something different.

By the concept "spiritual consciousness" Peirce means the immediate sense of firstness on the edge of the carnal consciousness that moves in the domains of secondness and thirdness. The signs and orders that impinge on bodily consciousness are so strong in their immediate impact, as tied to habit, that they drown out the gentle field of firstness that permeates us as a life-giving source.

Peirce spent his life in search of this providingness, this firstness of all firstnesses that makes each self possible, and that holds the self's trajectory in its healing embrace. Spiritual consciousness is a background continuum of feeling and awareness that stays with the self in this life and that makes the transition to the postworldly life possible. We have used three terms in this analysis and have argued that they are commensurate in meaning. The term "providingness" refers to the sustaining power of nature as it not only engages in continual creation, but supports the orders that have been created according to a measure that eludes human query. The term or phrase "natural grace" refers to the gift giving quality of providingness, that is, to its healing presence within each and every order. So far as we know, only the human process has some kind of direct or indirect access to the experience of natural grace *as* natural grace. Finally, Peirce's phrase "spiritual consciousness" refers to the almost spatial image of a surrounding field of sustaining grace that is felt at death and whenever the noise of bodily consciousness is momentarily stilled.

How does the self gain access to the providingness of nature, given to it through natural grace and experienced on the edges of signs and their portents? We have seen how the self comes to an awareness of the fissuring abyss at the heart of nature. Whenever the self experiences some kind of shipwreck, as often announced through archetypal dream material, it becomes open to the shock of the dark cleft at the heart of the world. The transition to an equal understanding of providingness comes in and through this shock. Tillich argued that one can only come to an awareness of what he called the "power of Being" through a prior experience of the shock of nonbeing. Ecstatic naturalism concurs with insight, as long as it is understood that the shock of nonbeing can come in less dramatic forms than those envisioned by Tillich.

When the above discussed dream ego looks into the abyss on its left, and then turns to the snake in the tree on its right, it encounters the shock of nonbeing. This is an intra-psychic experience, although it obviously has extra-psychic referents. The shock at the abyss, where meaning seems to be swallowed up, is also deeply entwined with the much less obvious yet equally powerful appearance of providingness at the heart of the dream. The dream ego (the dreamer's conscious attitude) is still sustained by the ground that stands beneath him. At the same time, he stands before the tree of life and death and witnesses a drama of death and resurrection that holds forth the possibility of continued meaning. The abyss and the ground are entwined, like the snake and the tree, thereby insuring that the dreamer will not be totally bereft of meaning possibilities.

Peirce's image is so evocative because it reminds us that we seem to have a built-in propensity to flee from the background consciousness that actually sustains us. To combine Peirce's framework with that of the dream we can see that the entire dream field, that is, its horizon of permission, its clearing away of the darkness of sleep, is the firstness, the providingness that makes *any* meaning possible in any respect for the dreaming self. The entire dream field is a kind of particularized spiritual consciousness that grants the light within which secondness and thirdness can find their measure. The horizon within which figures, events, colors, emotions, and activated complexes and archetypes unfold, is a providing that is infused with grace. Translate this concept to waking life, and we see that our conscious horizon, as linked to worldhood, is itself a gift of the spiritual consciousness that embraces us.

Grace has always been contrasted to sin in Christian dogmatics. This is a profound and absolutely binding insight. The current perspective insists that the human process is estranged from the whence of the potencies and from the whither of the spirit. In the

Introduction, the image of the "ontological wound" was used to denote the primacy of sin or estrangement in our understanding of the self. Natural grace, that is, the grace that comes from the heart of nature itself, is always present as the counter to our estrangement. Yet we are rarely aware of either our estrangement or the grace that sustains us. And we cannot come to an awareness of the one without a simultaneous, if cloudy, awareness of the other.

The initial experience of the ontological wound can produce a profound melancholy in the self, driving it toward what the tradition calls "concupiscence," that is, the attempt to devour the finite world and bring it into manageable shape, whether through sexual conquest, financial manipulation, or an intensification of experience by whatever means. The sudden awareness of estrangement opens up the haunting presence/absence of the lost object. This shock of the no longer begins to erode the self's confidence in the innumerable ersatz props in the domain of *nature natured*. As the self is grasped by the shaking power of the abyss, it struggles to reinforce the signs and orders that it mistakenly assumes are still within its control. The healing power of natural grace remains beyond reach.

However, the fissures that open up to the now decentered and anxious self begin to reveal the deeper and quieter light by and through which they are seen. All fissures are in and of a nature that is larger than any of its diremptions. The horizon within which they are seen is the side of grace that is turned toward us. Grace is not equivalent to the lost object. It is the almost silent, yet always available, clearing within which the drama of the loss and return of the lost object can take place. Providingness, the ontological source of natural grace, has its own voice, but it is one that can only be heard when we let go of the semiotic codes and structures that weave their way into our conscious and unconscious selves.

These codes have their own promiscuous momentum (Corrington 1994) that shakes and transforms the self in process. The experience of natural grace is continually being thwarted by the robust power of public interpretants that mark out a territory of their own against the night of the unconscious of nature. The quieter clearing provided by sustaining and natural grace is so filled in with mobile content that its light cannot often break through. Yet within the rush of interpretants to fill the world of *nature natured* with meaning, fissures and breaks emerge through which the light of natural grace *can* appear. As interpretant chains (or, as Peirce would say, "cables") are broken up and forced to turn back on themselves for a brief time, grace enters into the *be-*

tween to remind the sign-invaded self that it rests on a much more profound basis than the manifest world of signs. That signs are understood *as* signs is itself a gift of natural grace. Animals use signs without knowing that anything like a sign and its object relation exist. The human process is brought into the clearing where the sign can stand forth against and with its object as a sign that points to something in some respect.

Providingness sustains infinitesimals and their issue. It makes little sense to drive the concept of providingness back to the potencies, as they lie in a unique domain that is underneath the providingness that sustains the orders of the world. It makes more sense to say that the potencies are part of the 'how' that underlies providingness. They are intimately related to the innumerable providings, but are not identical to providingness. Infinitesimals, on the other hand, as the place where the potencies deliver their rhythmic powers, are sustained by the sheer providingness of nature that secures them against the threat of becoming absolutely null or zero.

We experience natural grace in the fullness of time, whereby the ravages of thermodynamic and entropic time give way, however briefly, before the life-granting powers of the pretemporal. The sheer sustaining power of the pretemporal is experienced in those moments in which the rush of interpretants gives way to a sense of clarity in which the horizon of meaning that surrounds the self enters into a deeper rhythm that allows its most fundamental structures to stand out in a dramatic way. Some of these structures, such as a compulsive pattern of behavior, will show their demonic features, while others will show their transformative prospects. The sudden gift of the pretemporal to the temporal does not eliminate the demonic, any more than it lifts the self into the 'pure' realm of transcendence. What does flash forth from the depths is the now clarified picture of what is within the horizon, and how its various powers are aligned.

The gift-giving power of the pretemporal, as a part of the 'how' of natural grace, opens the door to a deeper and more dramatic inversion as the posttemporal enters into the dialectic of timing. The pretemporal shows us where we are in our horizon, while the posttemporal empowers us to alter the relations of power within the horizon. The posttemporal is embedded in the spirit and moves the fragmented horizon of the self toward the fuller and richer field of meaning of the spirit itself. This is not to say that the spirit is a principle of semiotic plenitude, but that it is a clearing within which valuable meanings can be augmented and destructive meanings can be transformed so that their energies, which are needed by the self, can enter into a new gestalt of grace.

The demonic and the transformative belong to each other. No sense of the demonic can even begin to emerge unless it is understood that the demonic has the same roots as the transformative, namely, in the sheer power of the potencies. The demonic reaches down into the potencies and lives off of their churning momenta, while the transformative (the holy) reaches down into the potencies in a different way. The demonic structures, which come from the pretemporal, are without life-giving form. They ride on the back of the potencies and surge through the human process by destroying attained structures of meaning. Yet the holy dimensions of the self and its world also come from the potencies and share the numinous power of that which is not an order within the world. The difference between the holy and the demonic is that the holy is wedded to gestalts of power and meaning that unite the world of the potencies with the world of *nature natured*.

Returning for one last time to the dream images that have been amplified and probed above, we can see how any given archetypal image can participate in both the holy and the demonic, thereby also pointing to the mystery of how the pre- and posttemporal intersect with the temporal. The key image of the snake was seen to stand outside of the good and evil that belonged to the medical and legal professionals, who simply ignore its ambiguous presence. As a symbol of the loss of innocence and the power of the anima, the snake points to the abyss that opens up beneath the dream ego, making continued life within the protection of the persona impossible. But the deeper mystery of the snake image points to the healing power that can come from a cold-blooded creature that lies on the edges of our forms of civilized life.

The snake represents the power of sexuality to renew the self and its interpersonal life. On an even deeper level, the snake is a symbol of the healing power that comes from the intersection of the posttemporal and the temporal, especially as the temporal has been infused with the power of the pretemporal, a power that exists prior to the split between good and evil. The pretemporal shows the human horizon *that* it houses the demonic and the holy, but it does not provide any means for dealing with the split. The struggle between good and evil takes place within the temporal, as the self wrestles with the powers that it did not make but that shape its intra- and interpsychic life. The posttemporal empowers the self to transform the energy of the demonic into the liberating power of the holy. It is at this point that the snake becomes an image of healing.

The snake that injects the venom of wisdom, a venom that also comes from the potencies and is thus neither good nor evil, is the snake that lifts the consciousness of the dream ego into a new sphere of meaning in which the rigid parameters of the persona give way to a life that finally understands the demonic and the holy for what they are—powers of the potencies that must be honored before they can be transfigured into new meaning. The spirit enters into the snake image at the point where the pain of higher consciousness becomes most intense. The self is deeply tempted to withdraw to the earlier stage of dreaming innocence in which the shattering vision of nature's premoral abyss has not yet emerged. The spirit 'knows' the danger of succumbing to this temptation and provides the self with the courage to face into that abyss that shakes its persona to its roots. In many respects, the self is like the fig tree that is shriven by Jesus. Mere ego fruits are insufficient if the self is to face into the blast of the potencies that remain in eternal ignorance of good and evil.

The renewal of the self (fig tree) can only come through the spirit and the liberating vision of the posttemporal. On the quieter level of providingness, natural grace keeps the horizon of the self open for the very possibility of transformation and renewal. If this grace is, in Kant's terms, the condition for the possibility of transformation, then the spirit is the actualization of the dialectic that weaves the demonic into the holy on the edges of time.

Chapter Four
Nature's Self-Disclosure

We participate in innumerable orders within the domain of *nature natured*, even though we may be only aware of a very small number of them at a given time. The semiotic understanding of nature, once it has freed itself from its captivity to cultural and structuralist semiotic horizons, details the ways in which these orders communicate to us and leave their traces. Nature's self swims thorough vast currents of signs that shape the self in process and mark it as nature's own. It is a symptom of the profound alienation of our times that nature itself is envisioned as a cultural construct, merely awaiting the next liberating touch from the all-powerful sign user. The irony should be starkly evident. Perspectives that were allegedly created to free the self from the dominance of heteronomous forms of meaning have now led us into utter semiotic darkness in which the only light available comes from the ersatz signs that merely reflect back human projections. Deconstruction has shriven the self of its depth structures and has masked the innumerable connections between the self and the nature that spawned it. Were this process confined to the academy, we could simply see it as a peculiar sickness of an alienated social class. Unfortunately, the sickness runs far deeper and is a clear manifestation of the estrangement of the human process from the potencies of its whence and the spirit that is its whither.

The current intellectual climate is shaped by those who, following their own misreadings of Nietzsche, insist that nature is primarily concerned with hiding its secrets from the will-driven self. Nietzsche's perspectivalism, while philosophically inept, does not force nature into total closure, any more than, at the other extreme, does his understanding of the self-gathering will to more will of the Overman, show us how the human process actually negotiates between and among interpretants. Beneath his nominalism, and beneath his concept of the charismatic unfolding of projected signs and values, is a much deeper sense that nature, qua history, discloses its secrets to the self in ecstatic and transfiguring experience. His arch concept of the eternal return of the same would mean nothing were it not for his sense that it is the 'how' of time in the alleged post-Christian world. And this 'how' is not an arbitrary construct, but the true measure of time as he thought it was disclosed to him in an ecstatic experience.

This is not to say that we need only to return to a more insightful and balanced view of Nietzsche so much as to acknowledge that even in the work of one of the founding heroes of poststructuralism, we find the deep realization that nature, history, time, and self are fundamentally self-disclosive of their actualities and prospects. Nietzsche can say on the one hand that nature is a coy mistress, while on the other fully acknowledge that it is also generously self-revealing of its fundamental structures and patterns. Neither the concepts of the will to power nor the eternal return of the same are up for deconstructive negotiation. They give themselves to his thought on the edges of ecstatic experience.

Ecstatic naturalism, however, has no use for either of these concepts, but understands their role in a perspective that wrestled with the self-unfolding of nature in its depth structures. Even for Nietzsche, nature wants its most basic realities to become manifest to the sign-using self. Otherwise, all of his subaltern categorial structures would have no purchase, even in the most radical and deluded forms of deconstruction. Nietzsche can be seen as a precursor of ecstatic naturalism, provided that his primary structures are lifted out for analysis and reflection. This is not to say that we can equate the will to power with *nature naturing*, but that his arch concept is attempting to do something directly analogous to ours. Nor is this to say that his concept of the eternal return of the same is as phenomenological as is our distinction among the pretemporal, the temporal (understood entropically and modally), and the post-temporal. But it is to say that his daring reconstruction o time at least shatters the hegemony of *chronos* as the simple movement of triadic temporality.

Nature is no more a social construct than it is a static container or substance that can be mapped. At the very least, Nietzsche has made it harder to fall back on grooved and obvious concepts tha would deny the dynamism at the heart of the ontological difference. His notion of the death of God, when freed of its eulogistic and literalistic connotations, can emancipate philosophical theol ogy for a depth exploration of the ways in which God is found within nature and the ontological difference. The death of the God of theism prepares the way for an ecstatic naturalist God tha truly belongs to the 'how' of nature. By the same token, the death of the substantive self, and the birth of the ecstatic self on the edges of the unconscious of nature, can open up the ways in which nature discloses itself to the human process. The substantive self that was deconstructed by Nietzsche, did block the paths down into the heart of the ontological difference, and made it impossible for the self to understand the ways in which it participates in nature and its orders.

Our evocation of the 'true' Nietzsche, against the currently fashionable Nietzsche, makes it possible to reawaken the rhythmic patterns that connect the self to its whence and its whither. The self is supported by more than its own signs and finds its relation to nature, which is always 'in place' regardless of any thoughts about the relation, through a pervasive grace that sustains it as it moves from the original position into depositioning, repositioning, and back again. Nature continues to disclose itself to the human process even when the self is most resistant to acknowledging the connection. Grace, like Peirce's spiritual consciousness, need not be a thematic object of conscious intentionality in order to be deeply efficacious is sustaining the self and in quickening the selving process.

A. DISRUPTIVE GRACE

The concept of "grace" is one that both philosophers and semioticians abject, because it is held to assume some kind of supernatural invasion of the human that destroys the autonomy of the self. On a deeper level, it is held to be part of a dualism in which the human process is broken by some kind of metaphysical sense of sin that can only be 'fixed' by fiat. For many, this concept seems to hark back to a modernism that freezes the mobility of the self and that in turn reduces it to a kind of divine instrument. The self is merely the 'space' where God works out a drama of disobedience and reconciliation.

The philosophical process of the abjection of the concept of grace became most fully self-conscious in the later writings of Kant. In the previous chapter we noted how Kierkegaard inverted Kant's prior inversion of religion and ethics. For Kant, coming at the end of the German *Aufklärung*, religion was the chief instrument by which the ethical was thwarted by forces that were irrational and opposed to the unfolding of moral autonomy. He published a series of four essays in 1793 (reissued in 1794) that attempted to deconstruct religion, the heteronomous state, and the normativity of the Bible. His battle cry is clear (Kant 1793: 3):

So far as morality is based upon the conception of man as a free agent who, just because he is free, binds himself through his reason to unconditional laws, it stands in need neither of the idea of another Being over him, for him to apprehend his duty, nor of an incentive other than the law itself, for him to do his duty.

Kant had, of course, detailed the structure of the self in his 1781 *Critique of Pure Reason*, laying the foundations for his deconstruction of the role of religion in penetrating the depth structures of the human process. This framework carries over into the later work in which the autonomous moral agent contrasts private maxims with possible imperatives and selects the maxim that can be universalized to cover all rational beings, and in turn reversed to cover his or her own self. In this process of selection, the only norm is that of reason, and the only motive is that of duty. The two possibilities in Kant's universe are autonomy, which has nothing to do with religion except in the barest possible sense of some kind of Ideal; and heteronomy, in which forces *other* than autonomous and universal reason invade the self.

Put in simple terms, there is no role for grace in Kant's understanding of the moral self. He does make a surprising move that continues to vex scholars, in which he invokes an intelligible (or noumenal) self that lies outside of time and that provides the 'how,' through the evil or good will, for moral transformation. The irony is that Kant is compelled to bring in religious language, like that of "radical conversion," when talking about the inner heart of ethics. Yet he consistently refuses to draw the conclusion that moral transformation is impossible outside of grace.

Kant has set the tone for the philosophical abjection of grace by depriving the self of its connection with nature and with the unconscious. In many respects, the current philosophical climate is still deeply neo-Kantian with its refusal to acknowledge that there is anything outside of the self but Kant's "manifold." The previous chapters have shown in some detail the way past neo-Kantian misconceptions of nature's self. But even with this positive constructive work, there remains the problem of the abjection of grace. This abjection is based on a profound misunderstanding of the already configured structures that connect the self to both *nature naturing* and the innumerable orders of *nature natured*.

Kant primarily feared heteronomous invasion of the self from without. He abjected both grace and the spirit so that he could, in his eyes, protect the fragility of reason against the much larger forces that surround it. On the deepest level, his analysis of the transcendental derivation of space and time, as well as causality and the modal categories, represents a tragic denial of the supremacy of nature and its unconscious power. Put in sharp terms, Kant feared the unconscious, both of the self and of nature, and thereby quarantined the self against any invasion of something that could not be brought under the control of universal a priori reason (in the mode of the understanding). Lest we confine this primal abjection to the 18th century, we should note that the spirit of Kantian abjection can be found deep in the heart of the deconstructive rage against the reference relation and the power of that which can never be a cultural construct. The important point is that our *ideas* of nature can be constructed, but nature itself swallows up any and all constructions that would attempt to encompass all of the traits of *nature naturing* or *nature natured*.

The way past this impasse is to show the dynamic forms in which grace completes the selving process, making full human actualization possible. Without natural grace, and the deeper unfolding of grace in the spirit, the self would run the risk of falling back into unmediated origin or of remaining a blind captive among the interpretants of the world. With grace, the self can negotiate the volatile terrain connecting both 'sides' of the ontological difference of nature.

Semiotics abjects grace by focusing its attention on the attained world of interpretants and their innumerable connections. The condition is even worse in those perspectives that stress cultural codes as the sole medium of meaning within the world of communication. The Peircean analysis of interpretants is far richer and more subtle than the contemporary analysis of codes, yet it too falls prey to a certain blindness that refuses to see the true enabling conditions for any sign (representamen), object, and interpretant relation. Within the spaces opened out by sign activity, the power of grace can appear to move truncated meaning toward a more fulsome expression of the world and its orders.

Ecstatic naturalism is a perspective seeking to transfigure philosophy, semiotics, and theology around the depth structures of the spirit and nature. The transformation of philosophy focuses on the basic categorial structures that locate and define the world, the self, and the divine in an ecstatically transfiguring nature. The transformation of semiotics focuses on a more capacious understanding of sign activity as one of the primal 'hows' of nature as it 'seeks' to become more and more transparent to the human process and to the divine natures. The transformation of theology focuses on the specific traits of the divine life as they must be reconfigured in the light of the enlarged conception of nature and the ontological difference. In this sense, ecstatic naturalism is the vessel within and through which these three disciplines can be renewed. The ultimate goal is to realign the human process with the depth structures and potencies of nature.

With these historical and conceptual comments in mind, we are ready to proceed to an analysis of how grace works in and through nature's self, securing the self against closure and fragmentation. We have indicated that there are at least two forms of grace. The first is what we have called "natural grace," which comes from nature itself as it sustains its issue, for however brief a time. The second form is the grace of the spirit, which quickens the human process so that it can move into a deeper recognition of the ontological difference. The second form of grace will be treated in the next section, where it will be located within the eschatological momenta of the spirit.

Natural grace is ubiquitous. It cannot be earned, nor can it be canceled by acts of the self. Anything whatsoever in the domain of *nature natured* is already a recipient of natural grace if it has any traits at all. Any order having traits is an order that is different from all other orders. It is not often recognized that there is an intimate connection between natural grace and the principle of individuation. To be an individual at all is to stand out against the power of nonbeing and to prevail against nonbeing as long as nature 'deems' it appropriate. As we will see, natural grace supports individuation, and attendant metaphors of diversity and divergence, while the grace of the spirit moves toward healing forms of convergence in which the sheer uniqueness of given orders is gathered up into lines of reciprocity that do not cancel uniqueness, but bring individuality into a communal or aggregate structure that can provide a new measure for the individual.

To be at all, then, is to be sustained by a form of grace that honors individuality. This grace is so hard to see because it works in an extremely quiet way to support whatever is against nonbeing. As noted, non-human orders do not look into the face of natural grace, even if they are fully sustained by it. The human order can, if the conditions are right, face into the gift that usually has no name. This gift cannot be seen if the self confines its own self image to the Kantian realm of autonomous reason. Such a self-grounding reason can only see its own face reflected back. Further, autonomy, because of its flight from the unconscious or because of its obsession with cultural codes, abjects what must appear to it as alien and other. Strange as it may sound, the alienated self may even fear natural grace because it is a threat to its self-delusion that it is self-sustaining.

The transition from the closure of autonomy to the acceptance of the gift of natural grace can take place through many means. As noted, Tillich argued that the shock of nonbeing, manifest in such boundary situations as guilt, death, and anxiety, is one of the primary ways in which we are forced to let go of autonomy and then free to enter into what he termed "theonomy," namely the condition in which mere autonomy is opened to its depth in the ground of being. This ground integrates and overcomes the threat of nonbeing into itself, thereby transforming the self and its world of interactions. Ecstatic naturalism concurs with this analysis but also insists that there are many less dramatic roads toward the awareness of natural grace. In each case, however, this process must acknowledge a grace that is disruptive of the self and its current horizons of meaning.

Natural grace sustains each and every sign and order within the world. Yet it is beyond good and evil in that it does not 'acknowledge' any differences of value within the world that is sustained. In a rough sense, natural grace is equivalent to the traditional notion of the ground of being, provided that it is understood that this grace is not strictly equivalent to God. By being beyond good and evil, natural grace is in some sense indifferent to the foundlings that constitute the domain of *nature natured*. It sustains the orders and traits that prevail at a given time. It even supports the disruptive powers of entropy as they eat into ordered systems and render them less ordered through thermodynamic time. Entropy is no less real nor less 'valued' than order. Natural grace sustains either form of the actual without prejudice or teleological intent. Put differently, natural grace does not tell any order or any trait how to be, it merely lets it obtain for its due measure.

The human process can, and does, rage against this notion of "due measure" that often seems to cruelly mock human need and aspiration. What is the "due measure" of a cancerous growth, which has its own form of entropic decay? From the standpoint of the selving process, this is an appropriate and compelling question, while from the standpoint of natural grace, a question of this type represents a category mistake. We cannot ask sustaining grace anything about what is sustained. We can only accept the fact that the cancer is sustained by the same dimension of nature as is a profound creative product. It takes a great deal of courage to look into the heart of natural grace and to recognize that its giving of itself has no moral value per se. When Heidegger used the simple German phrase *es gibt* (it gives) to denote the how of being, he opened a door onto the simple giving over of grace that comes from nature itself. We can give thanks to this perennial giving, even if it is a thanks tinged with both melancholy and love.

Natural grace would seem on the surface to be a straightforward presence. It sustains the human process, and all we have to do is to turn into its light and be healed. But what does healing mean in a context that pushes beneath the very distinction between good and evil, the whole and the broken? Natural grace sustains the AIDS virus just as surely as it sustains the complexes that continue to haunt the self. It sustains the richness of the selving process and the war of one race or gender against another. It sustains the erotic embrace that shatters artificial boundaries, while allowing violence to break apart conflicted selves. It sustains the lie that can shatter community, while supporting the vision that can bring about justice. It sustains the voices that torture the schizophrenic, while supporting the liturgy that brings a community to the divine.

Why is natural grace disruptive of the human process? The disruption manifests itself when the self is suddenly forced to look into an ontological structure that has absolutely no relation to the axiological schemes that often quite rightly support human community. Grace cannot give us any directions for our moral life, any more than it can answer the question that so vexed Job. Good and evil orders and signs continue to play across and through the human landscape. The power of grace is found in each and every such order, regardless of how congenial any given order is to our depth structures. By accepting the ubiquity of natural grace we are asked to accept that the sustaining power of the world has refused to privilege the human process. The AIDS virus is no less 'valuable' to natural grace than is the world historical genius who establishes a new horizon of meaning. Can natural grace heal?

The transition from the stark realization of the absolute indifference of natural grace to its issue, to a sense of the healing powers of grace may take place slowly. It is crucial that the selving process work through this transition with some care. It is all too easy to ignore the disruptive aspects of sustaining grace and to leap to some sense of healing. Before the self can have a legitimate, and lasting, understanding of the depth logic of natural grace, it must face into the abyss that has no moral quality whatsoever. After all, what would it mean to say that natural grace is moral per se? We would have to argue that it is more moral to have a universe than not to have one. How would such an argument be made? From a position outside of the universe that could compare the difference between being and nonbeing? All we can do is to acknowledge that the world exists and that it is sustained by natural grace. It is not the world that is redemptive, but prospects within the world, prospects that the divine must also struggle with.

The healing aspect of disruptive grace begins to emerge when the relation between grace and origin is clarified. Natural grace connects each and every order to the pretemporal, to the domain of the world-spawning potencies and infinitesimals. The so-called 'negative' aspect of natural grace is tied to the three temporal orders. When the human process looks at the sheer fecundity of what is sustained, and quickly makes distinctions between the destructive and the healing, it works within the manifest side of grace that is tied to the orders of the world. From this perspective, fully entropic and filled with the anxiety of *chronos* as it eats its children, natural grace appears more demonic than holy. Yet once this necessary vision is integrated into the self, a second disruption may emerge in which the depth momentum of grace becomes clarified.

Natural grace not only sustains each and every order or sign against absolute nonbeing, but it also connects whatever is to its originating ground and abyss. Here, it is the ground relation that assumes priority. The ground reaches back into the pretemporal, a domain that does not recognize the power of entropy to eat away at the self. The pretemporal knows neither death nor decay. The self looks backward, as it were, into the ground and sees that there is a domain that has no temporal markers of any kind. This can be felt by the self on the edges of its field of awareness. Again, Peirce's concept of the spiritual consciousness enters to remind us that we do have indirect phenomenological access to a pretemporal grace that makes the temporal structures of the self actual.

As will quickly emerge in the next section, natural grace joins with the grace of the spirit to transform the self and bring it back to the ethical realm, but in a dramatic new way. The cure for the vision of an indifferent natural grace is to enter into the depth logic of that grace, as it opens into the pretemporal, and then to weave that vision into the grace of the spirit that is posttemporal. Natural grace alone would not bring us to the ethics beyond ethics. However, it does show us the utter scope of the sustaining power in the world, and thereby reminds the self of its finite yet self-transcending location within *nature natured*.

The self looks into the darkness of evil orders and powers and realizes that they are granted their own "due measure" in the world. This realization that the "rain falls on the just and the unjust" can shatter the ethical horizon of the self and its communities. Natural grace seems to be cold comfort in a universe that is slowly falling into ultimate disorder. Discussions of grace often take on a romantic cast as if the encounter with grace can solve all intra- and interpsychic problems. In the transition, more akin to a leap, to the second dimension within natural grace, the power of the pretemporal begins to enter into the self, reminding it of its lost object and of the fecundity of *nature naturing*. This opening is deeply disruptive to the self as it must, perhaps for the first time, let go of the blinding power of intra-worldly temporality.

The self has two senses of its whence. The theologian Schleiermacher invoked the deeper sense when he showed that the realms of thought and action have their roots in a primal feeling of absolute dependence that could be found at the heart of the psyche (Schleiermacher 1821). The felt whence of the self is very much akin to Peirce's spiritual consciousness in that it lies beneath each given sign and thought in the finite self. Thus the second sense of the whence is tied to the originating powers outside of the self. The first sense is tied to the immediate interpretants that surround the mobile sphere of consciousness. The self often lives as if this sense of the felt whence is the only one, tying each sense of origin to immediate or just past intrapsychic signs. The disruptive power of natural grace emerges only when the self suddenly sees that its immediate whence is finite and deeply time-bound.

The leap from the *chronos* of the intrapsychic whence to the pretemporal realm of the ultimate whence disrupts the interpretants that hover around the self. In certain mystical experiences, these finite forms of the whence of the self may go into momentary eclipse as the ultimate whence envelopes and shapes the sign-using self. Within the mystical state, the sheer presence of the whence of *nature naturing* drowns out any signs in the fitful domain of *nature natured*. Upon leaving this state, the self may experience a profound discomfort around the suddenly returning signs of the finite self. The ultimate whence reaches so deeply into nature's self that all finite forms of the whence are profoundly devalued, thereby leaving the self stretched across a painful abyss.

The selving process must then learn to negotiate between the two whences, as both represent aspects of disruptive grace. It is at this nexus that the healing power of natural grace begins to emerge into some clarity. The ultimate whence of nature enters into the self and allows it to participate in a conscious way in the surging potencies that are pretemporal. This in turn can reempower the finite forms of the whence that are tied to the originating powers of interpretants, be they emotional, energetic, or logical. Each given interpretant is transformed whenever it becomes permeable to the ultimate whence that is the carrier of natural grace for the human process.

For most selves, there is nothing akin to a mystical shattering of the finite whence, but a more subtle prospect in which some fitful sense of the ultimate whence can appear around the edges of interpretants. For Kristeva, who, of course would frame this problematic differently, the ultimate whence (*chora*) would appear in transgression and sexual release in *jouissance*. The moment of sexual ecstasy transgresses the boundaries that separate one self from another and a self from itself. For her, the psychoanalytic situation is the key to these ontological transitions:

> In this vein, several aspects of psychoanalysis cross the boundary between body and soul and explore various elements that transcend this dichotomy: for instance, the energy component of drives, the determination of meaning through sexual desire, and the inscription of the treatment within transference, which is understood to be a repetition of prior psychosensory traumas. Nevertheless, the linguistic mechanism remains at the core of treatment: as a signifying construct, the speech of both the analysand and the analyst incorporates different *series of representations*. (Kristeva 1993: 5)

The therapeutic context, shaped by the unique semiotics of language, moves across and through the boundaries that have foreclosed meaning in the past. The biological/personal whence appears in this nexus in which language invokes release of primal unconscious energy. In sustained ecstasy, finite forms of the whence, while still present, reveal that they are surrounded by an ultimate whence that empowers them to reveal their deeper treasures, at this stage only hinted at in the psychoanalytic relationship.

Asexual analyses of the self, such as Heidegger's in *Being and Time*, fail to show how bodily structures are channels of the ultimate whence in which the pretemporal spills over and into the temporal. Only the most reductive analysis would see sexuality in terms of nerve stimulation, rather than in terms of the opening power of the ultimate whence to reshape the self in process. This does not, of course, ignore the often tragic and ambiguous elements in human sexuality, but affirms that finite signs are transformed in such a way as to open up the possibility that natural grace can become more dramatically present.

Participation in the whence is ecstatic in the obvious sense that the self is compelled to stand outside of its current configuration, either to encounter new interpretants, or to reposition those interpretants in the ultimate whence. This ultimate dimension of the whence is disruptive of the self in the sense noted above, namely, in that it is shriven of its self-grounding so that it becomes open to the whence underlying each and every order of *nature natured*. Sustaining and natural grace enters into the horizon of the self whenever current interpretants are freed from self-closure so that they can reveal their ultimate rootedness in the pretemporal.

The self thus lives at this stage in a dialectic between the often blinding powers of the temporal orders and the quieter but deeper powers of the pretemporal. The power of temporality is never fully overcome by the whence of natural grace, but it is transformed. The self feels the ubiquity of the pretemporal, which refuses to be refracted into temporality, while seeing the dependent quality of the temporal. All temporal orders float over the elusive realm of the pretemporal and arch back toward the lost domain that made them possible in the first place. The self is tempted to choose between these two domains and will usually privilege one over the other. An ecstatic naturalist understanding of the Fall will point to the tendency of selves to live out of the temporal alone while abjecting the pretemporal and denying its ultimacy within the configuration of the whence.

This dialectic would remain static and incomplete were it not for another stage in the selving process that moves from natural grace to the grace of the spirit. Natural grace is ubiquitous, even when not acknowledged. It sustains each self, each interpretant, each order, and each structure of the world. At the same 'time' it sustains the depth structures of the self that live in and out of the pretemporal. However, the dialectic between the temporal and the pretemporal can only be fully grasped and experienced when the self enters into the second type of grace, that of the spirit, which emerges out of the posttemporal. Natural grace is quiet in its presence/absence, and needs to be evoked on the edges of 'ordinary' experience. The grace of the spirit is more dramatic in that it is deeply tied to conscious structures and emerges in the great betweenness structures that link selves to each other in community. At the same time, the spirit enters into the individual psyche to bring about a link between consciousness and the unconscious, so that psychic complexes and archetypes are brought into meaningful and conscious intersection with the conscious self. The ultimate whence of natural grace does not add new semiotic content to the self, whereas the wither of the spirit makes

Nature's Self-Disclosure

new content possible when the temporal groans toward the post-temporal.

B. Eschatology and the Heart of Nature

If the self were to remain in the dialectic between its current temporal configuration and the whence of the pretemporal, it would fail to find its way into transforming community. The experience of the whence of the potencies, while necessary, is not sufficient for the horizontal domain of personal intersection. If the ultimate model of intersection in the domain of natural grace is that of sexual ecstasy, in the domain of the spirit it is that of the loving and courageous communication of shared and divergent meaning. Put in psychoanalytic terms, it is the domain where the spirit can enter into transference and countertransference relations to bring about an openness to an ultimate whither that is not confined to the domain of the lost object. The momenta of both transference and countertransference are themselves part of the spirit's work within community, and only through the spirit can these great psychic powers be brought into a healing nexus.

The relation between selves within the spirit is also, and more deeply, a relation to nature. The most powerful evocation of the eschatological dimension of nature is found in Paul's letter to the nascent Christian community in Rome. In this epistle (written ca. 54–58 C.E.), he evokes a sense of the ultimate eschatological drama that awaits the world (NRSV Romans 8: 22–25):

> We know that the whole creation has been groaning in labor pains until now; and not only the creation, but we ourselves, who have the first fruits of the Spirit, groan inwardly while we wait for adoption, the redemption of our bodies. For in hope we were saved. Now hope that is seen is not hope. For who hopes for what is seen? But if we hope for what we do not see, we wait for it with patience.

As children of the spirit, selves are gathered up into the same process that works within the heart of creation itself. If we groan to be given spiritual bodies, as analogues to the resurrected body of Jesus, nature also groans to renew itself through the powers of *nature naturing*. In the previous chapter we discussed the enigmatic passage in which Jesus condemns the fig tree (a symbol for Israel) for not bearing fruit out of season. The Markan passage converges with the thought of Paul in that in both cases there is an implied appeal to the deeper and more mysterious forces of *nature naturing* that can surge forward to bring about an eschatological renewal of the world and its orders.

The selving process is indeed a child of the spirit when it lets itself become gathered up into the power of the spirit and its own form of grace. The spirit did not create nature, any more than it can literally stop the momentum of entropy. Yet the spirit emerges from the heart of the ontological difference to convey the power of the potencies to the drought-inflicted world of *nature natured*. All children of the spirit are children of nature and derive their healing energies from the grace of the spirit, itself an eject from the heart of nature. The spirit itself is eschatological through and through, but this must be sharply distinguished from any sense that it 'contains' an internal teleological pattern. Here we are again reminded of Buchler's distinction between providence and providingness. The spirit is, if the expression may be allowed, a unique form of eschatological providingness, not a manifest form of providence.

The spirit provides for an enhancement of all sign systems and all conscious sign users, but it does not hand over to selves some kind of life plan that can be decoded and rendered into a manifest code. The spirit enables and empowers, even while remaining mysterious as to its own whither. The most basic manifestation of the spirit is its unrelenting drive to connect the pretemporal and temporal to its own form of posttemporal rhythm. Put in terms of the ontological difference, the spirit moves some of the potencies of *nature naturing* into the pertinent orders of *nature natured*, thereby expanding them in unpredictable ways. Any serious encounter with the spirit will involve novelty and creativity for the sign-using self. Yet on an even deeper level, there will be genuine cosmic novelty that cannot be predicted from antecedent conditions. As noted in the previous chapter, the spirit is akin to a strange attractor that moves an unstable system into a new and higher form of stability that cannot be predicted from within the traits of the system.

Where is intelligibility in this process? The spirit must not be seen as some kind of providential mind that is filled with attained intelligibility (Peirce's thirdness). Nor must the spirit be seen as a conscious person that is directly aware of each and every self in a conscious way. It makes far more sense to see the spirit as a field of enabling energy rather than as a person (in the traditional trinitarian sense). The theologian Pannenberg, in dialogue with contemporary philosophy of science, has worked out some of the inner logic of this new conception of the spirit:

The concept of the force field, both in terms of its historical antecedents and in terms of its systematic implications, needs careful assessment by the theologian. The concept of a field of force could be used to make effective our understanding of the spiritual presence of God in natural phenomena. Einstein's field theory comprises space, time, and energy in such a way as to make thinking about the whole of time intelligible. This, it seems, would give priority to eternity in our conception of time. (Pannenberg 1993: 48)

In this perspective, which is very close to that of ecstatic naturalism, the spirit is neither a self, a body, a place, nor a consciousness. Rather, it lives between all bodies and selves as an enabling force field that makes true interaction between and among bodies possible. Pannenberg's sense of eternity is better understood in our terms as the domain of the posttemporal, namely, that which comes after the ravages of entropic temporality, thereby making it possible to heal the rifts of time.

The grace of the spirit enters into the quieter power of natural grace to unite the whence with the whither of its own life. This whither remains open in a radical way to the augmentation of meaning that comes from enhanced interpretants and the selves that house them. The whence ceases to be abjected by the self when the whither of the spirit opens up a power that enables it to withstand the presence/absence of the lost object. The lost object looses its demonic face, which had appeared as a kind of devouring mother, when it is quickened by the spirit. The loss of the material maternal is transfigured into a return of the enveloping maternal through the spirit that lifts the pretemporal into the eschatological power of the posttemporal.

We must be especially careful here to avoid literalistic images of the kingdom of meaning that awaits nature's self when it enters into the force field of the spirit. Given the fissures within entropic temporality, the self is tempted to project a completed utopian structure that will decisively end time as understood. Utopian expectation is not demonic in itself, but must be correlated to the actual work of the spirit, which does not destroy time and its issue in order to invite selves into the kingdom of meaning. That is, neither the pretemporal nor the temporal are canceled or effaced with the emergence of the posttemporal. Entropy will always exist in the cosmic structures that prevail. The lost object will always remain to some extent lost. The *fort-da* game of Freud's nephew, discussed at length in the first chapter, retains its truth even in the domain of the spirit. Children of the spirit will gain and lose the lost object as the posttemporal opens up the compelling vista of the not yet. The lost object will continue to be abjected and feared, even while longed for with increasing intensity. The grace of the spirit does not somehow wrench the lost object into the light of day, so much as give us the power and grace to enter into its complex approach/withdrawal. Insofar as the self can participate in both natural and spiritual grace, it will gain a new *kind* of access to the lost object that will enable the lost object to enter into the open draft of the not yet and take on a new and transfigured face.

The lost object (whence) of the self is entwined with the lost object of nature (the potencies). The presence of the spirit gives the self more fully back to its whence, even while bringing it closer to the undelimited potencies that underlie whatever is. Where is the eschatological dimension in this drama? The spirit is the carrier of the not yet. The not yet is not something that is already attained, merely awaiting an unveiling when the conditions are right. Rather, the not yet is truly open and cannot be filled in with utopian expectation. When Paul reminds us that "we hope for what we do not see," rather than for what we do see (i.e., a content-specific utopian expectation), he shows us the logic of the not yet. The kingdom of meaning has no analogues with anything in the domain of *nature natured*. The power of the not yet is to provide us with a continual process of opening onto the undelimited realm where the temporal opens its heart to the posttemporal. In opening its heart, the temporal does not cease to be (a confusion of the apocalyptic mind), but tastes of a time beyond the ravages of entropy and decay.

The true eschatological nature of the spirit, which opens both human selves and nature, is manifest when the children of *chronos* find and enter into the comfort of the posttemporal in which the whence is brought forward into its healing configuration. If the whence of natural grace is without a healing face, the whence that is birthed into the not yet is the all-embracing ground that nurtures its own foundlings. What was once the devouring mother or destructive father now becomes the welcoming parent that is part of the new being that is a gift of spiritual grace. The eschaton is not so much a place of places as it is a continual invitation to the enhancement of meaning within the flow of temporality.

The specific mechanism for this momentum as it takes place between and among selves is the transference/countertransference relation. In classical psychoanalytic theory the transference is activated within the confines of the analytic situation. The analysand (patient or client) will project a great deal of emotional energy onto the analyst, and in turn may provoke a countertransference from the analyst to the analysand. On a deeper level, the transference enables the analysand to reawaken aspects of figures from his or her past so that they can come alive through the transference projection onto the analyst. In its purist form, the transference passes through the catalyst (analyst) to the parent or relevant figure from the analysand's past. In its less pure form, the transference gets tangled up with both the analyst and the figure from the past, thereby brooking confusion about the true object of positive and negative projections. Insofar as the analyst enters into the enriched atmosphere of the transference, he or she may be coaxed into a countertransference in which unresolved complexes may be powerfully activated.

For both Freud and Jung, the transference/countertransference is the heart of therapy. Healing can only begin when there is a full flowering of the transference. For Jung, who had a more profound understanding of these dynamics, synchronistic experiences can take place when the transference and countertransference activate archetypal structures and bring them into a momentary constellation. The synchronistic experience, in which two separate causal sequences, one mental and one physical, are brought into meaningful connection, shatters the shells that had hampered the therapeutic relation. After the synchronistic event(s), both analyst and analysand are changed and moved forward into a larger horizon of meaning. Jung hinted that this process was itself a gift of the spirit as it moved between the two selves.

Structurally, transference can open up the creative tension between the ego and the deeper psyche. Often there is a bridging figure, such as the anima or animus, that serves to ply the path between the two very different orders of meaning and power. Ann Ulanov gives a precise analysis of this transaction:

> The reaching of the ego toward relation with the Self is the central issue in analysis for Jungians, whether with negative or positive effect. The movement of the ego toward Self is involved in any transference, but nowhere so strongly as when the contrasexual anima or animus is activated, stretching consciousness to make space for all that arrives from the unconscious. (Ulanov 1982: 75)

The ego would remain in its own egocentric universe were it not for the liberating power of the transference that brings it into the vicinity of the deeper heliocentric reality of the Self. What we have called "selving" reaches its highest intensity when the transference, working through the intoxicating power of the contrasexual archetype, moves the ego toward the source of meaning. The work of the transference is never easy precisely because it throws internal material out into conscious semiotic space, where its uncanny power must be acknowledged. To enter into a transference is to be seized by that which has no known whence or whither. In time, the inner cunning of the transference will become manifest as the psyche learns the difficult process of internalizing the projected material so that it can enter into the growth of conscious meaning.

It must be remembered that transference energies are never purely personal (Machtiger 1982: 99), but that they come from archetypal energies and powers that must be honored. The power of the transference is a gift of the spirit to the finite ego so that it can burst forth from its self-encapsulated world. It is as if the transference muddies up the waters of interpersonal life so that new growth possibilities may emerge. This means, of course, that transference phenomena are highly ambiguous, especially in their initial stages, and must be tended with great care. Should the transference not be seen *as* transference, the psyche runs the profound risk of wounding both itself and the other persons involved in the relation. Is this to say that all interhuman relations are transferential? Yes, insofar as the energy for entering into the rhythm of another life comes from projection and longing. When the transference field takes hold, the relation assumes proportions that are much larger than the persons involved. Put simply, every relation involves a minimal form of transference and countertransference energy. In certain unusual cases, for reasons that almost always baffle the ego, the transference energies may assume overwhelming and demoralizing proportions.

Ecstatic naturalism takes Jung's understanding of the centrality of the transference very seriously. All human relations involve projection and counter-projection. When any given relation moves into a new sphere of intensity, projection deepens into transference, which in turn may shake loose a strong countertransference. It must be remembered that the transference is a two-leveled phenomenon. On one level it is a projection of internal qualities onto the other, while on a deeper level it is part of the process whereby one self participates in the inner structures of another. Thus the transference, as a gift of the spirit, is both an externalization of hidden semiotic material (projection) and an erotic movement into the depth dimension of another self.

The spirit is, as noted, like a strange attractor in that it is not disclosed through static or periodic antecedent conditions, but moves by its own hidden logic. When we are brought into a transference relation it is as if we are lifted out of fixed and cyclic attractors and handed over to a force that has an elusive whither. In the analytic matrix, transference and countertransference energies have an unusual focus and intensity, yet these energies occur in many nonanalytic situations where the boundaries between selves are much murkier.

We must be careful, of course, in eulogizing all forms of the transference as if such energy is benevolent in each case. Jung warns us that the object of the transference must be an appropriate one:

> In the transference all kinds of infantile fantasies are projected. They must be cauterized, i.e., resolved by reductive analysis, and this is generally known as "resolving the transference." Thereby the energy is again released from an unserviceable form, and again we are faced with the problem of its disposibility. Once more we shall put our trust in nature, hoping that, even before it is sought, an object will have been chosen which will provide a favourable gradient. (Jung 1917: 63)

The movement of the transference in its initial stage is a return to conditions of origin in the domain where dreaming innocence gave way to autonomy. The carrier/recipient of the transference must be complex enough to move the projection toward a rich whither such that the self can withdraw the transference and internalize in a more conscious way the riches contained within it. Jung's own form of ecstatic naturalism places "trust in nature" that the appropriate object will show itself so that the transference can find a suitable field for its projective possibilities.

Why does transference exist at all, given that it merely complicates and frustrates communication between and among selves? The answer is clear. The transference is a powerful semiotic and emotional field that throws deep and abjected structures out into the world so that they may take on an external life of their own. In entering into a transference relation with another person I clothe him or her with my depth self. Insofar as my own projections converge with someone else's hidden semiotic fields, often in the form of contraries, they too will enter into the transference field and experience the fierce logic of these underground currents. The transference/countertransference force field, one of the 'hows' of the spirit, will transform both selves should there be enough courage and insight to sustain the energy of the field.

When the transference field is at its higher forms of intensity, the dream field may be activated. Dreams are rarely private, whatever 'private' would mean, and often enter into other selves and their internal semiotic fields. When two persons are caught in the mutual transference field, they may dream their way into each other's dream field. This is not to say that two selves actually change places, but that their co-implicated semiotic fields will have common themes and structures that can be mutually illuminating. That is, I may have a dream sequence that illuminates complexes that we both share. In telling the other person of my dreams, he or she may enter into a commensurate dream sequence that deals with our common needs and complexes. This is a form of erotic participation in the spirit in which meaning suddenly becomes interpsychic and sharable. Dreams, as the most important 'tools' of the transference force field, are prospective horizons of meaning that can hold open a *between* connecting two or more selves.

Consider the movement of contraries in the transference field. A biological male will have his contrasexual archetype in the anima, while a biological female will have her contrasexual archetype in the animus. In someone with an undeveloped anima or animus, there will be a strong need to project the incomplete complex or archetype onto another person. It is as if the anima and the animus are constantly sending out semiotic feelings, waiting for the right object to call them forth more fully. Insofar as this is a conscious process filled with planning and calculation, it is doomed to failure. The cunning of nature runs deeper. There may happen a purely chance encounter in which a man and a woman meet, e.g., on an airplane or at the theater, in which there is a sudden 'recognition' on the unconscious level that the anima and animus projections have found a home. The force field of the transference suddenly surges forward without warning and the two selves are caught in the matrix of the spirit. Consciousness of the inner logic of the encounter may come much later, if at all, and the future of the relation may be extremely tenuous at best. Yet the initial work of the spirit has been done and two persons are moved forward into new structures that, should the conditions be right, promise an enriched understanding of the complexes involved.

Nature's cunning takes many such dramatic forms and should never be underestimated. The grace of the spirit works with the products of this cunning, moving selves toward self-understanding and some sense of community. Natural grace is beyond good and evil, while the grace of the spirit has strong ethical dimensions. Yet the concepts of good and evil coming out of our encounter with the spirit are not always commensurate with those that have emerged from the controlling super ego. The spirit is primarily concerned with the enhancement of meaning, pointing us toward the kingdom of meaning on the edges of history. Consequently, the spirit often must shatter those boundaries that stand in the way of genuine individuation and emancipatory community. Put in different terms, the spirit must also provide a place for the demonic and its own forms of energy if it is to move selves toward a new form of power and meaning.

Thus we must be willing to redefine the concepts of good and evil if we are to enter into the rhythms of the spirit as it moves selves toward both their whence and their whither within the structures of community. Nature's self often flees from the obligation of the spirit and clings to the attained communal interpretants that have their own built-in reward systems. The power of the whence moves the self back to its own loss of innocence and compels it to reenact the movement of negativity in which it rejected the birthing ground. Tillich quite correctly correlated autonomy and guilt. To move away from the whence toward the autonomy of an original position is to incur guilt that cannot be dissolved through finite means. Ironically, the self throws itself into the lure of innumerable interpretants in order to drown out the voice that comes from the now rent and torn whence (lost object). No finite power can compel the self to look backward toward its origin. Only the whither of the spirit, which paradoxically moves in the opposite direction, can bring the self into a fuller awareness of the whence that underlies all of its internal and external signs.

From the standpoint of autonomy, the move back toward the whence may appear to be evil insofar as it means a shifting of energies and allegiances from cultural codes and norms to an undulating and darker rhythm that seems to have little respect for norms. The very concept of "undulation" has been clothed with patriarchal abjection because it points to a momentum that cannot be contained within the boundaries of the super ego. The mysterious rhythm of the whence haunts the autonomous and communal self, threatening seeming ruin should the iron grip of cultural codes give way to the potencies that speak from the heart of the unconscious of nature.

From our perspective, the return to the power of the whence (whether of the self or of nature) represents one of the goods of the spirit. Abjection of the whence is itself violent and manifests itself throughout the community in the form of heteronomous personal and social controls. With the appearance of the spirit, there is a powerful inversion of the valuation process. What was once seen to be a good, namely, social control of eros and transference, now shows itself to be opposed to the spirit and the kingdom of meaning. On the other side, what was once feared as an evil, namely, the loss of 'pure' autonomy in the face of the 'devouring' abyss, now shows itself to be a gift of the spirit as it aids the selving process. But here the plot thickens.

Ecstatic naturalism does not call for an anarchic destruction of social norms, insofar as these norms may be healing, but insists that they must receive their validation from the reappearance of the whence (on the other side of abjection), and the lure of the whither. The grace of the spirit transforms normative ethics and relocates the form of empowerment for ethics from the community to the ontological difference and the spirit. Human ethical systems can deal with finite goods and their position within interpretive and natural communities. The spirit, which is infinitely larger than the 'sum' of human selves, invokes dynamic goods that participate in the mobile infinity of the spirit's life. These goods enter into emancipatory communities, which are more closely aligned with the spirit than are interpretive or natural communities.

A natural community merely reiterates the signs that have been embedded in it and can be deeply heteronomous. Such a community will cling to antecedent powers and enshrine them in the form of "blood and soil." An interpretive community will quicken and deepen its interpretants but will not necessarily embed them in the eschatological lure that calls for personal and social justice. Horizons of meaning will expand and take on novel and rich interpretants, but there will be little openness to the inbreaking of dynamic and nonfinite goods. An emancipatory community will feel the power and lure of the spirit and will bend its dynamic goods in the direction of the kingdom of meaning. Members of such a community will live on the boundaries where the concepts of good and evil will be reconfigured in the light of the healing spirit.

Life in an emancipatory community will be both eschatological and ambiguous. The eschatological dimension will be manifest in the constant creative tension that moves all actions and all interpretations toward the whither of the spirit. The ambiguous dimension will be manifest in all human relations in which the spirit will both grant and withhold its gifts at the same time. Carriers of the spirit may even break the ethical structures that often hold communities together. From the biblical David to the misogynist activities of Martin Luther King Jr., carriers of the spirit often inflict deep wounds on the very community that they struggle to transform. There seems to be no answer to this profound ambiguity under the conditions of our estrangement, other than to endure the tensions between the promise of the kingdom of meaning and the lure of finite powers and goods.

If we move from finite human community to the vast canvas of nature itself, we see St. Paul's drama played out in a fuller way. The power of the potencies, always hidden yet always present in their absence, continues to pull the world back to the pretemporal. It is as if the world itself has a Freudian death drive to return to dreaming innocence. Jumping to the manifest orders of entropic time, the world spawns and destroys without any sense of moral constraint. Finally, in the whither, emerging out of the mysterious cleft of the ontological difference, the spirit moves some orders of the world toward the kingdom of meaning that transforms both the pretemporal and the posttemporal. Nature's self participates in this travail of nature, and finds its true measure only insofar as it enters into rhythms not of its own creation.

C. TRANSFIGURATION

It is extremely difficult to find a genuine sense of transfiguration that also honors the fitful and often destructive forces of *nature natured*. The spirit is embedded in the fissure opened up by the ontological difference and is thus of lesser scope than nature itself. Yet we have also referred to the spirit as infinite, especially as it relates to dynamic goods and the emergence of the kingdom of meaning. This sense of infinite must be understood to denote an nonencompassable quality within the spirit. Yet the infinity of the spirit is a 'lesser' infinity than that of nature. Neither nature nor spirit can be encompassed. Indeed, using Jaspers' term we can say that both nature and the spirit are "encompassing" per se. Yet the encompassing presence/absence of the spirit is of a very different reality from that of nature. We can refer to nature in the barest sense as the potencies on the one side and the 'sum' of all orders on the other. The spirit, on the other hand, is the movement *within* nature to transform those orders funded with meaning. Put in negative terms, there is nowhere where nature is absent, while there are innumerable orders bereft of the spirit.

Nature may *appear* to be absent from the standpoint of alienated consciousness, but, by definition, it can never be in eclipse as it is impossible to look anywhere at anytime without encountering orders and potencies. Even after bodily death, the self will still be *in* nature, although the dimensionality of its environment will be strikingly different. The spirit, however, moves to a depth logic that can never be fathomed by the human process. It is possible to look at vast portions of *nature natured* and fail to find traces of the spirit. When spirit is present, it works in a more direct way to manifest its unique form of prevalence to the human process.

The concept of "transfiguration" functions in the gospels of Matthew and Mark to denote the ontological change in Jesus as he is compared to the ancient prophets Moses and Elijah. In spite of the obvious polemical move to place Jesus on top of the new historical configuration, the ontological elements assume priority, with Jesus receiving a divine confirmation of his depth relation to the ground of being and the human process. In the NRSV translation of Matthew 17:2 it is asserted, "And he was transfigured before them, and his face shone like the sun, and his clothes became dazzling white." The disciples witness this cosmic drama and come to a fragmented understanding of the break that has now taken place in space, time, and history. The transfiguration has signaled that the most basic structures of *nature natured* have broken open to the potencies of *nature naturing*. Of course, this language, derived from medieval Latin, would have made no sense to Jesus' followers, yet the reality of the ontological difference was present to them nonetheless.

For ecstatic naturalism, the concept of transfiguration is the most pertinent for denoting the final consummation of the human process under the conditions of time. We need not literalize the concept nor limit it to one historical experience, even if that experience is held to be normative for many. What is far more pertinent is how the concept points to the mobile dialectic that finally brings together the lost object, the foundlings of time, and the spirit. The lost object appears in the symbolic guise of Moses and Elijah, while the foundlings of time are clearly present in the disciples. The transformation of Jesus into a kind of solar power and radiant epiphany points to the whither of the spirit in which the lost object and the children of *chronos* are shown their true reality.

The lost object—from the simple *fort-da* game of Freud's nephew, to the lost realm of dreaming innocence, to the material maternal—has remained embedded in the lost whence that has continued to haunt the movement of the self through the shoals of time and space. We have seen that it is impossible to go back fully to the lost object without the destruction of autonomy. Yet the inner transformation of the self also requires that the lost object return in some form to give depth to natural grace. The lost object cannot bring about this movement on its own, as it would merely devour the child of time. This is precisely why the spirit must enter into the human process to protect the self against the devouring aspects of the lost object while at the same time bringing forward the grounding and healing powers of the lost domain.

It is highly pertinent that Jesus cannot shine forth without the power of the ancient ones that grounds his radiance in antecedent conditions. It is, of course, a very painful matter as to whether or not Jesus is held to overcome the powers of his origin (Judaism). Christian anti-Semitism has often marred the biblical account of the transfiguration, and great care must be used in working through the ontological structures evoked by the biblical material. A more judicious reading would emphasize the utter necessity of the depth correlation of origin and goal, refusing to privilege either. In fact, goals, without the ballast and empowerment of origin, would quickly become demonic. The most ontologically precise way of describing the transfiguration is to say that it is something that happens to origin (Moses and Elijah), the children of time (the disciples), and the power of the whither (Jesus). In this triadic structure, all three dimensions are brought into a new correlation that has its ultimate foundation in the eternal fissure between *nature naturing* and *nature natured*.

How, then, do we translate this biblical/ontological structure into terms pertinent to the selving process? At the outset it must be clear that we are not advocating some kind of divinization of the human process. Schleiermacher edged in this direction with his Christological framework that saw Jesus as the *urbild* (archetype) of humankind (Schleiermacher 1821). For Schleiermacher, insofar as we attain religious self-consciousness in the form of absolute dependence on the infinite, we assume the ontological structure and power of Jesus. Ecstatic naturalism moves in a very different direction. The power of estrangement is simply too strong, with its attendant movements of transference and countertransference, for any such ontological comparisons to be made. The transfiguration awaiting the selving process is finite and deeply ambiguous, even though it does participate in basic ontological structures, structures that are sharply etched in the biblical account.

Shifting our language, we see how the spirit moves the lost object into a different dimension of meaning and power. The realm that was abjected by the self on its journey into the domain of interpretants, retained its power for the self, even while the self was busy erecting barriers against its return. The spirit enters into this necessary boundary to empower the self with new energy and insight. As the spirit coaxes the self through its own self-deluded protections, the whence enters into the rhythms of temporality to give the self back to its abjected past, a past that is ultimately pretemporal.

In terms pertinent to object relations theory, the spirit makes it possible for the self to enter into the depth logic of its transference so that abjected personal material can reappear to enter into the healing nexus of the spirit. Personal complexes, and actual persons from the past, can never be effaced, no matter how desirable this may be to the self. But this material can be invited into a new configuration in which some of the demonic forces can be entwined into the spirit.

The spirit does not abject the demonic. Indeed, it always contains the demonic within itself. It must be remembered that the demonic contains great energy and form shattering power. To abject the demonic is to run the risk of allowing that power a manifestation that will be destructive to the self and its communities. When the spirit takes the demonic into itself it gives it a place within which to unfold its fierce energy. Yet it is precisely here that the most astonishing transfiguration takes place. For in entering into the movements of the spirit, the demonic encounters a power that is greater than itself. The spirit transforms the energy of the demonic into healing energy. Of course, under the conditions of finitude, it would be a dangerous form of romanticism to assume that the spirit can always perform this miracle of transfiguration. On the simple personal level, the work of the spirit must be aided by strenuous efforts toward self-consciousness and realization. If there is a concept of original sin in depth psychology, it is the sin of unconsciousness in the face of the demands of the spirit. To fail to struggle with and for the spirit against the hegemony of the demonic is to fail the selving process on the deepest level. It is precisely here that the concept of an ethics beyond ethics manifests itself.

To live in the realm of norms alone is to fail to become conscious of the innumerable powers that circulate in and through the psyche. This is never to say that norms are simply evil, far from it, but it is to say that any norm that is allowed to prevail outside of its connection to the dialectic of the demonic and the holy is a norm that has no liberating or transforming power. Norms per se belong to the domain of temporality. When a norm becomes permeable to the whence and the whither, it assumes a potency within the self and the social orders that must be honored, even if that potency calls individuals into actions that may

NATURE'S SELF-DISCLOSURE

violate norms that abject the ground and the goal of the self. When the hegemony of the temporal is broken by the spirit, norms can emerge, or given norms can be transfigured, in such a way as to create an emancipatory community under the conditions of time.

There is a strong element of risk whenever the self is called by the spirit to move beyond the stated mores of the social order. Behind the momentum of the spirit, which invites us to move toward the edges of boundaries, whether in the transference relation or in other structures, lies the power of love that restructures all laws. Tillich, profoundly aware of the ambiguities of finite existence, argues that the power of love, in the dimension of agape, remakes the self and its communities:

> Every moral decision demands a partial liberation from the stated moral law. Every moral decision is a risk because there is no guarantee that it fulfills the law of love, the unconditional demand coming from the encounter with the other one. . . . The principle of *agape* expresses the unconditional validity of the moral imperative, and it gives the ultimate norm for all ethical content. But it still has a third function: it is the source of moral motivation. It necessarily commands, threatens, and promises, because fulfillment of the law is reunion with one's essential being, or integration of the centered self. (Tillich 1963: 47 & 48)

When the self moves beyond the norms of the social order, it can either make a pact with the demonic and its form destroying powers, or it can listen to the demands of the spirit. The heart of the spirit is the love that combines validity, norm, and motivation. As the principle of validation, the spirit of love transforms and then accepts the deepened law. As the giver of norms, the spirit of love provides the meaning horizon within which ethical conduct takes place. Most important, the spirit of love motivates the self to let go of cost/benefit analyses of social norms and enter into the prophetic demands of the new law on the other side of norms.

This ethics beyond ethics cannot be fathomed by looking at antecedent social and personal conditions. Like the spirit itself, the new transfigured laws serve as a kind of strange attractor, moving the self past one state of order into a higher order that emerges when the internal pressures have reached a breaking point. It is precisely on the boundaries of the law that the new law can begin to show itself. In one dimension, this involves opening the old law to its theonomous depths, while in another dimension it may involve a prophetic critique of the super ego and its constricting norms.

As there is a new law, so too is there a new self. The inner transfiguration of the selving process is tied to the law beyond law, to the ethics beyond ethics. Ecstatic naturalism works out of the primal intuition that nature is absolutely indifferent to all human laws. Yet out of the self-fissuring of nature the spirit unfolds to transform fragile human law into form granting powers that can recenter the self around the self-disclosure of the spirit of love. It is misguided to refer to this kind of love as only agapastic. In the self-disclosure of the spirit there is a fundamental wedding of agape and eros. The agapastic element is the grace giving moment in which the spirit gives the self the love that cannot be found in the human order. The erotic element is the invitation to participate in the rhythm of the spirit as it enters into the transference/countertransference world(s).

Erotic participation in the spirit shatters boundaries and opens the self to the unlimited richness of meaning that comes out of the spirit. The spirit is not an actual storehouse of attained meanings, but is a momentum that coaxes enriched meanings into the light of human consciousness so that they can transform the self and its communities. At the same time, the spirit enables us to see the creative empty space between meanings so that we can come to an understanding of betweenness per se. This frees us from the frenzied plenitude of interpretants, which, while necessary, often blocks out the more elusive light of the spaces opened out by the spirit.

The love of the spirit enters into the human process as the gift of grace that is both accepting and demanding, while at the same time inviting us to an erotic participation that moves us into a different reality where we become open to the other in a dramatic new way. In the vibrating betweenness, held open for us by the spirit, both self and law become transfigured.

But this process also entails a different relation to nature. The haunting image of the blasted fig tree returns one last time to remind us of how the depth rhythm of *nature naturing* enters into the laws and periodic structures of *nature natured*. Insofar as we cling to the norms and powers of the created orders, we violate a deeper logic that does not respect the measure of entropic temporality and conflictual space. In the domain of *nature natured* it makes no sense to ask a fig tree to behave other than it must according to the dispensation of *chronos*. Yet the spirit opens us to the interstices of the world where the potencies of *nature naturing* leave their traces. These pretemporal powers can transfigure the orders of the world, but only if the potentialities are right. As finite selves we can never develop a list of necessary and sufficient conditions for discriminating these potentialities in advance, but we can, as children of the spirit, recognize them when they emerge.

In our concluding remarks we will show the extremes of the human process as manifest in the dialectic of melancholy and love. As noted, moods represent fundamental access structures onto the orders of the world and have their fulfillment in the transfiguring shock that comes from the recognition of the ubiquity of the ontological difference. For many, melancholy has the last word, as it is directly tied to the lost object, which remains forever beyond recall. Were this the final answer, the human process would have no recourse but to endlessly reiterate the conditions of origin through memory and longing. The lost object would appear and reappear as a haunting presence/absence with no healing or grace-giving powers. The domain of temporality and language would thus be the domain where we develop masks that both hide and reveal the lost object, but that never bring us any closer to understanding its lure or its danger.

Is melancholy itself as straightforward as it seems? That is, does melancholy normally come from our embeddedness in temporality and finite spatial structures, or does it have a unique dimension that often eludes inquiry? Insofar as an analysis of the human process ignores the spirit, it follows that melancholy is a finite human mood that comes directly out of the frustrations of *nature natured*. When any given meaning or meaning horizon frustrates or betrays us, we can enter into the dark rhythms of melancholy. Or so it would seem. We can ask a deeper question: what is it that makes finite orders frustrating? There is certainly a sense in which instrumental structures frustrate us, and there is also a sense in which projected meanings can fail to find a proper location within events as they unfold. But these failures and frustrations do not generate true melancholy. The power of melancholy emerges when something much more shattering enters into our awareness.

Finite meanings come and go, but there soon emerges a sense that the entire structure of the world, from objects to interpretants, is hovering over something that is not a finite meaning, and that this 'something' represents a strong negation of all attained meanings. Schopenhauer brilliantly captured this sense of total negation in his delineation of the will and its relation to the phenomena of perception. His intuition remains compelling, in spite of his inept metaphysical structures, precisely because he recognized that there is no way to 'fill in' this abyss through the mere augmentation of finite structures in space and time. Only a very different axis of vision can still the metaphysical hunger that comes from this no longer.

How, then, do we move from finite frustrations to the kind of primal melancholy that puts the *entire* world into question? The answer is simple: we do not move at all, but we *are* moved by the spirit that gives us melancholy as one of its most treasured gifts. The transition from finite disappointments to the infinite power of melancholy is not a product of *nature natured* or any of its orders. It is a gift of the spirit that moves to free us from our absolute dependence on the world, so that we can begin to fathom the abyss of *nature naturing*. We certainly understand finite grounds and abysses in the temporal order. But it is only with the flowering of melancholy, which initially appears as a poisoned fruit, that we begin to understand what it is to have all grounds removed. Yet this process also brings us toward that deeper ground that we hunger for in the lost object.

The ontological wound of the self, a product of the self-fissuring of *nature naturing* as it spawns *nature natured*, becomes more acutely felt as nature's self enters into the elusive ground of the whence. Melancholy can never be felt for a finite object *within* the world, but always points to the nonfinite domain of the elusive whence that produces dissatisfaction with all finite orders of meaning. The spirit moves the self toward the abyss that opens up the whence, thereby producing an awareness of the ontological wound that fails to heal under the conditions of finitude. But the spirit moves in a healing way to both show the wound and point toward its possible amelioration in the posttemporal. Without the experience of melancholy, which opens up a sense of the ontological difference, the self would have no chance of finding either the pretemporal or the posttemporal.

Why does our initial encounter with the abjected and lost object produce melancholy rather than curiosity or joy? The reason for this should be clear: The lost object was once the source of all nourishment and empowerment for the self as it began its journey from its original position toward depositioning and repositioning. Like Peirce's firstness (which he likens to an egg), the lost object is remembered as the originating potency that made autonomy possible. The various nourishments in the world of *chronos* do not have the richness or sustaining power of the nourishments of the lost object. The transition, filled with negation and fear, from the infinite to the finite, leaves strong traces that can be reenergized whenever the finite world becomes empty of support and meaning. Whenever one of these traces is suddenly awakened, the self feels the full extent of its loss and hungers to return to the source. Of course, such a complete return is not possible. The no longer can only fully return if it is gathered up into the liberating power of the not yet.

How does the self move from melancholy to love? The love of the spirit is not felt or understood unless and until the self passes through the crucible of melancholy. The spirit pries the self loose from the tyranny of *nature natured* by opening it up to the continuing power of the no longer. When the self learns that melancholy is a gift, rather than a visitation of the demonic, it can enter into the rhythm of the infinite/finite correlation. The initial taste of the infinite produces longing, a longing that only grows in intensity as long as the only possible goal for its yearning is the lost object. Life would indeed be tragic, and destined for suicide, if this were the only locus for the spirit. The failure to find the lost object in its plenitude, rather than in pieces and fragments, would drive the self with an unrelenting logic toward self-annihilation in which the impossible tension between the desired and the actual would shatter consciousness and its fragile structures.

For many selves, this is the only possible outcome of the infinite/finite correlation. For reasons that remain locked in mystery, the spirit cannot move the melancholic self past its obsession with the lost object (material maternal), into the liberating breath of the not yet. No philosophical or theological perspective can ignore the fact that suicide has claimed, and will continue to claim, many of the foundlings of *nature natured*. This reminds us that the spirit is not omnipotent and that it must do its healing work under the constraints of finitude. Ecstatic naturalism, along with its celebration of the ecstatic transformations of the self and its world, remains in mourning for those children of *chronos* whose profound hunger for the infinite pulled them down without protection into the lost object and thus to their death.

But melancholy does not always have the last word. The protection against the destructive side of the lost object comes from the same spirit that opened the self to its infinity in the first place. If, for Martin Luther, divine wrath was the outer shell of divine love, for the current perspective, the melancholy for the lost object is the shell for the love that comes from the not yet of the spirit. Without the fire storm created by the infinite longing of melancholy, love would not have the healing potential to bring nature's self into the circle of the spirit and the kingdom of meaning. This kingdom, perhaps better termed a "community," awaits the self whenever its hunger for the infinite moves from the sustaining/destroying powers of the no longer into the momentum of the not yet. The community of meaning is not some kind of delimited space/time continuum, but a presence that encompasses selves and their communities, pointing them toward the mobile realm of the posttemporal.

Love, in both its erotic and agapastic forms, envelops the foundling of the world and quiets the destructive forces of the lost object. At the same 'time' it allows the necessary and healing forces of the lost object into the opening and creating clearing of the not yet. In its erotic dimension, love calls us to participate in the bodily rhythms that connect selves, and which connect the self to its world of objects and interpretants. In its agapastic dimension, love invites us into the grace of the spirit that makes us whole, while filling us with the demand for personal and social transformation. This love is not only a love that accepts us as we are, it is also a love that holds before us the obligation to enter into the postethical realm of the community of meaning in which norms are broken open to their theonomous depths. The love of the spirit can never efface its own gift of melancholy. But out of its heart it will bring our deepest melancholy into the tension filled dialectic with love so that the lost object and the not yet embrace each other under the conditions of time.

Bibliography

The following list of references contains: 1) All works cited in the text, 2) All works *directly* relevant to the writing of the text but not specifically cited, 3) My own publications, where pertinent, and 4) secondary literature on ecstatic naturalism.

BARTUSIAK, Marcia.
1993. *Through A Universe Darkly: A Cosmic Tale of Ancient Ethers, Dark Matter, and the Fate of the Universe* (New York: Harper Collins).

BIBLE.
1991. *The New Oxford Annotated Bible With the Apocrypha: New Revised Standard Version* (Oxford: Oxford University Press).

BRENT, Joseph.
1993. *Charles Sanders Peirce: A Life* (Bloomington: Indiana University Press).

BUCHLER, Justus.
1955. *Nature and Judgment* (New York: Columbia University Press).
1989. *Metaphysics of Natural Complexes*, second expanded edition, ed. Kathleen Wallace and Armen Marsoobian with Robert S. Corrington (Albany, NY: SUNY Press), based on the original 1966 edition.

CASSIRER, Ernst.
1929. *Philosophie der symbolischen Formen* (Berlin: Bruno Cassirer). English translation, *The Philosophy of Symbolic Forms*, in 3 vols., trans. Ralph Manheim (New Haven: Yale University Press, 1955).

CASTI, John L.
1994. *Complexification: Explaining a Paradoxical World Through the Science of Surprise* (New York: HarperCollins).

CORRINGTON, Robert S.
1982. "Horizonal Hermeneutics and the Actual Infinite," *Graduate Faculty Philosophy Journal*, vol. 8, no. 1 & 2, pp. 36–97.
1985. "Justus Buchler's Ordinal Metaphysics and the Eclipse of Foundationalism," *International Philosophical Quarterly*, vol. XXV, pp. 289–298.
1987. *The Community of Interpreters: On the Hermeneutics of Nature and the Bible in the American Philosophical Tradition* (Macon, GA: Mercer University Press).
1987a. *Pragmatism Considers Phenomenology*, co-edited with Thomas Seebohm and Carl R. Hausman (Washington: The Center for Advanced Research in Phenomenology and The University Press of America).
1988. "Being and Faith: *Sein und Zeit* and Luther," *Anglican Theological Review*, vol. LXX, no. 1, pp. 16–31.
1988a. "Semiosis and the Phenomenon of Worldhood," *Semiotics 1987*, ed. John Deely (Lanham, MD: University Press of America).
1989. "Faith and the Signs of Expectation," *Semiotics 1988*, ed. Terry Prewitt, John Deely, and Karen Haworth (Lanham, MD: University Press of America).
1990. "Emerson and the Agricultural Midworld," *Agriculture and Human Values*, (Winter), pp. 20–26.
1990a. "Transcendence and the Loss of the Semiotic Self," *Semiotics 1989*, ed. John Deely, Karen Haworth, and Terry Prewitt (Lanham, MD: University Press of America).
1991. "The Emancipation of American Philosophy," *APA Newsletter*, vol. 90, no. 3, pp. 23–26. (with a reply by Cornel West)
1991a. "Josiah Royce and Communal Semiotics," *The Semiotic Web 1990*, ed. Thomas A. Sebeok and Jean Umiker-Sebeok (Berlin: Mouton de Gruyter), pp. 61–87.

1991b. *Nature's Perspectives: Prospects for Ordinal Metaphysics*, co-edited with Armen Marsoobian and Kathleen Wallace (Albany, NY: SUNY Press), article, "Ordinality and the Divine Natures," pp. 347–366.
1992. "Ecstatic Naturalism and the Transfiguration of the Good," *Empirical Theology: A Handbook*, ed. Randolph Crump Miller (Birmingham: Religious Education Press), pp. 203–221.
1992a. *Nature and Spirit: An Essay in Ecstatic Naturalism* (New York: Fordham University Press).
1993. *An Introduction to C. S. Peirce: Philosopher, Semiotician, and Ecstatic Naturalist* (Lanham, MD: Rowman & Littlefield).
1993a. "Beyond Experience: Pragmatism and Nature's God," *American Journal of Theology & Philosophy*, vol. 14, no. 2, May, pp. 147–160.
1993b. "Nature's God and the Return of the Material Maternal," *The American Journal of Semiotics*, vol. 10, nos. 1–2, pp. 115–132.
1993c. "Peirce's Abjected Unconscious: A Psychoanalytic Profile," *Semiotics 1992*, ed. John Deely (Lanham: University Press of America).
1994. *Ecstatic Naturalism: Signs of the World*, Advances in Semiotics (Bloomington: Indiana University Press).
1995. "Peirce's Ecstatic Naturalism: The Birth of the Divine in Nature," *American Journal of Theology & Philosophy*, vol. 16, no. 2, May, pp. 173–187.

DAVIES, Paul.
1992. *The Mind of God: The Scientific Basis for a Rational World* (New York: Simon & Schuster).

DEAN, William.
1986. *American Religious Empiricism* (Albany: SUNY Press).
1988. *History Making History: The New Historicism in American Religious Thought* (Albany: SUNY Press).

DEELY, John.
1969. "The Philosophical Dimensions of the Origin of Species," *The Thomist*, XXXIII (January and April), Part I, pp. 75–149, Part II, pp. 251–342.
1982. *Introducing Semiotic: Its History and Doctrine* (Bloomington: Indiana University Press).

1987. "On the Problem of Interpreting the Term 'First' in the Expression 'First Philosophy'," *Semiotics 1987*, ed. John Deely (Lanham, MD: University Press of America), pp. 3–14.
1988. "Semiotics and First Philosophy," *Hermeneutics and the Tradition*, ACPA Proceedings, vol. LXII, ed. Daniel O. Dahlstrom (Washington, DC), pp. 136–146.
1990. *Basics of Semiotics* (Bloomington: Indiana University Press).

DELANEY, C.F.
1993. *Science, Knowledge, and Mind: A Study in the Philosophy of C. S. Peirce* (Notre Dame: University of Notre Dame Press).

DEWEY, John.
1927. *The Public and Its Problems* (New York: Henry Holt & Company).
1929. *Experience and Nature* (New York: W.W. Norton).

DRISKILL, Todd A.
1994. "Beyond the Text: Ecstatic Naturalism and American Pragmatism," *American Journal of Theology & Philosophy*, vol. 15, no. 3, September, pp. 305–323.

ECO, Umberto.
1976. *A Theory of Semiotics* (Bloomington: Indiana University Press).
1980. *In nome della rosa* (Milan: Bompiani). English translation, *The Name of the Rose*, trans. William Weaver (San Diego: Harcourt Brace Jovanovich, 1983).
1988. *Pendolo di Foucault* (Milano: Gruppo Editoriale Fabbri Bompiani, Sonzogno Etas S.p.A.). English translation, *Foucault's Pendulum*, trans. William Weaver (San Diego: Harcourt Brace Jovanovich, 1989).
1990. *The Limits of Interpretation* (Bloomington: Indiana University Press).

EMERSON, Ralph Waldo.
1844. "Experience," *Nature, Addresses, and Lectures* (Boston: Phillips, Sampson & Co., 1855). Reprinted in, *Nature, Addresses, and Lectures*, critical edition, ed. Robert E. Spiller and Alfred R. Ferguson, (Cambridge, MA: Harvard University Press, 1979).

FERGUSON, Kitty.
1992. *Stephen Hawking: Quest for a Theory of Everything* (New York: Bantam Books).

FISCH, Max H.
1986. *Peirce, Semeiotic, and Pragmatism*, ed. Kenneth Laine Ketner and Christian J. W. Kloesel (Bloomington: Indiana University Press).

FOUCAULT, Michel.
1975. *Surveiller et penur* (Paris). English translation by Alan Sheridan, *Discipline and Punish* (New York: Random House, 1977).

FREUD, Sigmund.
1920. *Beyond the Pleasure Principle*, English translation by James Strachey, from *The Freud Reader*, ed. by Peter Gay (New York: W.W. Norton, 1989).

GADAMER, Hans-Georg.
1960. *Wahrheit und Methode: Grundzüge einer philosophischen* (Tübingen: Mohr). English translation, *Truth and Method* (New York: Crossroad, 1982).

GRIBIN, John.
1993. *In The Beginning: After COBE and Before the Big Bang* (Boston: Little, Brown).

HANN, Lewis Edwin.
1991. *The Philosophy of Charles Hartshorne*, Library of Living Philosophers vol. XX (La Salle, IL: Open Court).

HARTSHORNE, Charles.
1948. *The Divine Relativity: A Social Conception of God* (New Haven: Yale University Press).
1973. *Born to Sing: An Interpretation and World Survey of Bird Song* (Bloomington: Indiana University Press).

HAUSMAN, Carl R.
1993. *Charles S. Peirce's Evolutionary Philosophy* (Cambridge: Cambridge University Press).

HAWKING, Stephen W.
1988. *A Brief History of Time* (New York: Bantam Books).
1993. *Black Holes and Baby Universes and Other Essays* (New York: Bantam Books).

HEGEL, G.W.F.
1807. *Phänomenologie des Geistes* (Hamburg: Felix Meiner Verlag, 1952). English translation, *Phenomenology of Spirit*, trans. A. V. Miller (Oxford: Clarendon Press, 1977).
1827. *Vorlesungen über die Philosophie der Religion* (Berlin 1832), English translation by R. F. Brown, P. C. Hodgson, and J. M. Stewart, with the assistance of H. S. Harris, *Lectures on the Philosophy of Religion*, One Volume Edition of The Lectures of 1827 (Berkeley: University of California Press, 1988).

HEIDEGGER, Martin.
1927. *Sein und Zeit* (Zuerst erschienen als Sonderdruck aus "Jahrbuch für Philosophie und phanomenologische Forschung" Band VIII). English translation, *Being and Time*, trans. John Macquarrie and Edward Robinson (New York: Harper & Row, 1962).
1929. "Was ist Metaphysik?," in *Wegmarken* (Frankfurt am Main: Vittorio Klostermann Verlag, 1967). English translation, "What is Metaphysics?," in *Martin Heidegger: Basic Writings*, ed. David Farrell Krell (New York: Harper & Row, 1977).
1929/ *Kant und das Problem der Metaphysik* (Frankfurt am
1973. Main: Vittorio Klostermann). English translation, *Kant and the Problem of Metaphysics*, fourth edition, enlarged, trans. Richard Taft (Bloomington: Indiana University Press, 1990).
1936/ Uberwindung der Metaphysik," in *Vorträge und*
1946. *Aufsätze* (Pfullingen: Neske, 1954). English translation, *The End of Philosophy*, trans. Joan Stambaugh (New York: Harper & Row, 1973).

1954. *Was Heisst Denken?* (Tübingen: Max Niemeyer Verlag). English translation, *What is Called Thinking?*, trans. J. Glenn Gray and F. Wieck (New York: Harper & Row, 1968).
1962. "Zeit und Sein," in *L'Endurance de la Pensée* (Paris: Plon, 1968). English translation, *Time and Being*, trans. Joan Stambaugh (New York: Harper & Row, 1972).

HOOKWAY, Christopher.
1985. *Peirce* (London: Routledge & Kegan Paul).

IRWIN, Alexander C.
1991. *Eros Toward the World: Paul Tillich and the Theology of the Erotic* (Minneapolis: Fortress Press).

JASPERS, Karl.
1935. *Vernunft und Existenz*, (Groningen), English translation by William Earle, *Reason and Existence* (New York: Noonday Press, 1955).
1962. *Der philosophische Glaube angesichts der Offenbarung* (Hamburg: R. Piper & Co., Verlag). English translation, *Philosophical Faith and Revelation*, trans. E. B. Ashton (New York: Haper & Row, 1967).

JUNG, Carl Gustav.
1917. "Die Psychologie der unbewussten Prozesse" (Zurich). English translation by R. F. C. Hull, *Two Essays on Analytical Psychology*, second edition, vol. 7 of The Collected Works (Princeton: Bollingen, 1966).
1925. *Analytical Psychology: Notes of a Seminar Given in 1925*, ed. William McGuire (Princeton: Bollingen, 1989).
1927. "Die Erdbedingtheit der Psyche" (Darmstadt). English translation by R. F. C. Hull, *The Structure and Dynamics of the Psyche*, second edition, vol. 8 of The Collected Works (Princeton: Bollingen, 1968).
1934/ "Archetypes of the Collective Unconscious," *Eranos-*
1954 *Jahrbuch* (Zurich). English translation by R. F. C. Hull, *The Archetypes and the Collective Unconscious*, second edition, vol. 9.1 of the Collected Works (Princeton: Bollingen, 1968).

1938. "Die psychologischen Aspekte des Mutterarchetypus" (Zurich). English translation by R. F. C. Hull, *The Archetypes and the Collective Unconscious*, second edition, vol. 9.1 of The Collected Works (Princeton: Bollingen, 1968).

1950. "Zur Empirie des Indivuationsprozesses" (Zurich). English translation by R. F. C. Hull, *The Archetypes and the Collective Unconscious*, second edition, vol. 9.1 of The Collected Works (Princeton: Bollingen, 1968).

1954. "Von den Wurzeln des Buwusstseins" (Zurich). English translation by R. F. C. Hull, *The Archetypes and the Collective Unconscious*, second edition, vol. 9.1 of The Collected Works (Princeton: Bollingen, 1968).

KANT, Immanuel.

1781. *Kritik der reinen Vernunft* (Riga, second edition 1787). English translation by Normen Kemp Smith, *Critique of Pure Reason* (New York: St. Martin's Press, 1929).

1793. *Die Religion innerhalb der Grenzen der blossen Vernunft* (Köningsberg). English translation by Theodore M. Greene and Hoyt H. Hudson with an essay by John R. Silber, *Religion Within the Bounds of Reason Alone* (New York: Harper Torchbooks, 1960).

KRIKORIAN, Yervant H., ed.

1944. *Naturalism and the Human Spirit* (New York: Columbia University Press).

KRISTEVA, Julia.

1974. *La révolution du langage poétique* (Paris: Editions du Seuil). English translation, *Revolution in Poetic Language*, trans. Margaret Waller (New York: Columbia University Press, 1984).

1985. *Au commencement etait l'amour: psychanalyse et foi*, (Paris: Hachette). English translation, *In the Beginning was Love: Psychoanalysis and Faith*, trans. Arthus Goldhammer (New York: Columbia University Press, 1987).

1987. *Soleil Noir: Dépression et mélancholie* (Paris: Editions Gallimard). English translation, *Black Sun: Depression and Melancholy*, trans. Leon S. Roudiez (New York: Columbia University Press, 1989).

1991. *Étrangers à nous-mêmes* (Paris: Libairie Artheme Fayard). English translation, *Strangers to Ourselves*, trans. Leon S. Roudiez (New York: Columbia University Press, 1991).
1993. *Les Nouvelles maladies de l'ame* (Paris: Librairie Artheme Fayard). English translation, *New Maladies of the Soul*, trans. Ross Guberman (New York: Columbia University Press, 1995).

KRUSE, Felicia E.
1990. "Nature and Semiosis," *Transactions of the Charles S. Peirce Society*, vol. XXVI, no. 2, pp. 211–224.

LACAN, Jacques.
1966. *Écrits* (Paris: Editions du Seuil). English translation, *Ecrits: A Selection*, trans. Alan Sheridan, (New York: W. W. Norton, 1977).

LECHTE, John.
1990. *Julia Kristeva* (London: Routledge).

LEIBNIZ, G. W.
1686. "Primary Truths," from English translation, *G. W. Leibniz: Philosophical Essays*, trans. Roger Ariew and Daniel Garber, (Indianapolis: Hackett, 1989).
1695. "A New System of the Nature and Communication of Substances, and of the Union of the Soul and Body," from English translation, *G.W. Leibniz: Philosophical Essays*, trans. Roger Ariew and Daniel Garber (Indianapolis: Hackett, 1989).

LEWIN, Roger.
1992. *Complexity: Life at the Edge of Chaos* (New York: Macmillan).

LIGHTMAN, Alan.
1991. *Ancient Light: Our Changing View of the Universe* (Cambridge: Harvard University Press).

MACHTIGER, Harriet Gordon.
1982. "Countertransference/Transference," as anthologized in *Jungian Analysis*, ed. Murray Stein (La Salle, IL: Open Court).

MANN, Thomas.
1924. *Der Zauberberg*, (Berlin: S. Fischer Verlag), English translation by H. T. Lowe-Porter, *The Magic Mountain* New York: Random House, 1927).

MARITAIN, Jacques.
1957. "Language and the Theory of Sign," *Language: An Enquiry into its Meaning and Function*, ed. Ruth Nanda Anshen (New York: Harper & Row), pp. 86–101.

MATES, Benson.
1986. *The Philosophy of Leibniz: Metaphysics and Language* (New York: Oxford University Press).

MOORE, A. W.
1990. *The Infinite* (London: Routledge).

MORRIS, Richard.
1993. *Cosmic Questions: Galactic Halos, Cold Dark Matter, and the End of Time*, (New York: John Wiley & Inc.).

NESHER, Dan.
1984. "Are There Grounds for Identifying 'Ground' with 'Interpretant' in Peirce's Pragmatic Theory of Meaning?," *Transactions of the Charles S. Peirce Society*, vol. XX, no. 3, pp. 303-324.

NÖTH, Winfried.
1990. *Handbook of Semiotics*, (Bloomington: Indiana University Press).

OLIVER, Kelly.
1993. *Reading Kristeva: Unraveling the Double Bind*, (Bloomington: Indiana University Press).

PANNENBERG, Wolfhart.
1988. *Metaphysik und Gottesgedanke* (Göttingen: Vandenhoek & Reprecht) translation by Philip Clayton, *Metaphysics and the Idea of God* (Grand Rapids: William B. Eerdmans, 1990).
1988a. *Systematische Theologie, band 1* (Göttingen: Vandenhoek & Reprecht), translation by Geoffrey W. Bromily *Systematic Theology*, vol. 1 (Grand Rapids: William B. Erdmans, 1991).

1993. *Toward a Theology of Nature: Essays on Science and Faith* (Louisville, KY: Westminster/John Knox Press).

PEIRCE, Charles Sanders.
Note: The designation CP abbreviates *The Collected Papers of Charles Sanders Peirce*, vols. I–VI ed. Charles Hartshorne and Paul Weiss (Cambridge, MA: Harvard University Press, 1931–1935), vols. VII–VIII ed. Arthus W. Burks (same publisher 1958). The abbreviation followed by volume and paragraph numbers with a period between follows the standard CP reference form. The designation W followed by volume and page numbers with a period in between abbreviates the ongoing *Writings of Charles S. Peirce: A Chronological Edition*, ed. Max H. Fisch, vols. I–V, (Bloomington: Indiana University Press, 1982–1993).

1866. "The Logic of Science; Or, Induction and Hypothesis," in, W 1.358.
1867. "On a New List of Categories," CP 1.545–567; W 2.49–59.
1867a. "Upon Logical Comprehension and Extension," CP 2.391–426.
1868. "Grounds of Validity of the Laws of Logic: Further Consequences of Four Incapacities," *Journal of Speculative Philosophy*, (2), 193–208, reprinted in CP 5.318–357, W 2.242.
1868a. "Questions Concerning Certain Faculties Claimed for Man," *Journal of Speculative Philosophy*, (2), 103–114, rerpinted in CP 5.213–263, W 2.193.
1868b. "Some Consequences of Four Incapacities," in CP 5.310–317; W 2.241.
1877. "The Fixation of Belief," *Popular Science Monthly*, (12), 1–15, rerpinted in CP 5.358–387, W 3.242.
1878. "How to Make Our Ideas Clear," *Popular Science Monthly*, (12), 286–302, reprinted in CP 5.388–410, W 3.257.
1878a. "The Order of Nature," *Popular Science Monthly*, (13), 203–217, reprinted in CP 6.395–427; W 3.306.
c.1890. "A Guess at the Riddle," CP 1.354–416.
1891. "The Architecture of Theories," *The Monist*, (1), 161–176, reprinted in CP 6.7–34.
1892. "The Doctine of Necessity Examined," *The Monist*, (2), 321–337, rerpinted in CP 6.35–65.

1892a. "The Law of Mind," *The Monist*, (2 July), 533–559; reprinted in CP 6.102–132.
1892b. "Synechism and Immortality," CP 7.565–578.
1893. "Evolutionary Love," *The Monist*, (3), 176–200, reprinted in CP 6.287–317.
c.1893. "Of Reasoning in General," of the "Short Logic," CP 7.555–558.
c.1896. "The Logic of Mathematics; An Attempt to Develop my Categories From Within," CP 1.417–520.
c.1897. "Fallibilism, Continuity, and Evolution," CP 1.141–175.
c.1897a. "Ground, Object, and Interpretant," CP 2.227–229.
1898. *Cambridge Conference Lectures: Reasoning and the Logic of Things*, edited by Kenneth Laine Ketner with and introduction by Kenneth Laine Ketner and Hilary Putnam (Cambridge: Harvard University Press, 1992).
1898a. "Detached Ideas on Vitally Important Topics," CP 6.66–87.
1898b. "The Logic of Continuity," CP 6.185–213.
1898c. "The Logic of Mathematics in Relation to Education," CP 3.553–562.
1900. "Infinitesimals," CP 3.563–570. Letter in *Science*, Vol. 2, pp. 430–33, March 16, 1900.
c.1902. "Syllabus," CP 2.72–77, 283–84, 292–94.
1903. "Degenerate Cases," CP 1.521–544.
1903a. "The Reality of Thirdness," CP 1.343–352.
1903b. "The Reality of Thirdness," CP 5.93–119.
1903c. "Variety and Uniformity," CP 6.88–101.
1905. "Issues of Pragmaticism," *The Monist*, (15), 481–499, reprinted in CP 5.438–462.
c.1905. "The Basis of Pragmaticism," CP 5.497–537.
c.1907. "Pragmatism," manuscript 318," draft of Lowell Lecture.
1908. "A Neglected Argument for the Reality of God," *Hibbert Journal*, (7), 90–112, reprinted in CP 6.452–493.
c.1910. "Notes for my Logical Criticism of Articles of Christian Creed," CP 7.97–109.

POINSOT, John.
1632. *Tractatus de Signis*, subtitled *The Semiotic of John Poinsot*, extracted from the *Artis Logicae et Secunda Pars* of 1631–1632. Bilingual edition ed. John Deely (Berkeley: University of California Press, 1985).

PROGOFF, Ira.
1956. *The Death & Rebirth of Psychology* (New York: McGraw-Hill Paperbacks).
1973. *Jung, Synchronicity, and Human Destiny* (New York: Delta).

RAPOSA, Michael L.
1989. *Peirce's Philosophy of Religion* (Bloomington: Indiana University Press).

ROYCE, Josiah.
1899. *The World and the Individual*, 2 vols. (New York: Macmillan).
1913. *The Problem of Christianity*, 2 vols. (New York: Macmillan Co.). Citations are from the 1968 edition ed. John E. Smith (Chicago: The University of Chicago Press).

SANTAYANA, George.
1923. *Scepticism and Animal Faith* (New York: Scribners).
1925. "Dewey's Naturalistic Metaphysics," *The Journal of Philosophy*, vol. XXII, no. 25, December 3. Reprinted in, *Dewey and His Critics*, ed. S. Morgenbesser (New York: The Journal of Philosophy, Inc., 1977), pp. 343–358.

SAFRANSKI, Rüdiger.
1987. *Schopenhauer und die wilden Yahre der Philosophie*, English translation, *Schopenhauer and the Wild Years of Philosophy*, trans. Ewald Osers (Cambridge, MA: Harvard University Press, 1990).

SARTRE, Jean-Paul.
1943. *L'Etre et le Néant* (Paris: Gallimard). English translation, *Being and Nothingness*, trans. Hazel Barnes (New York: Philosophical Library, 1956).

SAVAN, David.
1987. *An Introduction to C. S. Peirce's Full System of Semeiotic* (Toronto: Toronto Semiotic Circle).

SCHLEIERMACHER, Friedrich.
1821. *Die Glaubenslehre* (Berlin), English translation of second edition by H. R. Mackintosh & J. S. Stewart, *The Christian Faith* (Philadelphia: Fortress, 1928).

SCHOPENHAUER, Arthur.
1819. *Die Welt als Wille und Vorstellung* (Leipzig). English translation, *The World as Will and Representation*, 2 vols., trans. E. F. J. Paine (Indian Hills, CO: The Falcon's Wing Press, 1958).

SEBEOK, Thomas A.
1991. *Semiotics in the United States* (Bloomington: Indiana University Press).
1991a. *A Sign is Just a Sign* (Bloomington: Indiana University Press).

SHEA, William M.
1984. *The Naturalists and the Supernatural* (Macon, GA: Mercer University Press).

SHERIFF, John K.
1989. *The Fate of Meaning: Charles Peirce, Structuralism, and Literature* (Princeton: Princeton University Press).

SINGER, Milton.
1984. *Man's Glassy Essence: Explorations in Semiotic Anthropology* (Bloomington: Indiana University Press).

SMOOT, George, with DAVIDSON, Keay.
1993. *Wrinkles in Time* (New York: William Morrow).

TEILHARD de CHARDIN, Pierre.
1955. *Le Phénomene Humain* (Paris: Editions du Seuil). Citations are from English translation, *The Phenomenon of Man*, trans. William Wall (New York: Harper & Row, 1961).

THORNE, Kip S.
1994. *Black Holes & Time Warps: Einstein's Outrageous Legacy* with a forward by Stephen W. Hawking (New York: W. W. Norton).

TILLICH, Paul.
1912. *Mystik und Schuldbewusstsein in Schellings philosophischer Entwicklung* (Berlin), English translation by Victor Nuovo *Mysticism and Guilt-Consciousness in Schelling's Philosophical Development*) (Lewisburg, PA: Bucknell University Press, 1974).

1919. "Über die Idee einer Theologie der Kultur," in *Religionsphilosophie der Kulture*, (Berlin: Reuther & Reichard). English translation in *What is Religion?*, ed. James Luther Adams (New York: Harper Torchbooks, 1973).
1925. "Religionsphilosophie," in *Lehrbuch der Philosophie* (Berlin: Ullstein). English translation in *What is Religion?*, ed. James Luther Adams (New York: Harper Torchbooks, 1973).
1933. *Die sozialistische Entscheidung* (Potsdam: Alfred Protte), English translation by Franklin Sherman, *The Socialist Decision* (New York: Harper & Row, 1977).
1951. *Systematic Theology, Vol. I* (Chicago: University of Chicago Press).
1952. *The Courage to Be* (New Haven: Yale University Press).
1957. *Systematic Theology, Vol. II* (Chicago: University of Chicago Press).
1963. *Systematic Theology, Vol. III* (Chicago: University of Chicago Press).

von UEXKÜLL, Jakob.
1940. "Bedeutungslehre," *Bios 10* (Leipzig). English translation as, "The Theory of Meaning," in *Semiotica* vol. 42, no. 1, 1982, trans. Barry Stone and Herbert Weiner, pp. 25–82.

ULANOV, Ann B.
1982. "Transference/Countertransference: A Jungian Perspective," as anthologized in *Jungian Analysis*, edited by Murray Stein (La Salle, IL: Open Court).

WALDROP, M. Mitchell.
1992. *Complexity: The Emerging Science at the Edge of Order and Chaos* (New York: Simon & Schuster).

WEST, Cornel.
1989. *The American Evasion of Philosophy: A Geneology of Pragmatism* (Madison, WI: The University of Wisconsin Press).

WHITEHEAD, Alfred North.
1929. *The Function of Reason* (Boston: Beacon Press).

1929a. *Process and Reality* (New York: Macmillan Publishing Co., Inc.). Citations are from *Process and Reality: Corrected Edition*, ed. David Ray Griffin and Donald W. Sherburne (New York: The Free Press, 1978).

WHITMONT, Edward C. & PERERA, Sylvia Brinton.
1989. *Dreams, A Portal to the Source* (London: Routledge).

WITTGENSTEIN, Ludwig.
1921. *Logisch-philosophische Abhandlung* (Annalen der Naturphilosophie). English translation, *Tractatus Logico-Philosophicus*, trans. D. F. Pears & B. F. McGuiness with an introduction by Bertrand Russell (London: Routledge & Kegan Paul, 1963).

WOODCOCK, Alexander & DAVIS, Monte.
1978. *Catastrophe Theory* (London: Penguin)

Index

—A—

abductive, 42
abject, 16, 45, 49–50, 57, 59, 67, 74, 76–77, 82–85, 88, 93, 106, 114, 116, 133–135, 142, 145-146, 149, 151–152, 155–156, 160
absence, 4, 16, 19, 30, 32, 37, 40, 66, 86, 97–98, 111, 127, 142, 145, 153, 159
absolutely, 44, 69, 119, 126, 128, 138, 158
abyss, 38, 56, 84, 92, 93, 98, 112, 113, 114, 115, 118–122, 124, 126–127, 129–130, 138–140, 152, 159–160
agape, 3, 4, 18, 61, 93, 95, 157–158, 162
alienation, 49, 113, 131
ambiguity, 114, 153
amplification, 113–114
analysand, 79–81, 141, 146–147
analysis, vii,3, 5–6, 14, 20, 25, 27–28, 37, 39, 42, 45–46, 56, 62, 64–65, 71, 75, 90–91, 95, 110, 112, 118–119, 125, 132, 134–137, 141, 147, 149, 159
analyst, 79–81, 114, 141, 146–147
anima, 116–117, 129, 147, 150
animus, 147, 150
anticipatory, 59
anxiety, 3, 10, 137, 139
apocalyptic, 104, 146
archetype, 36, 78, 81, 112–113, 115–119, 121–122, 126, 129, 142, 147–148, 150, 155
assimilate, 9, 47, 79
associational, 34
asymmetrical, 91, 93, 98, 110
attractor(s), 105–109, 111, 114–115, 144, 148, 157; periodic, 105–107, 109, 111, 115, 148, 158; strange, 43, 44, 105–107, 109, 111, 113–115, 136, 144, 148, 157
autonomous, 3, 36, 46, 74, 82, 84, 87, 134, 136, 151; autonomy, 3, 15, 24, 37, 39, 40–42, 55, 82, 88, 108, 133, 134, 136–137, 149, 151–152, 154, 160

—B—

Bartusiak, Marcia, 163
being, 3, 6, 20, 24, 27, 37, 46, 48–49, 53, 67, 74, 84, 87, 89, 92, 100, 102, 105, 115, 121–123, 126–127, 134, 136–139, 141, 146, 154, 157, 164, 168, 175
Berkeley, Bishop, 168, 174
between, vii, 2, 4, 6, 7–16, 18–20, 24, 26, 28–30, 32–33, 34, 35, 39, 43–45, 47, 48, 51–57, 62, 64–65, 68, 70–73, 75, 78–79, 82–89, 93–95, 97, 99, 100, 103–111, 114, 117–118, 120–122, 125, 128–129, 131, 136, 138–139, 140–147, 149, 150, 153, 155, 158, 161, 173
Bible, 113, 133, 152, 155, 164

big bang, 102, 167
birthing, 29, 33, 36, 70, 92, 93, 112, 151
bodily, 17, 29, 42, 46–47, 68–69, 116, 125, 141, 153, 162
Brent, Joseph, 106
Buchler, Justus, 8, 27–28, 123, 144, 163–164

—C—

Cambridge, 32, 166–167, 171, 173–175
cartesian, 1, 2
Cassirer, Ernst, 163
Casti, John L., 106, 164
catastrophe, 104, 106, 108–111
categorial, 1, 2, 52, 75, 90, 91, 124, 132, 135
category(ies), 2, 24–26, 88, 99, 116, 135, 137, 173, 174
chance, 39, 150, 160
chaos, 55, 59, 109, 111
chaotic, 51, 59, 101
chora, 29, 42, 88, 141
Christ, 52
Christian, 3, 53, 110, 126, 132, 143, 155, 167, 174, 175
Christological, 155
chronos, 15, 30, 132, 139, 140, 146, 154, 158, 160–161
cleft, 1, 16, 28, 89, 97, 113, 126, 153
closure, 20, 24, 44, 48, 50–51, 54, 59, 79, 82, 86, 94–95, 131, 136–137, 142
code(s), 3, 5–6, 9–10, 12, 16, 25, 28–31, 35–36, 38, 41, 43–44, 46–47, 55–57, 59, 61, 64, 75, 82, 84–85, 88, 114, 127, 135–136, 144, 151
community(ies), 3, 13, 32, 44, 46, 47, 62, 108, 120–121, 138, 140, 142, 143, 150–153, 156–158, 161–162; communal, 16, 20, 65, 119, 136, 151
complex, 5, 7, 9–11, 14, 16, 18, 30, 32, 39, 40–42, 46, 48, 50, 52, 58, 65, 68, 71, 73, 78, 81–84, 88, 92, 97, 104, 109, 111–113, 117, 146, 149, 150

complexes, 4, 19, 24, 27–28, 73, 82–84, 87, 93, 100, 111, 123, 125–126, 138, 142, 147, 150, 156
complexity, 1, 6–7, 11, 12, 111
concupiscence, 73, 127
consciousness, 1, 7, 9, 10, 13, 19, 29, 34–35, 42, 46, 48, 52, 55, 62, 66, 73, 76, 77, 79–81, 83, 85, 87, 88, 94, 125–126, 130, 133, 139, 140, 142, 145, 147, 153, 155, 156, 158, 161
continuum, 32–33, 35, 101–102, 105, 106, 125, 162; continua, 103; continuity, 35, 83, 106, 124
contour(s), 5, 7, 10, 11, 20, 23, 25, 28, 42–43, 50, 55, 58, 74, 94, 107–108, 118, 122, 124
Corrington, Robert S., vii, 12, 26, 32, 40–41, 127, 163, 164,
countertransference, 80, 143, 146–149, 155, 158
creatio, 36
creation, 32, 36, 101–103, 121–122, 125, 143, 153
cunning (of nature), viii, 38, 41, 44, 57–58, 148, 150
cusp (Catastrophe Theory), 30, 47, 100, 106, 110–111, 114

—D—

Davidson, Keay, 176
Davies, Paul, 165
Davis, Monte, 104, 178
Dean, William, 165
decentering, 44
Deely, John, 11, 164–166, 174
Delaney. C.F., 166
demonic, 18, 21, 26, 31–32, 44, 58, 67–70, 75, 82–84, 93–94, 108, 122, 128–130, 139, 145, 151, 155–157, 161
deposition, vii, 3, 7, 10, 12, 25–26, 39–45, 47–51, 55–57, 61–62, 73–74, 76, 78–79, 81–83, 85–86, 88, 118, 121–122, 133, 160
Descartes, Rene, 107
desire, 37, 45, 51, 63, 70, 73, 141

INDEX

devouring, 127, 154
Dewey, John, 119, 145–146, 152, 155, 166, 175
dialectic, 6–7, 13, 16, 26, 38–39, 41, 43, 49–50, 55, 57, 61, 66, 68, 70, 83–85, 92–95, 107–109, 118, 120, 122, 128, 130, 142–143, 154, 156, 159, 162
diremption, 97, 112, 119, 127
discontinuity, 11, 32, 104–105, 124
divine, 13, 21, 52–53, 95, 97, 124, 133, 135, 138–139, 154, 161, 165, 167
dreams, 4, 47, 77–81, 113, 117, 118, 122, 150, 178
Driskill, Todd, 166
drives, 15, 29, 36, 43, 45, 63, 74, 113, 141

—E—

Eco, Umberto, 166
economy, 29, 83, 103, 111, 118
ecstasy, 12, 63, 141, 143
ecstatic, vii, 2, 3, 5, 8, 13, 16, 18–20, 32, 33, 36, 42, 52, 55, 61, 63–64, 73, 84, 97, 99, 103, 106–107, 110, 119, 121, 123–126, 132, 135, 137, 142, 145, 148–149, 152, 154–155, 158, 161, 163, 165–166
eject, 6, 23, 28, 35–36, 97, 102, 144
Elijah, 154–155
emanation, 36
emancipatory, 26, 151–152, 157
embeddedness, 11, 43, 95, 159
embodiment, 4, 14, 19, 23–25, 29, 50–51, 54, 58, 61–62, 90, 109, 111
emergent, 44
Emerson, Ralph Waldo, 36, 164, 166
emptiness, 57, 99, 100
encompass, 33, 54, 59, 75–76, 80, 86, 94, 103, 109, 153, 162
en-soi, 48
entropy, 57, 59, 68, 82, 98, 103, 110, 137, 139, 144–146
enveloping, 59, 145
eros, 3–4, 18, 61, 93–95, 102–103, 107–108, 111, 138, 148, 150, 152, 154, 158, 162, 169

eschatology, 48, 54–55, 71–72, 87–88, 91–93, 95, 136, 143–146, 152
estrangement, 110, 122, 127, 131, 153, 155
eternity, vii, 15, 19, 33, 36–37, 52, 61, 95, 97, 111, 114, 119, 130, 132, 145, 155
evil, viii, 32, 41, 82, 113, 117–122, 129, 130, 134, 137–139, 150–152, 156
evolutionary, 11, 34, 44–45, 48, 55, 77
existential, 30, 109
existents, 35

—F—

feeling, 19, 33, 45, 68, 73, 78, 104–108, 110, 113, 125, 140, 150
Ferguson, Kitty, 166
finitude, 4–3, 6, 13, 23–24, 28, 31–33, 45–54, 56, 59, 61–63, 65–66, 68–69, 71, 76, 78, 80–82, 84–85, 93–95, 98–100, 109, 111, 120, 127, 139, 140–141, 148, 151–153, 155, 156–161
firstness, 1, 6, 15, 17, 25, 37–39, 41, 45, 51, 55, 62, 65, 72, 75, 88, 90, 99–100, 106–108, 122, 125–126, 136, 140, 142–143, 145, 160–161, 165–166
Fisch, Max, 167, 173
fissioning, 112
fissure, vii, 1, 4, 6, 15, 19, 28–33, 37, 39–41, 45, 68, 87, 93–94, 97–98, 100, 112, 114–122, 124, 126, 145, 153, 155, 158, 160
fitful, 18, 140–141, 153
force field(s), 5, 38, 46, 66, 76–77, 79–82, 87, 89, 99, 107–109, 113, 125–126, 128, 139, 144–145, 148–150
Foucault, Michel, 29, 166–167
Freud, Sigmund, 6, 14, 17, 25, 31, 33, 37–39, 41, 49, 74, 77–78, 109, 145, 147, 153–154, 167

—G—

Gadamer, Hans-Georg, 167

Gelassenheit, 27
gestalt, 34, 37, 129
Geworfenheit, 27
glottocentrism, 43
God, 53, 97, 115, 118, 123–124, 132–133, 137, 145, 165, 167, 172, 174
gods, 36, 116
grace, 3, 4, 20, 31, 41, 43, 55, 57, 63, 86, 93, 119, 124–128, 130, 133–146, 150, 152, 154, 158–159, 162
Gribin, John, 167
ground, 2, 6, 19, 20, 26, 28, 38, 43–44, 52–54, 56, 64, 78, 90, 92–94, 111, 126, 137, 139, 146, 151, 154–156, 160

—H—

habit, 34, 37, 44, 125
Hann, Lewis, 167
Hartshorne, Charles, 110, 167, 173
Hausman, Carl, 164, 167
Hawking, Stephen W., 109–110, 167, 176
Hegel, G.W.F., 26, 42, 66, 168
Heidegger, Martin, 3, 27–28, 46, 74–75, 84, 124, 137, 141, 168
hermeneutics, 18, 42
heteronomy, 131, 133–134, 151–152
holy, 53
Hookway, Christopher, 168
horizon(s), 17–18, 49–51, 56, 59, 63, 65–73, 75, 79, 81, 94, 97, 113, 119, 122–124, 126–131, 137–139, 142, 147, 150, 157, 159

—I—

incarnation, 13, 19, 51, 53–54, 72, 90
indebtedness, 27
indeterminacy, 101, 110
indexical, 43
indifferent, 12, 40, 48–49, 55, 88, 94, 118–119, 123, 137–139, 158
individuation, 15, 55, 115, 136, 151
inertia, 5, 11–12, 18, 32, 41, 46, 48, 50, 52, 69

infinite, 14, 20, 24, 43–44, 49, 51, 53–55, 57, 59, 65, 75, 82, 89, 92, 98–99, 101, 103–104, 152–153, 155, 160–161
infinitesimal, 3, 20–21, 32–36, 38, 45, 47, 56, 59, 95, 97–104, 106–113, 119–120, 122, 124, 128, 139
information, 53
integration, 44, 61, 157
intention, 5, 19, 46, 52, 65–66, 86, 116
interpretant, 2, 4, 9–10, 12, 16–17, 19–20, 26–27, 29–30–31, 37–38, 40–44, 51–53, 55–59, 62–64, 71–74, 80, 82, 85–95, 97, 103, 105, 127–128, 131, 135, 140–142, 145, 151–152, 155, 158–159, 162
interpretation, 8, 32, 38, 64, 78, 121
interpreter, 2, 4, 9, 10, 13, 18, 20, 39, 43, 53, 56–59, 62, 85–90, 92–94
interpretive, 19, 44, 65, 152
Irwin, Alexander C., 169

—J—

James, William, 114, 167, 177
Jaspers, Karl, 59, 153, 169, 1
Jesus, 113, 120–121, 130, 143, 154–155
jouissance, 141
Jung, Carl Gustav, 6, 14, 19, 39, 41, 67, 77, 81, 113, 115–116, 118, 147–149, 169, 171, 175, 177

—K—

Kant, Immanuel, 30, 70, 118, 130, 133–134, 168, 170
Kierkegaard, Søren, 118, 133
Krikorian, Yervant, 170
Kristeva, Julia, 3, 42, 86, 88, 141, 170–172
Kruse, Felicia E., 171

—L—

Lacan, Jacques, 171
lack, 16, 72, 78–79, 113, 116, 120, 122, 124
Lechte, John, 171

Leibniz, Gottfried, 28, 72, 80–81, 171–172
Lewin, Roger, 171
Lightman, Alan, 171
logos, 53
Lowell Lectures, Peirce, 52, 174
lure, 51, 74–75, 107, 109, 112, 151–153, 159
Luther, Martin, 152, 161, 164, 177

—M—

Machtiger, Harriet Gordon, 171
Mann, Thomas, 171
Maritain, Jacques, 172
Mark, Gosepl of, 120, 154
Marx, Karl, 49
maternal, 3, 14–16, 24, 28–33, 35–47, 55–57, 59, 61, 82, 86, 88, 90, 92–94, 102, 145, 154, 161
Mates, Benson, 172
matricide, 15, 29, 41, 42
melancholy, 1, 3, 4, 10, 16, 27, 36, 38, 41–45, 57, 61, 63, 74, 89–91, 93, 127, 138, 159–162, 170
mirror, 29–31, 37–42, 43, 46, 80, 85, 108
Moore, A.W., 172
morphogenesis, 104
Morris, Richard, 172
Moses, 154–155

—N—

narcissistic, 15, 26, 108
natura, 29
naturalism, vii, 2, 3, 5, 8, 13, 16, 18–19, 32–33, 36, 42, 52, 55, 84, 97, 99, 107, 110, 119, 121, 123–124, 126, 132, 135, 137, 145, 148–149, 152, 154–155, 158, 161
naturalist, 20, 23, 27, 52, 106, 124, 132, 142, 165, 176,
nature, vii, viii, 1– 4, 6, 9, 11–17, 19–20, 23, 26–33, 35–36, 38–40, 42–43, 45–46, 50, 52, 54–57, 59, 61–66, 69, 72–74, 77–82, 84–88, 90–102, 104–105, 109–113, 115, 117–125, 127–137, 139–140, 142–146, 149–151, 153–155, 158–161, 163–166, 171–173
negativity, 23, 151
Nesher, Dan, 172
Nietzsche, Friedrich, 36, 131–133
norms, 118, 121, 151–152, 156–158, 162
nothing, vii, 3, 27, 69, 71, 101, 120, 132, 134, 141

—O—

object(s), vii, 2–3, 5, 9, 12, 14, 16–17, 19–20, 26–28, 30–32, 37–39, 41–44, 46, 48–49, 52–53, 55–57, 59, 61, 66–68, 70, 72–73, 88–94, 97–98, 105, 127–128, 133, 135, 140, 143, 145–147, 149–151, 154, 155–156, 159–162
Oedipal, 3, 29, 42
Oliver, Kelly, 172
Olivier, Sir Lawrence, 58
openness, 58, 63, 67, 143, 152
origin(s), 3, 13–16, 19, 23–25, 27–29, 31–32, 36, 40, 42, 47–51, 54, 57, 61–62, 70–72, 80, 83, 85, 88–90, 92–95, 103, 106, 123, 135, 139–140, 149, 151, 155, 159
other, vii, 2–3, 5, 9, 11–12, 15–17, 20, 23–25, 27–32, 34–35, 39–40, 43, 45, 50, 52, 54–55, 62, 64, 66, 69–71, 79–81, 84, 87–88, 90–91, 93, 95, 97, 99, 100–102, 104–105, 109, 113–115, 118, 122, 124, 127–129, 131–132, 134, 136, 142, 148, 150, 152–153, 157–158, 162, 168
othering, 15, 19, 28–29, 35–36, 62, 81, 88–89, 98–104, 107–110, 112, 120–122, 124
otherness, 13, 46, 94, 98, 107–109, 118

—P—

Pannenberg, Wolfhart, 144–145, 172
panpsychism, 35
panpsychist, 1, 11, 48
pansemioticism, 56

patriarchy, 24
Peirce, Charles Sanders, 2, 12, 14, 19,
    20, 32–36, 40, 45, 48, 52–54, 57,
    72, 88, 90–92, 99, 100–101, 103,
    105–109, 125–127, 133, 139, 140,
    144, 160, 163, 165–169, 171–173,
    175–176
Peircean, 1, 2, 9, 32–33, 135
Perera, Sylvia Brinton, 178
persona, 115, 129, 130
phenomenological, 2, 5, 6, 13, 17, 20,
    26–27, 66, 89, 103, 110, 132, 139
phenomenon, 3, 10, 25, 27, 50, 65, 112,
    148
philia, 3
phylogenetic, 29, 64, 82, 84
Poinsot, John, 174
position, vii, 4–7, 9, 12, 17, 19, 25, 28–
    –36, 39–41, 45–46, 49, 51, 57–58,
    62, 72, 80–81, 85–86, 88, 91–92,
    113, 115, 133, 138, 151–152, 160
positioning, 7, 9–10, 24–29, 31, 35,
    39–40, 61, 85
postmodernism, 49
postspatial, 30, 32
potencies, 2, 6, 11–12, 14–17, 19, 27–
    31, 33, 36, 39, 42, 45, 50, 54–56,
    61, 73, 77, 79, 81, 85, 95, 97–103,
    109–113, 118–119, 120–122, 126,
    128– 131, 136, 139, 140, 143–144,
    146, 151, 153–154, 156, 158, 160
pragmatic, 44
pragmaticism, 33
pragmaticist, 16, 25, 27, 33, 36, 40, 54
preconscious, 30
pre-Oedipal, 3, 5, 14–15, 25, 33, 35–
    36, 39, 40, 61, 73, 85
prepositioned, 11, 28–29, 32–33, 35–36
presemiotic, 1, 2, 4, 6–7, 11–13, 27, 29,
    35–36, 38, 40–41, 46–47, 49, 54,
    56–57, 73, 80, 97
presence, 2, 4, 9, 13, 16, 19, 24, 28, 30–
    32, 40, 43, 47, 49, 54–55, 64, 66–
    68, 82, 86, 89–90, 92–93, 95, 97–
    99, 110, 111, 115, 122–125, 127,
    129, 138, 140, 142, 145–146, 153,
    159, 162

prespatial, 2, 30–31, 33, 36, 79, 81, 99,
    100–101, 103–104
pretemporal, 14, 30–31, 36, 49, 56, 59,
    61, 81, 89–92, 98, 100–101, 103–
    104, 109–112, 122, 128–129, 132,
    139–145, 153, 156, 158, 160
prevalence, 154
primal, 2–4, 9, 19, 23, 25, 27, 45, 47,
    51, 64, 66, 68, 85, 98, 102, 110–
    112, 115, 135, 140–141, 158, 160
primordial, 45
products, 5, 7, 10–11, 20, 23, 46–52,
    57–59, 61–62, 65, 77–78, 87–88,
    93–95, 113, 150
Progoff, Ira, 174
projected, 55, 67, 131, 148–149, 159
provide, 7–8, 10, 12, 20, 23, 25, 55–59,
    77–79, 83–94, 97, 103–104, 109,
    112, 118, 123–124, 127, 129–130,
    132, 134, 136–137, 144, 146, 149,
    151, 157
providingness, 3, 80, 110–111, 119,
    123–128, 130, 144
psyche, 82–84, 103, 111, 116–118,
    140, 142, 147–148, 156
psychic, 24, 81, 86, 103, 109, 116, 118,
    125–126, 142–143
psychoanalysis, 3, 6, 14–16, 17, 24, 36,
    40, 42, 54–55, 86, 106, 141, 143,
    146, 165

—R—

randomness, 106, 109
Raposa, Michael, 175
reason, 53, 134, 136, 160
reasoning, 32, 174
reconstruction, 11, 52, 70, 132
relevance, 3, 6, 11, 20, 25, 28, 33, 36,
    50, 64, 88–90, 97
relevant, 13–14, 17, 24, 49, 53, 147,
    163
religious, 2, 15, 56, 87, 118, 134, 155
repetition, 31, 40, 54, 59, 83, 88, 93,
    141
reposition, vii, 7, 10, 12, 25–26, 39,
    50,–53, 55–59, 61–62, 73, 75, 78–

INDEX

79, 85–86, 88, 115, 118, 121–122, 133, 142, 160
representamen, 37, 42, 91, 99, 103, 110, 135
resistance, 23, 43, 50–51, 54–55
resurrection, 4, 42, 52, 121, 123, 126
Richard III(Shakespeare), 58, 168, 172
Royce, Josiah, 53, 72, 164, 175

—S—

Safranski, Rüdiger, 175
Santayana, George, 175
Sartre, Jean-Paul, 48, 175
Schleiermacher, Friedrich, 140, 155, 175
Schopenhauer, Arthur, 70, 159, 175, 176
Sebeok, Thomas A., 164, 176
secondness, 32–33, 38, 43, 50, 62, 65, 72, 81, 88, 100–101, 125–126, 136, 139–140, 142, 170, 175
selving, 40–44, 46, 51, 53–55, 57, 97, 109, 111–112, 115, 124–125, 133, 135, 137–138, 140, 142, 144, 147, 152, 155–157
semiotic, vii, 1–7, 10–13, 15, 17–21, 24–38, 40–59, 61–67, 69–77, 79–86, 89–92, 94–95, 97, 99–100, 102–104, 107–109, 112–114, 117, 120, 123–125, 127–128, 131, 142, 148–150, 164–165, 174–175–176
series, 1, 6, 8–9, 11–12, 14, 19, 27, 34, 42–43, 47, 49, 56, 63–66, 71–73, 78–80, 86, 88, 93, 103, 109, 111, 118, 133, 141
sexuality, 102, 129, 141
shadow, 7, 67–70, 73, 75–76, 113–117, 120
Shea, William M., 176
Sheriff, John K., 176
shipwreck, 66–67, 70, 75, 77, 126
shriven, 119, 130–131, 142
signified, 43
signifier, 43
signs, 4–5, 9–13, 16–20, 24, 26–28, 34, 36–39, 41–45, 49–58, 61–62, 64–66, 70–71, 73, 79–80, 82, 85–86,
88, 90, 92–93, 100, 103–104, 111, 123–128, 131, 133, 138, 140–141, 151–152
Singer, Milton, 176
Smoot, George, 176
space, vii, 2, 10, 16, 20, 23, 29–31, 33, 35, 39, 43, 45–47, 51, 54–59, 64–66, 68–70, 77, 79, 81, 83–85, 87, 99, 100–104, 108–109, 111–112, 119, 121–122, 133–135, 145, 147–148, 154, 158–159, 162
spatial, 2–3, 6–7, 16, 27–28, 30–31, 33, 35, 40, 50, 81, 99, 100–101, 103, 107, 109, 125, 159
spatio, 32, 38, 43, 81
spirit, vii, viii, 3–4, 9–10, 13, 16, 18–20, 23, 31, 39–40, 42–43, 51–59, 61–62, 85–95, 97, 109, 111–112, 114–115, 119–122, 125–126, 128, 130–131, 133–136, 139, 142–162, 165, 168, 170
stigma of finitude, 48, 111
stone, 116
structuralism, 132
supernatural, 133
suspicion, hermeneutics of, 18, 42
sustaining, 25, 51, 74, 102, 125, 127, 128, 133, 136–139, 142, 160–161
symbol, 52–53, 69, 114–117, 119, 120, 129, 143
symmetrical, 48, 91, 93
sympathy, 45, 70
synchronistic, 147

—T—

Teilhard de Chardin, Pierre 176
teleology, 7–9, 39, 40, 51, 62, 75–81, 84–88, 94, 97, 102–103, 106, 109, 115, 123, 137, 144; developmental, 7–10, 36, 39, 40, 54, 62, 74, 76–87, 94, 106, 109, 111, 115
telic, 108
telos, 28, 43, 97
temporal, 14–16, 25, 28, 30–32, 38, 40, 43, 49, 54, 56, 59, 61, 81, 87–95, 98, 100, 103, 109–112, 114, 119,

122, 128–130, 132, 139, 141–142, 143–146, 153, 156, 160
temporality, vii, 14–16, 26, 30, 49, 56, 79, 89–92, 95, 98, 110–111, 132, 140, 142, 145–146, 155–156, 158–159
theology, 24, 41, 52, 122–124, 132, 135, 161
theonomous, 157, 162
theonomy, 137
thirdness, 2, 5, 50–51, 54–55, 58–59, 62, 80, 85, 87–88, 90, 100, 125–126, 144, 157
Thorne, Kip, 176
thrownness, 27–28
Tillich, Paul, 28, 55, 111, 126, 137, 151, 157, 169, 176
time, vii, 2, 5, 7–8, 10, 14–15, 19, 23–24, 27, 30–32, 35, 37, 39, 43, 45–46, 48–49, 51, 53, 55–56, 58–59, 62–63, 66, 68, 72, 74, 79, 81, 87–95, 98–106, 109–112, 114, 119, 121–122, 126–137, 140, 142, 145–146, 148, 152–155, 157–159, 162
transcendence, 3, 6–7, 9, 23, 50, 53, 56, 59, 61–69, 70–72, 75–76, 78, 85, 88, 93, 95, 109, 128, 164
transcendent, 54, 85, 88, 94
transference, 79–80, 141, 143, 146–150, 152, 155–158
transfiguration, vii, 4, 40, 54, 63, 69, 73, 95, 153–157
transfigure, 1, 2, 4, 6, 13, 15–18, 20, 23, 27, 30–31, 36, 39, 42, 54–55, 59, 61–62, 69, 83, 86–88, 91–93, 104, 111, 130, 132, 135, 145–146, 154, 157–159
transgression, 30, 141
triadic, 29, 54, 132, 155
trinitarian, 52, 144
trinity, 52–53

—U—

Ulanov, Ann, 147, 177
unconditional, 116, 134, 157
unconscious, 4–10, 12–13, 16, 19, 20, 28, 34–35, 62, 67–68, 71, 73–88,
94, 98–103, 112–120, 123, 125, 127, 133–136, 141–142, 147, 150–151
unconsciousness, 156
utopian, 145, 146

—V—

vector, 12, 19, 23, 39, 45, 49, 64–65, 71–72, 77–78

—W—

Waddington, C.H., 104
Waldrop, M. Mitchell, 177
West, Cornell, 164, 177
whence, 28, 36, 40, 45, 95, 97, 110–111, 120, 122, 124, 126, 131, 133, 140–143, 145–146, 148, 151–152, 154, 155–156, 160
Whitehead, Alfred North, 177
whither, 36, 40, 45, 95, 97, 109–111, 120, 126, 131, 133, 143–145, 148–149, 151–156
Whitmond, Edward C., 178
wholeness, 28, 85, 112
Wittgenstein, Ludwig, 178
womb, 28, 29, 41, 67
Woodcock, Alexander, 104, 178
world, 1, 2, 4, 5–8, 10–12, 15–17, 20–21, 23–24, 27–37, 39, 41, 43, 45–46, 48, 50–53, 55–56, 62–63, 66, 72, 74, 81, 83, 85, 88–90, 93, 95, 97–104, 107, 109, 111–115, 121–122, 124, 126–129, 132, 135, 137–139, 142–144, 148–149, 153, 158–162
worldhood, 104, 107, 124, 126
worldly, 7, 20, 53, 91, 98, 111, 113–114, 125, 140
wound, 1, 2, 15, 28–31, 37, 93–94, 127, 160

—Z—

zero, 20, 32, 98, 105, 128
Zuhandensein, 47

About the Author

Robert S. Corrington is associate professor of philosophical theology in the Graduate and Theological Schools of Drew University. He has written 45 articles in the areas of American philosophy, semiotics, theology, and metaphysics and has authored four other book-length studies, *The Community of Interpreters* (Mercer University Press); *Nature and Spirit: An Essay in Ecstatic Naturalism* (Fordham University Press); *An Introduction to C.S. Peirce: Philosopher, Semiotician, and Ecstatic Naturalist*, (Rowman & Littlefield) and *Ecstatic Naturalism: Signs of the World*, Advances in Semiotics, (Indiana University Press). He co-edited *Pragmatism Considers Phenomenology* (The Center for Advanced Research in Phenomenology and the University Press of America); Justus Buchler's *Metaphysics of Natural Complexes, second expanded edition* (SUNY Press); and *Nature's Perspectives: Prospects for Ordinal Metaphysics* (SUNY Press). He has also written a full-length play, *Black Hole Sonata*. He is a past president of the Karl Jaspers Society of North America. In addition, he has served on the executive boards of the Semiotic Society of America and the Highlands Institute for American Religious Thought. Dr. Corrington is the recipient of the Church Divinity, Douglas Greenlee, and John William Miller prizes.